Changing Education Through ICT in Developing Countries

Marianne Georgsen
Pär-Ola Zander

AALBORG UNIVERSITY PRESS

Changing education through ICT in developing countries
Edited by Marianne Georgsen and Pär-Ola Zander

© The authors and Aalborg University Press, 2013

Cover layout: Skinstad
Text layout: Søren Cort Hansen
Printed by Toptryk Grafisk ApS, 2013

ISBN: 978-87-7112-079-0

Published by:
Aalborg University Press
Skjernvej 4A, 2nd floor
9220 Aalborg
Denmark
Phone: (+45) 99 40 71 40
Fax: (+45) 96 35 00 76
aauf@forlag.aau.dk
forlag.aau.dk

This book is financially funded by eLearning Lab at the department of Communication and Psychology, Aalborg University.

All rights reserved. No part of this book may be reprinted or reproduced or utilized in any form or by any electronic, mechanical, or other means, now known or hereafter invented, including photocopying and recording, or in any information storage or retrieval system, without permission in writing from the publishers, except for reviews and short excerpts in scholarly publications.

Contents

Foreword..9
    By Jacques Steyn

Introduction..13
    Fundamentals of Education and ICT for Development
    By Pär-Ola Zander & Marianne Georgsen

Part I - ICT in Higher Education..31

    Developing the Qualifications of the ICT Workforce through
    Problem-based Learning   33
    By Mayela Coto, Sonia Mora & Marianne Lykke

    Transformation of the Universities in Developing
    Countries to Support ICT for Development   61
    By Heilyn Camacho

    Exporting a Scandinavian Learning Model to Egypt and
    Vietnam: Challenges and Implications   83
    By Sandra Safwat Youssef Fahmy, Ann Bygholm & Kirsten Jæger

Part II - Approaches to development................................103

    Application of PLA Methods in Educational Technology Research:
    A Rural Bangladeshi Case   105
    By Saifuddin Khalid & Tom Nyvang

    An ICT Implementation Strategy for Primary Schools in Fiji   129
    By Vinesh Chandra & Ramila Chandra

    The Unheard Voices at Dhaka University   153
    By Marianne Georgsen & Pär-Ola Zander

Part III - Learning with ICT...171

    Learning as Negotiating Identities: Applying Wenger's
    Identity Theory to Inform Designs for Learning to Use
    ICT in a Developing Country Context   173
    By Aparna Purushothaman

    Pre-Service Teachers' Learning Experiences with E-Portfolios
    or ICT and Language Development   195
    By Mahbub Ahsan Khan & Muhammad Kamarul Kabilan

Biography

Ann Bygholm, PhD, is Professor in Human Centered Informatics at the Department of Communication, Aalborg University. Her research is within the fields of learning in higher education and health informatics. The overall research interest concerns the relations between ICT and working/learning practices, and the implications of mediating and affording work/learning practices with ICT. She is a member of the ICT4D group. Email: ann@hum.aau.dk

Dr. Heilyn Camacho is associate professor at Informatics School, Universidad Nacional (UNA), Costa Rica. She worked previously as the co-ordinator of a Continuing Education Programme on the Management of ICT at UNA. She completed her PhD at Aalborg University, within the area of developing ICT competences in SMEs. Her current research interest relates to industry-government-university interactions, action learning and ICT4D. Email: hcamacho@hum.aau.dk

Ramila Chandra is an academic librarian at the Bremer Institute of TAFE in Brisbane, Australia. She obtained her Master of Information studies degree from the Charles Sturt University in Australia in 2013. Her professional interests include developing strategies that facilitate effective utilization of print and digital resources. She has worked on setting up and managing libraries in Australia and Fiji. Email: ramila.chandra@tafe.qld.edu.au

Dr Vinesh Chandra is a Senior Lecturer in Education at the Queensland University of Technology in Brisbane, Australia. His teaching areas are in ICT and Technology. His research interests include the investigation of technology rich learning environments and teacher education. Dr. Chandra has worked on ICT and technology focused projects for schools both in Australia, China and Fiji. Email: v.chandra@qut.edu.au

Dr. Mayela Coto is a professor in the School of Informatics, Universidad Nacional, Costa Rica. Since 1986 she has taught various computer science courses at two major universities in Costa Rica. She was the coordinator of the Master of Educational Technology and currently is the Research Coordinator of the School of Informatics. Her main research interests are educational software, learning, engineering education, communities of practice and CSCL. E-mail: mcoto@una.cr

Dr. Sandra S. Fahmy (MD) is a medical doctor and also a PhD Scholar at E-learning Lab, Aalborg University. Dr. Fahmy is currently the Education and Training director of "International Business School of Scandinavia", a privately owned Danish Business School. She has 5 years of teaching experience to post graduate students in different countries as Denmark, Egypt, Vietnam, Malaysia, Bangladesh and UAE and her research interests are aimed at developing innovative e-learning course designs that would suit her students' cultures and needs. Email: ssafwat@hum.aau.dk

Dr. Marianne Georgsen is senior consultant and research associate at the School of Continuing Education, University College VIA, Denmark. Her research interests are ICT4D, innovative teaching and learning with ICT, and professional development and capacity building. She is an external member of the ICT4D research group at Aalborg University. Email: mage@viauc.dk

Dr. Kirsten Jæger is an associate professor at Department of Culture and Global Studies, Aalborg University. Her research areas are international education studies and intercultural health communication. Email: kirstenj@cgs.aau.dk.

Dr. Muhammad Kamarul Kabilan trains English language teachers at USM. He has presented numerous academic papers relating to English language education and published various international journals. His main research interests are the use of Internet for ELT, professional development of English language teachers and creative and critical thinking in ELT. Email: kabilan@usm.my

Md. Saifuddin Khalid is a Ph.D. Candidate at eLearning Lab, Department of Communication & Psychology, Aalborg University. For about four years he has taught at School of Engineering and Computer Science, Independent University, Bangladesh, where he holds a lecturer position. His research interests in educational technology include the adoption and integration of ICT in secondary and higher educational institutions. Email: khalid@hum.aau.dk

Dr. Mahbub Ahsan Khan obtained BA (Hons.) and MA from Jahangirnagar University and taught 5 years in secondary level and Bangladesh Open University. From 2000 he has been working at the Department of Language Education, Institute of Education & Research, University of Dhaka, where he is now an associate professor. In 2010, he obtained PhD from Universiti Sains Malaysia (USM). Email: makhanrajib@gmail.com

Marianne Lykke, PhD, is professor and Knowledge Group leader for e-Learning Lab (eLL), Department of Communication and Psychology, Aalborg University. She holds a professor-2 position at HIOA in Oslo, and is visiting professor at Åbo Academy University, Åbo. Her research concerns technologies for knowledge sharing and learning in organisations. She is member of several editorial boards, and has published in several international journals. She has made consultancy in a large set of enterprises and government organisations. Email: mlykke@hum.aau.dk

Dr. Tom Nyvang is an associate professor at Department of Communication and Psychology, Aalborg University, where he acts as head of the board of the bachelor and master programs in Human Centered Informatics. He is part of the ICT4D group at Aalborg University and his main research interests are ICT and organizational change and design for learning. Email: nyvang@hum.aau.dk

Aparna Purushothaman is a PhD Scholar at E-learning Lab, Aalborg University. Her research interests include the digital divide, action research and communities of practice. Email: aparna@hum.aau.dk

Sonia Mora Rivera, obtained a BA in Computer Sciences and a master degree in Educational Technology. She has worked for over 25 years in university teaching mainly at the School of Informatics, Universidad Nacional of Costa Rica. Currently she is working on pedagogical approaches applied to programming. Email: sonia.mora.rivera@una.ac

Dr. Pär-Ola Zander is an associate professor at Department of Communication & Psychology, Aalborg University. He has previously taught at Aarhus University, Lund University, and Asian University for Women, and is now the leader of the ICT4D group of Aalborg University. His own research interests relate to learning, participatory design and collaborative technologies. Email: poz@hum.aau.dk

Foreword

This book, investigating educational matters in the less developed regions of the world, with a focus on the role of information and communication technologies in education, is a timely book. As Zander and Georgsen point out, in the past too much development focus was on economic issues and development, too little on education.

The contributions in the book might assist in releasing the stranglehold the economic development bias has in discussions on ICT4D. If we are not homo economicus, perhaps the focus of investing in developing underdeveloped regions should be channeled into other domains of human endeavors. Navigating through all domains of human activity requires some level of knowledge. Knowledge, especially knowledge about the complexities of modern life, is dependent on education, while ICT is certainly the most powerful tool that could assist for all to participate in acquiring knowledge. Perhaps it is time to stop giving money to developing nations, and rather concentrate on developing their educational systems.

Perhaps education might bear fruit only in the long run after a generation or two, while donors want to see quicker results. However, after more than half a century of attempts to uplift the poorer regions economically, and investments of many hundreds of millions of dollars (some estimates even claim trillions of dollars), there is not much to show for all this money. The economies of particularly African countries are worse off than they were in the first half of the 20th century, before economic development began

Francis Bacon (1561 - 1626), an Englishman who lived at the beginning of the modern era and who made the case for the scientific method of induction, lived at a time of transition in the history of humankind. His most famous dictum is "Knowledge is power", or more precisely Nam et ipsa scientia potestas est, translated as For also knowledge itself is power. These words appeared in Meditationes Sacrae (Sacred Meditations, but in English known as Of Heresies) published in 1597. These words come from a section with a subtitle "You err not knowing the scriptures not the power of God." This saying in its religious context does not seem to apply to general knowledge, or scientific knowledge, but it must be remembered that the early critical thinkers in the West did not break away from the religious conceptual framework dominant in Europe at the time. They broke away only from the religious argument favoring the authority of religious tradition. For these early scientists, if they could be called that, the world was rational and open to investigation because it was created to be so. By understanding the world rationally one is empowered. Thus, knowledge is power.

Knowledge is power is a modern dictum too. It is obvious that given the complexities of the world, without understanding it, it would be hard to manipulate it to the extent that humans have done. In previous and earlier eras during the history of humankind, important knowledge might have been rudimentary – knowledge such as which plants could be eaten without negative consequences – but nevertheless knowledge is important for our continuous existence.

The early farmers had the knowledge to genetically manipulate domesticated plants (the grasses we eat today, such as wheat) and animals (to increase dairy production and rendering meat to eat) by selecting the most fruitful for reproduction. We take such matters for granted, but knowledge about these matters were not inborn. Our ancestors needed to acquire such knowledge by learning from the experience of caretakers, thus through education.

We still acquire knowledge through education. Of course, today's cultures are manifold more complex than earlier ones, and the degree of specialization requiring specialized knowledge is astounding. Ever since we moved from the plains into more permanent dwellings and villages, and acquired the ability to provide a surplus in agricultural goods, specialization entered societies more formally. Learning basic living skills was done through some form of apprenticeship. Higher learning, if we might label it thus, or the learning of more abstract matters, was restricted to the learned elite. This imbalance continued throughout the history of civilizations. Even in the mighty Roman Empire perhaps as little as 5% of the population could read and write and were educated.

Formal schools have been in existence for millennia, but always served the elite, or at best served the ideology of either some political or religious group, its main function to promote the world view of the ruling elite. Since the common era began, schooling in Europe was done by Christian churches. In England, for example, schools independent of the Church of England were established only recently. These so-called public schools only came into being in the early 1800s, thus about 200 years ago, during the Industrial Revolution. They were of course anything but public as they still served the elite. However, in the ethos of this time, the British parliament also made available money for the construction of schools for the poor, and education slowly but surely became available to larger numbers of populations.

The example of Britain was given here, but similar advancements in schooling and education could be found all over Europe and the USA. For the greater part of the twentieth century the Euro-American regions dominated to world's economy, and lead in technological and scientific advances. It would be a very hard argument to make to deny the important role education of a few consecutive generations of people played in this growth. Citizens of developed regions are today the most educated and wealthy people in the history of humankind. The middle classes of these regions today have better lives than the nobility of earlier eras: better health, easier transportation and communication, access to a wider variety of cuisines, and better education.

Educational technology has developed quite significantly through the ages. Whereas our remote ancestor "teachers" perhaps scribbled with sticks in the dirt, later generations used clay tablets, papyrus and paper. The latter is still a very powerful means for distributing knowledge. Considering modes of teaching and learning, there are aspects handled much better with technology.

Assuming that the humanist notion of global equality is a good value to strive for, and given the complexities of modern life, it is essential to make use of powerful technologies to get the job of education done more efficiently. Statistics seem to point to a positive correlation between level of schooling and economic wealth. Further assuming that economic wealth enables better achievement of general well-being, perhaps higher levels of education might be a catalyst in economic development.

Successful contemporary economies result from a complex web of interwoven and interrelated systems and subsystems that support one another in order to enable societies to live in the modern world. Knowledge of each of these subsystems is necessary to sustain their operations. Such knowledge can only be obtained through education and training. It is no trivial claim to state that modern societies are built on knowledge. It follows from this that educational systems need to be in place for societies to be economically successful. Vast regions on this globe are economically poor, while such poverty is often correlated with poor education levels.

It can be argued that the development of previous eras of unprecedented economic growth (such as the early western industrial revolution, and the Golden Age of development of the late 1800s), might not have happened if it were not for the explosion of knowledge to which the inventors had access. Such knowledge was theoretical as well as technical. Theory enabled engineers to calculate the stresses and optimum performance of structures and machines, while technical tinkering and experimenting fine-tuned the products. This gave us the steam engine, first a static one, later a mobile one, or in the parlance of the day, locomotive engines. The internal combustion engine followed, and in the previous century the jet propulsion engine. These advances, based on knowledge, changed human life forever. Manufacturing for the masses, with which we are so at ease and acquainted today, would not have been possible without steam, and later electricity. Neither would the world have become such a small place as our technologies overcame the barriers of time and space to a useful extent. None of these developments emerged magically from a vacuum. Bit by bit knowledge was expanded, and the new technologies are built on many layers of earlier technologies, none of which later generations would have known if not for education.

As humans we all aspire to the good life – whichever way this is defined. Such general well-being depends on having appropriate knowledge to be used to take the necessary action to achieve that state of living. We cannot acquire such knowledge from thin air. As humans we need educational systems that enable us to acquire knowledge that could be used for our own good.

The technological developments of which we taste the fruit today would not have been possible without the growth of knowledge and technical skills of the past few centuries. While in ancient times content to be learned was relatively little, today's complex societies require much more complex knowledge, and thus even more intense education. The days are gone when the village whiz knew just about everything, and younger generations learned from the village wise men. We live in the era of specialization. Whether it is a good thing or not, this changed the nature of learning. It also changed the role of "teachers". For one thing, no teacher can know everything available today, as perhaps the village wise of ancient times could master with the available knowledge of their time. Fortunately modern ICT tools allows for access to huge knowledge sources.

There are certain aspects that are much better handled with modern information and communication technologies. Early 21st century universities are under pressure, and there is much debate about which direction to follow with ideas such as multiverses and MOOCs. What is clear though, and what has been clear for at least half a century, is that educational technology is a more efficient tool for certain aspects of teaching than traditional tools. A village, or even a city, might have a large bricks and mortar library. But the stock of such a library can never compare with having the largest library in the history of humankind – the internet - literally available at one's fingertips. Surely such access facilitates the potential for self-empowerment. Combine this access with the facilitating role of a domain expert – the teacher – and human potential might be released, thus empowering the individual achieving such learning, who in turn will have an effect on those with whom the learner has contact.

Without increasing the pace of education in the poorer and less developed regions of the world, inequities such as the divides of many forms will remain for many generations. To improve the quality of life of the majority of the global population who are still disenfranchised requires a massive educational effort. Although ICT is neither a magic spoon, nor the final remedy, it is still the most efficient and best tool we have to facilitate mass education.

> Knowledge is power. Or put differently, the power of knowledge improves the human condition. ICT is the most effective means to achieve knowledge. Hence ICT as educational tool is essential for empowerment, especially so for lesser developed communities.

Using some poetic license, the common saying (of which the origin is unknown, and has been attributed to a various people, including a variety of ancient Chinese wise men): "Give a man a fish, and you feed him for a day; show him how to catch fish, and you feed him for a lifetime", can be rephrased "Give a man money, and tomorrow he needs more. Give him knowledge and he can develop himself and make his own money."

Jacques Steyn
Professor, Head of the School of Information Technology, Monash South Africa

Fundamentals of Education and ICT for Development

Pär-Ola Zander, Aalborg University
poz@hum.aau.dk

Marianne Georgsen, VIA University College
mage@viauc.dk

Introduction

It seems certain that the educational systems across the world will be very different in the future compared to today, as will their technical support. Many coinciding trends are to blame or praise for this; an increasing number of learners, the deregulation and privatisation of educational institutions, and the globalisation of opportunities for learning. And not least: A ready stream of new technologies often claiming to be the solutions to the latest challenges. This is being widely discussed by academic communities throughout the world.

However, discussing how learning activities are changing is one thing; another is to take a stance as to what it could and should change into. This question is closely related to a discussion about development of society in general. The purpose of this book is to provide a space for articulation of *where* information and technology (ICT) can take learning and educational activity - in a global context. Very few recent books concentrate on this. The issue can often be fruitfully addressed at the local level and within the context of a given organisation or network. Several of the chapters in this volume discuss the issue of ICT in education in specific interventions. The authors invite us to think about issues of theory, method, stakeholders, and the change of learning activities and education in general.

However, a discussion of the direction in which change should occur in order to be desirable necessitates some notions on what development is, and what education can do for development. A second question is what role ICT plays in development, which is the focal question of the young research field of ICT4D (information and communication technology for development). We do not think these issues can be exhaustively dealt with here (this has been dealt with in more depth elsewhere, see Unwin, 2009; Walker, 2006; Willis, 2005). Here we outline some existing stances towards development and technology to which the contributions to this volume can be related. It should be noted that all authors do not relate in the same way - we will return to this at the end of this chapter.

What is the Goal of Development?
The notion of development has been addressed by a very wide range of think-

ers, ranging from philosophy ("has humankind developed, or does it essentially stay the same, despite superficial change?"), to developmental psychology ("how do cognitive functions develop in interaction with the environment?"). This also relates to other concepts of change, evolution, progress, etc. However, initially, we will concentrate on the research discourses of development studies, pedagogy and informatics as ICT4D research intersects with all these approaches. We will now disentangle the various goals of development; if development is a process, then what possible goals does it pursue?

Much ICT4D research is funded by donor agencies that also fund sub-areas of development studies (of economics, health, agriculture, etc.), and this is one of several reasons why the development research discourse exerts a strong influence on the theorisation of development. A very common way to theorise development in this discourse is still to point to an increase in the Gross Domestic Product (GDP) and variants of this[1]. In the GDP approach, development is thus made synonymous with economic development. This approach is entrenched in current governance, development and aid politics, and in research funding programmes. This remains so, despite heavy critique from large parts of academia and in the media as well as increasing political dissatisfaction. Even when alternative measures are preferred, the infrastructure for obtaining the data is made for GDP, and it will be used as a proxy for other indicators (Morse, 2004). The defence of the GDP approach is arguably founded on the premise that economic progress may not, admittedly, be the only aspect of development. However, the following points count in favour of using economic progress as a parameter for measuring a well-developed society:

1. It is relatively easy to measure, and therefore development studies (and ICT4D) can get a solid empirical basis;
2. It is relatively easy to govern through various redistribution interventions;
3. Especially in the poorest areas, an increase in economic prosperity will generally also result in improvements in other areas of life.

Nevertheless, the economic approach to development has been both criticised and widened. The United Nations now use the Human Development Index (HDI) as a key measure on development, and the closely associated human development approach as its general approach, originating from the work of Nobel laureate Amartya Sen, amongst others (Haq, 1995; Sen, 2001). The HDI adds two aspects to that of economy: a long and healthy life, and knowledge. The latter is operationalised into adult literacy and the enrolment ratio in primary, secondary and tertiary education, and life expectancy. This index leads to a measure which is broader and can capture more nuances of human life. Although GDP largely correlates with HDI when comparing the developmental levels of countries, some differences are also manifest; e.g. Equatorial Guinea is economically well-developed but relatively underdeveloped according to HDI; in Cuba, the situation is the reverse (UNDP, 2011).

Other alternative approaches to development exist, although they are found

---

[1] Recently, e.g. UN and many other bodies have switched to the concept of Gross National Income (GNI), and there are also multiple other measures, national and capita-based.

in the periphery of the main debate. The Gross National Happiness (GNH) approach from Bhutan deserves to be mentioned because of its unusual merging of Buddhism and sanctioning from a national state (Bates, 2009). It is interesting as an example of a development approach whose foundation lies not in a Western tradition but in Buddhist philosophy. Focusing on happiness rather than income as the overall measure places an even stronger emphasis on non-material values than the HDI approach. When operationalised, however, its focus on happiness becomes similar, in many ways, to the human development approach (Christensen, 2011).

It is also instructive for the understanding of development to study its critics. This is, however, marginalised in the present ICT4D discussions. Although not endorsed by any authors in this book, the anti-theses to development are also relevant. One primitivist position is to point to the virtues of life and society in the Stone Age through paleontological anthropology (Zerzan, 1994) and thus question if modern (Western) civilisation has actually developed or merely changed. Another position agrees that change is indeed happening, but probably or perhaps even inescapably towards climate disasters and the breakdown of civilisation (Jensen, 2006). To this can be added scepticism towards equating partial improvements in society with improvements at large. Undeniably, within the last century, humanity has experienced enormous technological progress. But taking into account all war atrocities, environmental disasters and social problems of the same century, it is difficult to say that humanity has developed on e.g. the ethical or organisational level. Such aspects of development are often obscured by technological and intellectual development (Keohane, 1982).

Although the "anti-developmentalists" have not convinced us to abandon the research program of ICT4D, it is also true that numerous examples of naïve development research have been seen. Misguided replacements of some knowledge systems of indigenous tribes, with the implementation of modern ways of living and technological support that fits modern life but not the knowledge of the indigenous tribe is one such example (Rodil, Winschiers-Theophilus & Jensen, 2012). Primitivist and postmodernist perspectives may serve as watchdogs for this type of simplistic ICT4D projects.

Postmodern perspectives come in at least two variants. One emphasises local knowledge and is sceptical towards the large-scale re-engineering of societies. Easterly (2007) can be taken as a representative of this position (sometimes characterised as postmodern development). Adherents to this position may try to advance development on a micro scale, without assuming knowledge about the macro processes of "development". This may include development in which the subjects of research have co-influence on development and where different research projects have different notions of development, without this being a sign of the immaturity of the research field or the quality of the research projects. If Easterly's reasoning is taken one step further and considered in line with postmodern developments in other fields, the measure on development itself can be more locally constructed, rather than being seen as having a universal, context-independent meaning.

Another version cautions that development has been institutionalised; that development actors ultimately depend on the unequal relationship between the North and the South for their existence. Furthermore, the language of development may be loaded by language created under the era of colonialism (Gardner & Lewis, 1996). This perspective urges us either to maintain a sceptical stance towards development, or at least to closely examine the underlying language, power and production of knowledge that are intertwined with a given notion of development (Escobar, 2012). To take an example from within education, consider who decides that an actor possesses deep knowledge within a field. Knowledge becomes acknowledged when certified by universities, and the certification is stronger, the more prestigious the university is. Projects that strive to improve universities of the South without addressing the system in which knowledge becomes recognised may actually legitimise the power structures of the knowledge economy.

A related critique of the conceptualisation of development comes from post-colonialism, post-development and more recently and specifically, post-colonial computing (Irani et al, 2010). In post-colonial computing, the mainstream development paradigm is depicted as reductionist. Poverty, overpopulation, pollution, etc., are reduced to problems to which there is a technical solution (better markets, education on contraception and clean technology), rather than seeing these phenomena as endemic of a global system. The post-colonial computing paradigm also comes with awareness that the funding agencies of development have historically been aligned with the dominant actors that form the relations between the North and the South (i.e. market actors, the IMF, etc.). So, not only should we be careful when engaging in furthering development. We should also examine our assumptions and not too soon take for granted that technology is the solution, or that the donor agent funding our research in case of a conflict of interest is actually siding with the researchers' agenda. And when this is not the case, what then is the strategy?

This disentanglement of the various stances on development is an invitation to readers to think about the contributions in this book as well as their own ICT4D practice, and how and if they are transcending the challenges of primitivism and postmodernism. The chapters of this book mostly concentrate on particular cases, rather than spend a great deal of space explicating their positions as regards development. As in much intellectual activity, the definition of development is not a step that is made once and for all. Subsequent questions follow, all of them with complex political, theoretical, and methodological considerations: Should priority be given to reducing poverty in order to decrease global inequality? Or should priority be given to maximising development, even if inequality is the consequence? What if the post-developmentalists are right and development cannot be directed on a global scale? Will this mean that the results of interventions are impossible to predict, and even assess, beyond their local impact? This is not the place to elaborate on these issues; we are merely noting them for future reflection before proceeding to zoom in on technology and its relation to development.

ICT and Development

Now we will sketch the way in which we see that ICT relates to development. When practicing teachers, policy-makers and learners engage in learning activities, they draw on a number of resources. What, in this regard, are ICT's distinct properties? Why should this be discussed as distinct from other classes of resources or infrastructures?

- ICT can standardise human practice (Walsham & Sahay, 2006). So-called Enterprise Resource systems (e.g. SAP R/3) render report and production more globally uniform. Standard procedures can be sent out digitally. Remote surveillance can be used to "correct" unwanted behaviour. This has vast economic and cultural consequences. ICT can deliver and manipulate information - and often ubiquitously. The availability of a vast body of information through a smartphone is made possible through the combination of internet, telecommunications, search engines and cheap storage.
- Computation and simulation enable predictions and learning about many issues. These have been put into use to improve health, economic growth, and well-being in many areas.
- ICT can interconnect individuals at a previously unseen scale (just like railroads once did). It enables people who were previously unconnected to align their interests (Walsham & Sahay, 2006) and cooperate for a variety of purposes; intellectual exchange, business, love, political matters, etc. While not everyone agrees that it is always development in the right direction, actors use it to change the present organisation in and of society. In education, e-learning and blended learning are the most salient examples, but there are many other ways to interconnect people for learning and development, e.g. social networks, online directories, and location-based services that raise awareness about potential peers for information exchange, to name a few. And the question of getting access to information technology in order to do all this should not be overlooked (see also Purushothaman, this volume).
- Aesthetic experiences are enabled that can be used for learning or pleasure.

Furthermore, ICT may not be inherently unique, but has nonetheless reshaped the development and will reshape it in new areas:

- The ICT industry has transformed several economies (India, South Korea to name some notable examples), and has risen to become one of the most important sectors of the industry.
- Its convergence with entertainment and its diffusion and adoption has changed everyday life fundamentally in the developed world; consider the number of hours people in the developed world spend interacting with TV, computers, and mobile technology. Finally, as a design material it is very flexible. Jonas Löwgren has coined it "the material without properties" (Löwgren & Stolterman, 2004). This means that when we are faced with a new challenge, this material is so "open-ended" in its appearance and in its social aspects and content that it constitutes a candidate solution, at least partial, to any challenge. This becomes a tremendous challenge when theorising ICT for change.

Any one-page description of ICT and development will be bound to contain some simplifications and omissions. Nevertheless, our main point comes across: ICT plays an integral part when it comes to understanding development and is not a peripheral phenomenon. However, it is also complex to understand ICT theoretically. And it is important to emphasise that although ICT has a huge potential for development, it is not easy. Although initially successful, very few ICT programs have proven to be sustainable - especially in Africa (Kleine & Unwin, 2009). The challenges have perhaps even been a reason for ICT4D to establish itself as a research field, worthy of enquiry.

In the following, we will focus on the role of education for development, and among other things outline a number of challenges for education in developing countries in particular. We look briefly at primary education and secondary education; and – partly as a consequence of our research focus - we elaborate some on the topic of higher education. In a discussion about education in developing countries, adult education plays an important role as well, since a large proportion of the adult population has none or very little formal training or education. Although we wish to highlight this important difference between educational systems in developing and developed countries, we do not deal with the topic of adult learners in particular in the following.

How Primary Education Contributes to Development

Primary education is the first stage in the formal educational system. It is commonly defined as the 6 first years of schooling, but it varies greatly from nation to nation, sometimes ranging up to 10 years. From a development perspective, primary education:

- Is perceived as central. The United Nations' well-known Millennium Development Goals (MDGs) and later UN policy documents identify primary education as an important constituent of the goals; in fact, most of the MDGs can be addressed through the improvement of education.
- Supplies citizens with basic skills required for functioning in adult life, which increases personal freedom (in the sense of realising one's potential).
- Contributes to economic development on the secondary level. Basic skills (reading/writing) are required for accessing information and innovation, and spreading this further. Historically, this has been a common argument for focusing on primary education, even if it is also challenged: "...economic growth is positively related to the (1960) starting level of average years of adult male school attainment at secondary and higher levels but is insignificantly related to years of primary attainment (...) there is a strong effect of secondary and higher schooling on the diffusion of technology." (World Bank, 2005).
- Creates "social cohesion" in the sense of community and belonging to society. Primary education helps citizens understand their own roles in society so that they can understand where they can contribute (Selinger, 2009). Strictly speaking, this is not development, but an important means for avoiding regression.
- Is a prerequisite for many other functions for development that require

literacy (e.g. critical thinking, democratic consciousness, participation in public debate, problem solving, etc.).
- Is directly addressed in HDI measurements by adult literacy and knowledge.
- Is currently placing some groups in society at a disadvantage globally. It must be noted that in developing countries, less than 2% of the children with disabilities go to school (Lynch & Casely-Halford, 2003). This means that they are excluded from the development processes offered by school. Education will have only an indirect developmental impact on disabled people in developing countries - until they are included.

Merely attending education is not enough. UNESCO (2004) reports that as many as 60% of the children attending basic education do not acquire basic literacy or numeracy skills. UNESCO points to the fact that huge challenges persist (UNESCO, 2004) with better motivation, resources, teaching content and teacher skills development as candidate solutions. There is consensus that ICT can be useful for educational reform and for learning in primary education (Trucano, 2005). Some brief examples include multimodal modes of instruction, eBooks, Internet search for information rather than the use of physical resources as tools for self-directed learning, and the incorporation of digital educational content into existing teaching materials.

However, Selinger argues that basic needs must be fulfilled before ICT and educational reform are considered. Basic needs include "access to clean water, availability of basic shelter, personal safety, health of students, affordable costs for schooling, and sufficient and well-trained teachers" (Selinger, 2009, p. 217-218). This means that educational change with ICT has no relation to development in failed states or disadvantaged communities where life is too full of struggle for basic needs. However, with a growing divide between rural and urban areas in developing countries, the situation is becoming more complex. In many developing countries you find use of ICT in primary education in urban areas, despite the fact that schools in rural areas often are ill-equipped and lack the very basics to function properly.

How Secondary Education Contributes

Secondary education is the schooling that takes place after primary education. In some places this starts after 6 years of schooling, in others after 10 years. It precedes higher education, and thus occupies a middle position. With regard to development, in many ways it can be seen as continuation of the primary education described in the last section. It cannot always, however, be managed in the same way, and technologies do not necessarily work equally well:
- Secondary education is more heterogeneous than primary education
- The secondary education curriculum changes more often than that of primary education
- Secondary education generally consists of a smaller number of larger schools
- Its managers and teachers have undergone longer training and are more

specialised
- Secondary education is generally recommended to be more privately funded than primary education (World Bank, 2005)

Secondary education is more important for school-to-work transition. Some secondary education is vocational in nature, and needs to be more in tune with the immediate needs of the labour market, although the distribution of responsibilities between employers and the educational system is a complicated issue.

So far, investments in primary education have resulted in an equal distribution among the citizens of the returns. With secondary education, asymmetric distribution can be observed; the societal elite as a group gets a larger share of the returns. (World Bank, 2005)

Educational technology can catalyse all developmental functions stated so far. Networks for information exchange between employers and teachers can be created. Standardised course content (SCORM is one established standard example) enables institutions to share digital material and therefore keep costs at a reasonable level - even if the labour market is experiencing shifting demands. Many students can still not afford to use built-in cameras in smart phones for filming their daily work and then analysing it in school but will be able to do so with shrinking production costs. Distance education can to some degree mitigate the inequalities noted in distribution, if it is introduced to the more rural (and also often poorer) areas. Even if we have not explicated how this works in detail, or described the challenges these initiatives will face, we hope we have made our point clear. However, the shift in context means that there will be differences in the specific tools applied.

This discussion of secondary education is relatively short. The developmental functions of higher education that are described in the following section apply to a lesser degree also to secondary education[2]. The developmental policy discourse in SE is more complex as it features a "double discourse" of both primary education and higher education. In summary, secondary education derives its legitimacy mainly from its *total* contribution *both* to basic literacy *and*, in more complex terms, to higher education.

The Contribution to Development by Higher Education

Higher education is much more heterogeneous than the other main types of education. Some of them encompass a multitude of roles, aptly called 'multiversities' by Kerr (2001). 'University' is, we propose, an empty concept. The first question must be: What type of university? This is perhaps even clearer when considering the empirical basis for talking about what a university is and is not. Universities as a phenomenon are so heterogeneous that they are hard to even count. It is difficult to even discover an examination tool that can reliably tell

---

[2] This "continuum view" of secondary education is of course a simplification that obscures some idiosyncrasies of secondary education. Secondary education is more efficient than other types of education in reducing infant mortality (World Bank, 2005). A second interesting idiosyncrasy is that the connection to the community is arguably at its weakest in secondary school years. Secondary pupils are more likely to have their own culture (World Bank, 2005). Primary Education pupils are part of their parent's culture, and higher education students are (as a group), to a larger extent, in the process of finding their own places in the surrounding culture, with jobs and family.

us how many universities exist in the world. The main ranking lists (e.g. THE, QS[3]) solve this problem by subjectively choosing a subset in most (but not all) countries. (E.g. in 2012, QS did not even include the Nepali Tribhuvan university, despite the fact that this is one of the largest universities in the world). It is easy to grasp the variety this concept represents by thinking about interesting extremes within higher education, such as:

- Naropa University in the United States: strong orientation towards spiritual development and personal self-realisation rather than traditional research preparation.
- Kaboi Technical Training Institute: vocational education at the higher education level with no research ambitions and an emphasis on manual work, entrepreneurship and vocational skills.
- Almeda University: Issues non-accredited "university" degrees with controversial pedagogies or means of issuing degrees (some would say fraud)
- Danish Menighedsfakultetet [Lutheran School of Theology]: Officially accredited in 2012[4]; no postgraduate education; very narrow in scope; dedicated mission; 70 students.
- Quaid-e-Azam University in the 1960s: Only master & PhD education in "strategic" subjects such as theoretical physics, and an elitist orientation.
- Tribhuvan university: hundreds of thousands of students and distributed all over the country.
- European Humanities University: Transnational university with a mission to provide liberal arts education and democratic values to Belarus, against the will of the Belarus regime.

This heterogeneity complicates the discussion of the role of higher education in development. The mission of higher education is often described to be that of facilitator of the spread of innovation, and a component in the skill set required for innovation. Arguably, this is not always the main function, and we must strive not to restrict our thinking to the usual examples (high tech start-ups, new practitioner procedures that save lives). Universities are often claimed to be drivers in economic transformation, but empirical research does not indisputably put universities as significant players in such a position. Brennan et al (Brennan, King & Lebeau, 2004) conducted a multiple-case study of the role of universities in countries undergoing radical transformations. The study largely showed that if the universities played a role at all, it was often a question of them following the transformation rather than being anticipatory and proactive.

This may have several consequences. One is to say that many modes of university organisation are irrelevant and a few are relevant (e.g. so-called Triple Helix systems). Another is that research should rather focus on non-economic issues. In any case, it is hard to recommend investment in higher education unconditionally.

---

3 Quacquarelli Symonds, a company which publishes a widely recognised ranking list of universities. THE (Times Higher Education) publishes similar lists.
4 Not by Denmark, though, but by Great Britain.

Even if the university is no multiversity, its dominant functions may still be to:
- Supply a qualified and adaptable labour force, including scientists, professionals, technicians, teachers, civil servants and business leaders
- Provide capacity to access existing stores of global knowledge and adapt this for local use
- Actively support, perhaps even lead, innovation, beyond mere dissemination
- Promote social innovation rather than innovation, e.g. to provide foundations for democracy (Dirckinck-Holmfeld & Segura, 2010; Walker, 2006).

The university also has more equivocal functions like:
- Socialisation into the ruling elite, with knowledge of little practical value.
- Political functions, both subversive (student revolutions) and preserving the ruling order. Universities are often praised in festive speeches as the Providers of 'protected spaces' for critical debate, and rightly so. But history is also full of examples of universities that have acted as supporters of shaky regimes as well as places where opposition could be vented (Brennan et al., 2004). And 'protected spaces' has sometimes acted as birth grounds for ethnical hatred (in DR Congo and Nigeria) (Brennan et al., 2004). Some universities are more beneficial for development than others (Castells, 1994). However, even if a university is suboptimal as regards a given development paradigm, it can still promote development in *some* dimensions. For instance, a university in China may not be very active in the promotion of democracy, but may still be very important for the professional skills needed in the society, and thus contribute to the capabilities of its region.

A further complication is that higher education is hard to understand as an isolated system within national borders. Individuals who receive higher education and then move abroad clearly diminish the return of investments in higher education for some countries. And especially in the lower end of the LDCs (Least Developed Countries) and/or areas of conflict, it is probably fair to argue that these countries rely more on foreign than domestic higher education. The possibility of distance learning, where Massive Open Online Courses (MOOCs) are the latest development, enables people who would normally not be able to take part in university activities to follow courses. This makes it difficult to analyse higher education at the national level. Universities also contribute to the process of internationalisation and thus transform every culture by providing a bridge between all cultures; by their very nature they seem to defy national borders. The resemblance between 'university' and 'universal' is no coincidence.

The complications described in this section may cause the reader to doubt if universities have a strong role within development, beyond that of spinoff companies and the forming of bright administrators. However, the historical evidence of the relevance of universities to development is clear. Universities have often been a key tool for governmental societal transformation. Two historically prominent examples will suffice:

1. The land-grant colleges in the USA. It is also worth noting that in the 1850s, the U.S. emerged as a major power in terms of production, but was far away from its position today in academic matters. It greatly supported broader access to higher education, and to a liberal arts education that escaped the shortcomings of world-detached ivory tower studies as well as overly instrumentalist institutions that reduce higher education to professional development. Several of the land-grant colleges later rose to become globally famous prestigious universities. 2. Japan underwent a radical transformation in the late 1800s through the so-called Meiji modernisation. This also included radical reform of the educational system, which became a strong tool for unifying the country and nurtured a spirit of ultra-nationalism. Its educational objective also reached beyond economic or individual development; it aimed to create sufficient numbers of academics to run the modern state bureaucracy and produce and develop the military technology necessary to counter the threat of imperialism from Western powers.

It has been reported that universities are often not very well-functioning in many developing countries. The UNESCO Science report (UNESCO, 2010) points to the fact that many countries have universities which are very teaching-oriented, and that research and development unfold in other places. The report points to the many Arab universities and Asian developing countries like Nepal, in which this situation is prevalent at the national level. In India, the Indian Institutes of technology (IIT) are known as India's echelons of academic excellence, but they are actually very teaching-intensive and less productive of research (UNESCO, 2010). Although few people would argue that universities should be the only places where new knowledge is generated, the innovation model of universities needs to be better understood. The problem may rather lie in the relation between higher education and society than within a particular university (Sanchez, this volume). For instance, it is interesting to note in Latin America that although the countries there have an acceptable scientific sector that produces economically valuable knowledge, industry demands very little local knowledge and in general has a non-innovative economy (UNESCO, 2010).

As higher education is so heterogeneous, it is difficult to make theoretically powerful statements of what ICT can do to support development in general. Nor is it likely that higher education will be more standardised because of the increased use of ICT - rather it enables new organisational forms, leading to diversity. It is, we argue, often better to discuss at a concrete, case-specific level, but this does not relegate the relation between ICT and development to secondary importance. Many current governments channel large sums of money into the digitalisation of higher education. The results of these investments are important. Change projects involving ICT are generally high risk projects (Rizzuto & Reeves, 2007), and knowledge about the utilisation of educational technology would reduce risk.

Furthermore, it is clear to us that higher education ecology has the prospect of future radical change. The present mode of organising higher education is challenged with a massive increase in student numbers, a focus on innovation, globalisation, competing ways of pursuing knowledge outside of the formal system, and privatisation. Global distance education, educational technologies and new pedagogies enabled by ICT cannot be neglected when trying to understand this change. Also, beyond single case studies, higher education and ICT4D have been studied very little as compared to primary and secondary education.

Education is Systemic

The discussion so far should not give the impression that the levels of education are three factors, each of which contributes to development. The resource distribution is a case in point. Currently, the investments are generally allocated in this way: Primary education receives many resources, secondary receives the least, and higher education occupies the middle position (Bloom (2003) in World Bank, 2005). This lack of resources combined with the increased throughput from primary education has caused secondary education to become the bottleneck in many developing countries (Polgreen, 2007; Unesco, 2006, p. 11), creating a lack of skilled workforce and low diffusion of innovations. The reason is that there are many primary education lobbyists, as well as university lobbyists, who insist that society needs research and the highest possible intellectual debate, but secondary education is bereft of such lobbyism (World Bank, 2005). The report continues by stating that "historically, the countries that have experienced the most rapid and sustainable increases in educational attainment, as well as outstanding economic performance, have pursued balanced upgrading of the primary, secondary, and tertiary levels of education" (p. 18, ibid). Of course, some resource, activity and curriculum coordination should take place between the different levels of education. And a neglected research topic seems to be studies that look for signs of relative overinvestment and underinvestment in education.

Furthermore, education is a very open system related to learning and innovation. The concept of Triple Helix has attained much interest, first in the west, and has today reached a certain level of maturity also in the developing world (Saad & Zawdie, 2011). The idea is that the responsibility for innovation lies not solely in one sector, e.g. the industry, but in the collaboration between state, higher education and government.

Particularly the higher education sector is often engaged in inter-institutional collaboration, and is not confined to national competitive advantage. Inter-institutional collaboration can be very fruitful when involving several partners in multiple countries (Gregory, 2009). The HISP project, reported by Gregory is a very good example of successful capacity development, where a health informatics program was implemented across countries and interrelated with the development of information systems in a complex model of inter-institutional and inter-sector collaboration. Cooperation between universities and across the North and South is a very interesting area for changing education for development.

The openness of the educational systems, in particular in higher education, and the increasing role of ICT in this, suggest that there is room for approaches that are open to unexpected stakeholders, and which integrate the pedagogical and research levels. Networked learning (e.g. Dirckinck-Holmfeld, Hodgson, & McConnell, 2011; Steeples & Jones, 2002) is such an emerging approach, which we will expand on a little since it is the background of the training of many of the authors of this book. Instead of assuming the constraints of educational approaches, geographical distance and administrative borders, networked learning takes as its mission to overcome this, with technology as a principal candidate solution. This is also a way to overcome the individualist bias; that a lot of learning and development may be located in the (cross-boundary) network, rather than in the individual. It has emerged as an approach of pedagogy and learning design rather than within development studies. Very little is known so far about the way in which networked learning works in practice in developing countries (Munguatosha, Muyinda, & Lubega, 2011), but a few examples exist, with the ELAC project as perhaps the most noticeable forerunner. In the ELAC project, a learning infrastructure was set up, and a number of pilot courses with networked learning underpinnings were carried out in several Central American countries. The project reported a successful organisational uptake of the pedagogical and technological tools of networked learning (Dirckinck-Holmfeld & Illera, 2006).

As the discussion shows, the system of education and its connection to development form a system which becomes complex; perhaps even too complex to change in a 'big planning' approach. We are well aware, however, that we have not yet touched upon a multitude of critical issues, such as life-long learning, informal learning, teacher education, capacity building in general, and the practical de-skilling which education sometimes brings about.

Intervening with Technology in Education

There is scope for interventionism by researchers in all parts of the educational system. Although not dominant, this is a relatively common approach, especially in its action research variants (Zeichner, 2001). However, interventionism is somewhat rare within ICT4D - somewhat surprising, given the change-oriented agenda of this particular approach (Walsham & Sahay, 2006). Interventionism is an integral part of development studies and related approaches. Yet its nature is seldom explicated and perhaps not even very well understood by the researchers themselves (Koponen, 2004)[5]. The chapters of this book thus stand somewhat out from the mainstream of ICT4D research by either being interventionist, or at least by creating theory that easily lends itself, to interventionist research, or serves as the foundation of this. For the most part, the chapters' stance can be characterised as placing emphasis on the agency that can be found locally, and we try to analyse the reasons why agency is relocated to the West when this happens in projects. They are not interventions in which a model of instruction or a technology is devised in the West and subsequently deployed and enacted in developing countries. It is often true that a research idea emerges in the west, but it is important that the scope and goals of the project are open to negotiation with the partners, whether they be practitioners or

---

5 At the time of writing, Koponen was the chair of development studies at University of Helsinki.

researchers, so that consensus can be reached about the research objectives and outputs (Fals-Borda & Rahman, 1991). However, we have also provided a complementary view; in this book, Safwat et al actually deal with the straightforward export of the model of a Danish blended learning MBA program. Without uncritically assuming that education is culturally neutral, the authors provide rich empirically based descriptions of the prospects of educational export. We hope that the reader will see this as a starting point for thinking about debates between post-colonial computing and ICT-enabled education. Being interventionist while avoiding the traps of naïve modernism is not easy and it is possible that the methodologies and institutional viewpoints in this book will be regarded as naïve in a decade from now.

Interventionist ICT research in learning and education can be of several types and take place at various levels. On the individual level, it can examine the conditions for the ways in which individuals develop via new use of and practices with ICT. On the meso level, different strategies for reforming an institution of education, and ways in which this interacts through technology are the topics of research. The participatory approach to interventionism can stretch into the design process. An example of this is participatory design, in which users are engaged in co-designing and perhaps even leading the process of the educational technologies that they, or other users, are later to take into use. Here design should be understood broadly, and does not only encompass graphical interface design or new functionality of ICT, but also organisational design, i.e. the envisioning of new work practices, collaborations, and cultural practices - perhaps even on the societal level[6]. The reader may dismiss this as utopian social engineering, and we do not take a position here on the prospects of radical societal change. We merely note that many 'interventionists' have ambitions that go beyond the single organisational context, and that they cannot be assumed to be engaged in social engineering. Engineering evokes connotation of precision and prediction, which design does not evoke. A particularly noteworthy example is complex participatory approaches that combine the development of IT systems with educational programs within areas that are deemed critical for national and international capacity building. The HISP program is such an example. One of its legs consists of the development of a health management information system that keeps track of a variety of patient and staff information and functionality for displaying this[7], and which is today used in many countries. Its other leg is the building up of educational programs within health and information systems. Both legs enjoy mutual synergies and are not only interventionist but also user-involving (Braa & Hedberg, 2002; Gregory, 2009). This is particularly worth mentioning since it is a form of research and interventionist practice that is quite unique to the field of educational change through ICT.

---

6 The prospect of ICT4D that changes society as a whole is really just a specific version of the general debate of the possibility of radical, fundamental change of society within the public discourse of politics and within the human sciences.

7 http://www.dhis2.org

The Structure of the Book

In the previous sections, we have considered key concepts and elements in the research field ICT for development, and more specifically some of the relations we see between development, education and ICT. The introduction is meant to widen the horizon both in terms of theoretical and epistemological perspectives and in terms of scope of the empirical work reported on in many of the following chapters. Potential authors were invited to contribute to the book in the following way:

> "This book is a joint project for members of the research group on ICT for Development at Aalborg University and other interested parties outside our own organisation. The motivation for the book is to document ongoing and completed research within the field of ICT for development, with a specific focus on education, teaching and learning. We welcome conceptual as well as theoretical and empirical contributions".

We are very pleased to present nine chapters of original work, which consider recent developments in the theory, practice and application of ICT for development.

The contributions to the book responded very well to our call for chapters, which asked for contributions dealing with education, teaching and learning. There is also an extensive geographical coverage in the chapters: Studies are reported from Bangladesh, Costa Rica, Denmark, Egypt, Fiji, India, Malaysia, and Vietnam. The introduction above has made it clear that changing education with ICT (for development) is a very big territory to map theoretically as well as through empirical research. The chapters in this volume do not illustrate or discuss all aspects. From the chapters it is evident, however, that the particularity of the cases is very complex, and that they do not always sit easily within an attempt to categorise research systematically into ICT4D, or into specific levels of education. The chapters deal with the following topics (and most chapters deal with more than one topic, allowing them equal priority in their studies):

- Approaches to user involvement and participation in development
- Knowledge and its role in development, particularly in higher education
- Digital literacy and ways of developing it
- Pedagogic approaches
- Learning cultures in globalised education
- Teacher training and education.

We have organised the chapters into three sections:

1. ICT in higher education
2. Approaches to development
3. Learning with ICT

ICT in Higher Education

In this section, Coto, Lykke and Mora present a study on how problem based learning was introduced into the National University of Costa Rica in order to develop students' skills in problem solving. This chapter is followed by a second study from Costa Rica by Camacho, in which the triple helix model is explored as a means of developing ICT education and in turn the entire ICT sector in the country. The third chapter by Safwat, Bygholm and Jæger examines the internationalisation of higher education with blended learning, thus avoiding brain drain and increasing access to the expertise in demand in the South. All chapters are examples of using ICT to develop or even transform the way in which knowledge is produced, with the ambition of changing society.

Approaches to Development

In a way, all chapters would fit into this section, since they all - more or less explicitly – deal with different approaches to development. However, we have chosen to present three chapters which clearly address this issue in this section. The contribution by Khalid and Nyvang is based on empirical work carried out in rural Bangladesh. The chapter presents and discusses the specific methods used to involve local stakeholders in the process of implementing educational technology. This is followed by a Fijian study reported by Chandra and Chandra in which the focus is on the implementation of ICT in primary schools in Fiji. A three-fold approach is proposed in which the organisational level (community, school leadership, teachers), the learning design level (content, pedagogy, and technology), as well as the issues of sustainability are addressed. The third paper in this section (by Zander and Georgsen) discusses how users can be involved in ICT development projects relevant to their own work practices. At University of Dhaka in Bangladesh, a group of administrative workers participated in design workshops, and the authors discuss the scope for participatory approaches in technology development amongst users with no or little education and with an often presumed lack of analytical skills.

Learning with ICT

The final of the three sections presents two papers which deal with ways of learning digital skills or, we might add, ways of using ICT for personal learning. In the first paper by Purushothaman, the theoretical concept of identity (from Wenger's theory on communities of practice) is discussed as a framework for learning to use ICT. An empirical study from an Indian university serves as the background for discussing learning as identity building. Furthermore, this study is the only one in the book to target women only.

The second chapter in this section is by Khan and Kabilan, and this reports on a pedagogical intervention carried out by the first author in a teacher's training program in Malaysia. The students in the program were introduced to digital learning portfolios, and the study shows how these were used both as a personal learning tool as regards ICT in general, and as technique to developing the learning and teaching approach of the students (and future teachers).

References

Bates, W. (2009). Gross national happiness. *Asian-Pacific Economic Literature*, 23(2), 1–16.

Braa, J., & Hedberg, C. (2002). The Struggle for District-Based Health Information Systems in South Africa. *The Information Society*, 18(2), 113–127.

Brennan, J., King, R., & Lebeau, Y. (2004). *The role of universities in the transformation of societies: an international research project: synthesis report*. London: Association of Commonwealth Universities and The Centre for Higher Education Research and Information.

Castells, M. (1994). The university system: Engine of development in the new world economy. In J. Salmi & A. Verspoor (Eds.), *Revitalizing higher education* (pp. 14–40). Oxford: IAU Press.

Christensen, L. K. (2011). Gross National Happiness - a new approach to development? *Unpublished manuscript*.

Dirckinck-Holmfeld, L., Hodgson, V., & McConnell, D. (2011). *Exploring the theory, pedagogy and practice of networked learning*. New York: Springer.

Dirckinck-Holmfeld, L., & Illera, J. (2006). *SP4 Learning approaches - Conceptual framework of the innovative teaching and learning methods* (No. 4). Aalborg, Denmark. http://old.ell.aau.dk/fileadmin/user_upload/documents/research/ELAC/AAU_ELAC_publications/ELAC-SP4-Deliverable-4.1.pdf

Dirckinck-Holmfeld, L., & Segura, O. (2010). ICT and Learning for Development in Latin American Universities. In O. Segura & B. Johnson (Eds.): *Systems of Innovation and Development – Central American perspectives*.

Easterly, W. (2007). *The white man's burden: Why the west's efforts to aid the rest have done so much ill and so little good*. Oxford: Oxford University Press.

Escobar, A. (2012). *Encountering development: The making and unmaking of the third world*. Princeton: Princeton University Press.

Fals-Borda, O., & Rahman,, A. M. (1991). *Action and knowledge: Breaking the monopoly with participatory action research*. London: Apex Press.

Gardner, K., & Lewis, D. (1996). *Anthropology, development, and the post-modern challenge*. London: Pluto Press.

Gregory, J. (2009). A complex model of international and intercultural collaboration in health information systems. In S. Poggenpohl & Sato, K. (Eds.) *Design integrations - research and collaboration* (pp. 247–273). Intellect Ltd.

Haq, M. ul. (1995). *Reflections on human development*. New York: Oxford University Press.

Irani, L., Vertesi, J., Dourish, P., Philip, K., & Grinter, R. E. (2010). Postcolonial computing (p. 1311-1320). ACM Press.

Jensen, D. (2006). *Endgame*. New York: Seven Stories Press.

Keohane, N. (1982). The enlightment idea of progress revisited. In G. Almond, Marvin Chodorow, & R. Pearce (Eds.), *Progress and its discontents* (pp. 21–40). Berkeley: University of California Press.

Kerr, C. (2001). *The uses of the university* (5th ed.). Cambridge, Mass: Harvard University Press.

Kleine, D., & Unwin, T. (2009). Technological Revolution, Evolution and New Dependencies: what's new about ict4d? *Third World Quarterly*, 30(5), p. 1045–1067.

Koponen, J. (2004). Development intervention and development studies. In T. Kontinen (Ed.), *Development intervention - actor and activity perspectives* (pp. 5–14). Helsinki: DTPage Oy.

Löwgren, J., & Stolterman, E. (2004). *Design av informationsteknik: materialet utan egenskaper [design of information technology: The material without properties]*. Lund: Studentlitteratur.

Lynch, P., & Casely-Halford, L. (2003). *A Review of Good Practice in ICT and Special Educational Needs for Africa*. Imfundo KnowledgeBank Initiative. http://www.comminit.com/?q=ict-4-development/node/216802

Morse, S. (2004). *Indices and indicators in development: An unhealthy obsession with numbers?* London: Earthscan.

Munguatosha, G. M., Muyinda, P. B., & Lubega, J. T. (2011). A social networked learning adoption model for higher education institutions in developing countries. *On the Horizon*, 19(4), p. 307–320.

Polgreen, L. (2007). Africa's Storied Colleges, Jammed and Crumbling. *The NY times*. http://www.nytimes.com/2007/05/20/world/africa/20senegal.html?pagewanted=all&_r=0

Rizzuto, T. E., & Reeves, J. (2007). A multidisciplinary meta-analysis of human barriers to technology implementation. *Consulting Psychology Journal: Practice and Research, 59*(3), 226–240.

Rodil, K., Winschiers-Theophilus, H., & Jensen, K. (2012). Enhancing cross-cultural participation through creative visual exploration. In *PDC'12* proceedings (pp. 81–90). Roskilde: ACM Press.

Saad, M., & Zawdie, G. (2011). *Theory and practice of the triple helix system in developing countries: Issues and challenges*. New York: Routledge.

Selinger, M. (2009). ICT in education: Catalyst for development. In T. Unwin (Ed.): *ICT4D - information and communication technology for development* (pp. 206–248). Cambridge: Cambridge University Press.

Sen, A. (2001). *Development as freedom*. Oxford: Oxford University Press.

Steeples, C., & Jones, C. (2002). *Networked learning: Perspectives and issues*. London: Springer.

Trucano, M. (2005). *Knowledge maps: ICT in education*. Washington: World Bank. http://www.infodev.org/en/Publication.8.html

UNDP. (2011). *Human development report 2011: Sustainability and equity: A better future for all*. New York: United Nations.

Unesco. (2006). *Strong foundations: early childhood care and education*. Paris: UNESCO.

UNESCO. (2004). *Education for all: The quality imperative*. Paris: UNESCO.

UNESCO. (2010). *UNESCO science report 2010: The current status of science around the world*. Paris: UNESCO Publishing.

Unwin, T. (2009). Information and communication in development practices. In T. Unwin (Ed.): *ICT4D - information and communication technology for development* (pp. 7–38). Cambridge: Cambridge University Press.

Walker, M. (2006). *Higher education pedagogies: A capabilities approach*. Maidenhead; New York: Society for Research into Higher Education & Open University Press. Retrieved from http://site.ebrary.com/id/10175267

Walsham, G., & Sahay, S. (2006). Research on information systems in developing countries: Current landscape and future prospects. *Information Technology for Development, 12*(1), p. 7–24.

Willis, K. (2005). *Theories and practices of development*. London: Routledge.

World Bank. (2005). *Expanding opportunities and building competencies for young people: a new agenda for secondary education*. Washington: World Bank.

Zeichner, K. (2001). Educational action research. In P. Reason & H. Bradbury (Eds.), *Handbook of action research* (pp. 273–284). London: Sage Publications.

Zerzan, J. (1994). *Future primitive: And other essays*. Brooklyn, New York: Autonomedia.

Part I

ICT in Higher Education

Developing the Qualifications of the ICT Workforce Through Problem-based Learning

Mayela Coto, Universidad Nacional
mcoto@una.ac.cr

Sonia Mora, Universidad Nacional
smora@una.ac.cr

Marianne Lykke, Aalborg University
mlykke@hum.aau.dk

Abstract

The ICT sector has an important role in the development of Costa Rica, and consists of a mix of multinational and local companies. Such development requires a large workforce related to computer science and informatics, with skills in the areas of problem solving, team work, mathematics, business administration, and foreign languages.

While computer engineering have a tradition of deductive teaching which is strong in Costa Rica, studies show that problem-based, inductive teaching is a preferable alternative. This chapter presents a case study where the School of Informatics at the National University of Costa Rica analyzed and tried out how a problem-based learning approach (PBL) may contribute in developing student skills to real-life problem solving. The project used a design-based research methodology and gradually introduced PBL in a sequence of five programming courses with the purpose to examine and evaluate how PBL can be used to develop the desired real-life problem-solving skills.

The results show that the process of implementing PBL is not straightforward. The alignment of current curricula with deductive teaching methods is very strong, and inductive approaches require significant changes in the mindset of faculty and students. The results also show that the PBL approach has the potential to reduce failure rates, but is needed to consider carefully some key issues if we want to help develop in computer engineering students the skills the country needs

Introduction

When we started writing this chapter, we considered the concept of "development". What does it mean, and in terms of what indicators should we describe Costa Rica as a developing country? Because of our backgrounds, values and culture, our general understanding of development is based on a humanistic approach. For us, it is not possible to understand a human on the basis of economics alone. In that sense, our concept of development focuses on people and on providing them with acceptable minimum living conditions.

The Human Development Index (HDI) has the explicit purpose of changing the focus of development from national income accounting to people-centered policies. In this sense, development is considered more than the GNP growth; it is "a process of enlarging people's choices, to live a long and healthy life, to be educated and to have access to resources needed for a decent standard of living" (Nielsen, 2011; UNDP, 1990). Due to this multivariate approach, we have selected the HDI system in order to discuss and reflect on the concept of development in this chapter.

In terms of the HDI, Costa Rica is a developing country, belonging to the group of High Human Development Countries with a HDI of 0.773. The country ranks in the 62th position out of 187 worldwide. In regional terms, this index is above the average of 0.758 for countries in the high human development group and also above the average of 0.741 for countries in Latin America and the Caribbean (UNDP, 2012).

In the last decades the ICT sector has had an important role in the development of the country. At present Costa Rica is the fourth largest exporter of technology worldwide, according to data from the Costa Rican Investment Promotion Agency (CINDE, 2011b). The exports of high-technology products represented 41% of its total exports in 2009. For the period of 2011-2012, Costa Rica ranked #1 in Latin America for the Foreign Direct Investment (FDI) and Technology Transfer components of the Global Competitiveness Index (GCI). Multinational companies such as Intel, Hewlett Packard, Microsoft, Fujitsu, Sykes, Amazon, Oracle, Cisco, AvVenta, Amazon, Convergys, Dell, and IBM have operations and offices in Costa Rica (CINDE Costa Rica, 2011a). In addition, a growing number of local companies have been established to provide ICT products and services worldwide (Mata, Matarrita, & Pinto, 2012).

There are many reasons for the increasing interest in investing in Costa Rica; one of them is the investment that the country has made in education as part of its development strategy, believing firmly in the key role played by this indicator on competitiveness and development (Villalobos & Monge-González, 2011). The Costa Rican government is required to allocate at least 8% of the country's GDP to education, which has brought significant benefits to the country. Through the years, it has allowed the creation of a skilled workforce. Other factors are a reduction of taxes and trade barriers of technological products and a solid foreign trade policy. Both of them have created very good conditions for attracting high-tech foreign investment (FDI) (Villalobos & Monge-González, 2011).

It is clear that the growing number of multinational and local companies in the ICT sector required a large qualified workforce. Costa Rican universities produce highly qualified individuals as well as entrepreneurs especially in high technology areas (CINDE, 2011c). However, currently the country is facing challenges responding to these new demands. These challenges are in terms of the supply of ICT workers (Mata, Matarrita, & Pinto, 2012), and in terms of skills development (Monge& González, 2007; Villalobos &Monge-González, 2011).

According to Mata, Matarrita and Pinto (2012), the growing number of multinational and local companies in the ICT sector has provoked a deficit of ICT skilled workers in particular in careers related to computer science and informatics. Their study on the demand and supply of ICT workers in the period 2007-2009 reveals a tight labor market for this sector. Regarding the qualification of the workforce, Monge and González (2007), relying on a study conducted by Cespedes and González (2002), reveal a low level of satisfaction of the companies with employees' skills in the areas of problem solving, science and mathematics, business administration, and foreign languages. The authors conclude that a better way to respond to the demands of the ICT sector is creating more dynamic curricula and strengthening relationships between universities and companies to jointly establish the priorities for professional education.

The Costa Rican government continues to establish aggressive policies to attract foreign direct investment and to demand to the universities to react quickly and demonstrate that their curricula contribute to graduate professionals with abilities to meet the needs of this growing ICT sector. In particular, they are focusing on careers within computer science, computer engineering, informatics, systems engineering and related areas.

The School of Informatics at the Universidad Nacional has decided to address this challenge by a project that analyzes and tries out how a problem and project-based learning approach (PBL) can contribute in developing student skills in real-life problem solving. This question is investigated together with the challenge of reducing dropout and failure rates, which are, in particular, very high in programming courses. By reducing these rates the school aims at increasing the number of ICT graduates per year. These assumptions about the feasibility and usefulness of problem-based and project-based learning are examined in a case study with the following research questions:

1. How can a problem-based and project-based pedagogical (PBL) approach contribute in computer engineering curricula with the purpose of developing student skills in real-life problem solving, reducing dropout and failures rates?
2. How can this pedagogical approach be implemented in computer engineering curricula with the purpose of developing student skills in real-life problem solving and reducing dropout and failures rates, and does it work?

The case study involves an educational intervention in five programming courses, and it takes place through four semesters. The project has the support of the Office of the Vice-president for Academic Affairs as a pilot project at UNA, and it is expected that its results can be disseminated to other disciplinary areas.

This work presents a summary of the findings of the first two cycles of this intervention. The chapter is organized in eight sections. Section 2 presents a brief description of problem-based and project-based learning and some experiences at the university level. Section 3 introduces the methodology of the study. The analysis of the context and the design of the educational intervention are discussed in section 4, and the results from two cycles of intervention are presented in section 5 and section 6. Section 7 contains reflections on lessons learned and outlines future work, and section 8 presents final conclusions. An early version of the context analysis and initial design solution has previously been published in Spanish in (Coto, Mora & Lykke, 2012).

Problem-based and Project-based Learning: An Inductive Approach to Teaching

In order to effectively develop the new set of skills demanded by the ICT sector, we need to change the teaching. In computer engineering, teaching has traditionally been deductive (Prince & Felder, 2006), meaning that faculty presents a theme through a lecture which sets the general principles, shows illustrative examples, offers students practical work on similar applications, and then tests their ability to do the same kind of reasoning through exams. This approach is very common at Costa Rican universities. However, studies establish that a preferable alternative for the learning process is to begin with real-life questions to be answered, a realistic case study or a complex problem that must be resolved in the real world. When students analyze data and try to solve a problem, they create and see a need to know principles, facts, rules and procedures. This need has a strong impact on motivation for learning, because students can understand the purpose of what they are learning. This approach is known as inductive teaching and learning (Prince & Felder, 2006).

According to Prince and Felder (2007; 2006), problem-based learning and project-based learning, among others, are inductive methods of teaching and learning. They are student-centered, have constructivist principles, involve active learning and promote collaborative learning. Both approaches achieve a higher motivation and greater responsibility in the learning process.

Problem-based learning is promoted when students are faced with a real problem as a starting point for the acquisition and integration of new knowledge. Prieto (2006) points out that this approach can improve the quality of learning in universities in different ways as it encourages skills such as: problem solving, decision-making, teamwork and communication skills. It also fosters the development of information searching competences and research management capacity, because students are motivated to understand and investigate a problem before proposing a solution. On the other hand, a project-based approach is based on the idea that students can develop projects that can be applied in real-life as a starting point for their learning process. This means setting aside the traditional teaching and following an approach in which interdisciplinary activities promote and stimulate collaborative and student-centered learning.

The effectiveness of PBL (problem-based learning) approach has been analyzed in different studies in the university context. Dochy, Segres, Van den Bossche and Gijbels (2003) reviewed 43 empirical studies of the effects of PBL in the acquisition of knowledge and the development of problem solving skills. With regard to the first element, the results showed that students acquire more knowledge in short time if they are using a traditional teaching approach.

However, students who have experienced the PBL approach are capable of retaining the knowledge through a longer period of time. In addition, with regard to the acquisition of skills, the effect of the PBL approach was strongly positive, according to the authors.

In the same vein, Prince (2004) concludes that faculty who adopt PBL does not perceive a significant improvement in the academic performance of students, but possibly obtain a positive effect on their attitude towards learning, habits of study, the retention of knowledge and the capacity to apply it, as well as the development of critical thinking and skills to problem solving, particularly if the experience is accompanied by explicit training on these processes.

Nuutila, Törmä and Malmi (2005) observed a significant decrease in the dropout rate in a study on the application of PBL in initial programming courses. The authors state that, in addition to programming, students acquired skills related to collaborative work, independent study and communication. The research study followed the students in advanced programming courses, and data show that the average score of those coming from the PBL course were slightly better than the others. Similarly, Hamalainen(2004)reports findings from a course of theoretical concepts from computer science and concludes that the dropout and failure rates decrease when students follow a PBL approach compared to a conventional one. According to the author, students generate a greater commitment to a PBL course than to a traditional one.

In this way, research in pedagogical approaches identifies PBL as a helpful approach to solve partially some of the problems that students in computer engineering face. According to Mills and Treagust (2003) other inductive approaches as project-based learning may be more appropriate, because it better reflects the professional behavior of a computer engineer. Kolmos(2004)mentions that the latter approach facilitates the development of competences on project management and collaboration, both of them essential for computer engineers.

The use of projects as part of teaching and learning is well known in the area of computer engineering. Usually, they focus on the application of knowledge and, possibly, on the integration of previously acquired knowledge (Mills & Treagust, 2003). However, we should consider that project-based learning presupposes an integral educational strategy and not just a complement in the learning process. When a curriculum is organized in projects, most of the courses are linked with the development of a specific project. There are few examples of study programmes where the entire curriculum is organized in projects. The best example of a curriculum almost completely based on the PBL approach is Aalborg University in Denmark, where projects and courses related to these make up 75% of the curriculum (Mills & Treagust, 2003). Other universities using projects as the main focus of their engineering curricula include Roskilde University in Denmark; TU Berlin, Dortmund, Bremen and Oldenburg in Germany; TU Delft and Wageningen University in the Netherlands; Monash University and Central Queensland University in Australia; and Olin College in the United States (Prince & Felder, 2006).

To obtain the advantages of both the project-based and problem-based approach, they are sometimes used jointly, meaning that a problem is presented as the starting point of the learning process, while problem solving takes place through a project. This is the approach of Aalborg University in Denmark where students have an active role in the construction of knowledge in order to make them feel more committed to their own learning and to ensure high quality standards. This form is known as the PBL model of Aalborg University (Barge, 2010) or Project-Oriented Problem Pedagogy (POPP). Its basic principles are: problem solving as the point of departure of the learning process; projects as the way to address the problem; and integration of theory and practice. The students have a level of influence on the selection of the problem, and how to organize the project. Students collaborate in groups of three or more students with feedback from peers and faculty (Barge, 2010; Kolmos, 2004).

These characteristics are particular useful for computer related careers. The ability to solve problems is vital in computer engineering, and many of the activities of professionals in computer engineering are framed in the development of projects. Furthermore, ACM (2011) identifies a set of skills that future graduates must have, among them, problem solving, effective communication, effective group work, professional responsibility and the capacity of lifelong learning. In the same vein, Hissey (2000) and Mills and Treagust(2003) point out that professionals in computer engineering should be able to cope with continuing technological changes, work in uncertain situations, respond to diverse and sometimes contradictory needs, and understand the social, legal, ethical and cultural aspects involved in the exercise of their professional practice.

In the present research project, we have designed an educational intervention with the goal to investigate how principles from PBL may contribute, to some extent, to the demands of the Costa Rican ICT sector. We take as our point of departure the premise that PBL can help prepare students for real-life problem-solving, increase intrinsic motivation in students, reduce dropout rates, improve professional qualifications, and, in this extent, contribute to increase the number of graduates who are needed in the ICT sector.

Methodology for Implementing the PBL Principles in the Programming Area

In the project, we have chosen to introduce gradually the PBL principles in a sequence of five programming courses (Introduction to Programming, Programming I, Programming II, Programming III and Programming IV).With this objective in mind, a design-based research methodology was selected because it facilitates a framework for the study, design and evaluation of tools and educational strategies (Design-Based Research Collective, 2003). According to Wang and Hannafin (2005), the goal of the methodology is to improve and evaluate educational practices in real contexts. It is a flexible but systematic process guided by theories and design principles sensitive to the context, and it is based on a participatory process of collaboration between researchers and practitioners.

Design-based research can be seen as a model of five phases (Coto, 2010; Reeves, 2006) where participants are part of a joint and iterative process of analysis, design, development and implementation. The first phase "analysis of the problem" requires researchers and faculty to undertake an analysis of the context, in this case the curriculum programming courses. The second phase "design solutions with a theoretical framework" involves the creation of prototypes of solutions based on the principles of PBL, the learning objectives of the programming courses, student and faculty perspectives, and the review of the literature. The third phase "evaluation and implementation of the proposed solution in practice" refers to an iterative process of implementation and refinement of the initial design principles and the prototype solution. The fourth phase "documentation and reflection on the design principles" refers to the process of retrospective reflection on the design and its results. This process of reflection allows for iteratively refining the design principles as well as documenting the strengths and weaknesses. The last phase "dissemination and adoption in broader contexts" concerns the adoption and sustainability of the innovation process, as well as the dissemination to other contexts at the Universidad Nacional.

The process is guided by theoretical principles and knowledge of the "culture" of the academic context, and it is based on a participatory process of collaboration between researchers from Aalborg University and the School of Informatics, as well as faculty and students of the latter. The intervention is carried out in the area of programming. One of the advantages of design-based research is that it allows continuous monitoring of the changes, analyzing any discrepancies between the design and participant responses, and from this we are able to propose changes to achieve a more efficient approach of faculty and students.

Below, we will present some of the results obtained in the first two phases: analysis of the context, and design of the initial solution. Furthermore, we will present preliminary results of the evaluation and implementation phase.

Phase I: Analysis of the Context

It is considered fundamental to the project to design prototype solutions with probability of success. As Guskey (2002) suggests, a significant change in attitudes and practices of faculty mainly occurs once they have obtained evidence of the improvement of learning in their students. This model supports change as a process based on positive experiences for faculty.

To achieve the design of "successful" solutions, it was necessary to have a good understanding of the context. This entails to analyze the UNA pedagogical model that is the institutional framework for this process, to analyze faculty and students perspectives and their readiness to confront a process of change, and to analyze the actual conditions of the programming courses.

The Pedagogical Model of UNA

Since 2008, the Universidad Nacional has employed a pedagogical model which is based on an understanding of teaching and learning as a social, historical and cultural process that goes beyond a mere transmission of knowledge. Teaching and learning are thus based on (1) the analysis and questioning of the reality; (2) research and practical work concerning the context in which a student and his career develops; (3) the development of skills for innovation and problem solving, (4) the negotiation of conflicts; (5) interdisciplinary group work; and (6) making decisions based on reliable and timely information (Universidad Nacional, 2007).

The UNA pedagogical model does not point out any specific didactic strategy. UNA expects that its application will be enacted through diverse strategies of teaching and learning in accordance with the object of study, its nature and its practice. These general and flexible principles entail some practical difficulties, especially for faculty without pedagogical background. In the daily practice, the interpretation and reification of the pedagogical model rest heavily on the faculty understanding of its principles; on their own experiences of education; on their conceptions of teaching and learning; on their pedagogical knowledge, experience and skills to implement different didactic strategies; on the influence of their disciplinary context and on the negotiation that takes place in classrooms among faculty, students and practice.

In the project, PBL is understood as one possible concretization of the UNA pedagogical model. Both models are aimed at student centered teaching and learning, where the main role of the faculty is the facilitation of the learning process. In both, teaching is understood as a complex and multidirectional process through which knowledge is constructed and shared.

Faculty Perspective

In order to learn the faculty perspective, a workshop was conducted with the goal to identify the challenges of working with PBL as pedagogical approach. Eight academics from different disciplinary areas (programming, databases and information systems) participated in the workshop. The academics were divided into three groups. Each group was asked to brainstorm on goals that faculty wants to achieve, barriers that can obstruct goals, and on actions that should be implemented to reduce the gap between goals and barriers. The results were grouped by similarities and are shown in Table 1.

Table 1. Faculty perspectives about change towards POPP

BARRIERS
A rigid curriculum administration
Little possibility of collaborative work among professors
Students have low motivation
Low motivation at work
The pedagogy is not conceptualized as a fundamental vehicle to improve students' learning.
GOALS
Improve the organizational climate
Training professors in formulating and solving problems
Have a curriculum aligned with society's needs

Promote a working environment more geared to common goals, collaborative work and the pursuit of excellence
Improve the link University - industry
ACTIONS
A gradual strategy for change that will be able to anticipate future requirements
Design a continuous pedagogical training that allows the development of professor relevant teaching skills
Improve the curriculum

From a faculty perspective, the intervention should consider a rigid curricular administration and the existence of a group of academics who do not fully believe in pedagogy as a vehicle to improve faculty performance and student learning. This leads to promoting a gradual change with successful experiences to motivate professors to introduce small changes and to share their knowledge and experience, in such a way that contributes to improving the communication and learning processes among them. It is also important to monitor students' learning in order to obtain information that leads to an improvement in the curriculum.

As a complement to the previous information, a questionnaire was designed and administered to 14 professors from all the disciplinary areas and curricula levels. The questionnaire assesses professors' perception on the decision level of the students, project development, group work, assessment and motivation, which are all fundamental principles of the POPP approach. The following percentages are calculated on the basis of the number of professors who responded to each question. The response rate is indicated individually for each question below:

a. *With respect to the decision level of students*: 100% of professors provide in their courses a detailed definition of problems and projects. 62% of them argue that students are not mature enough to choose or define a well-working problem to solve. As such, students have almost no level of influence on this matter. On the other hand, 100% of professors say that the problems/projects they provide in classroom, always require research from the students. This can be a bit contradictory when 90% at the same time asserts that they provide everything students need to solve the project in their courses.

b. *With regard to project development*: 64% of professors consider that they offer real-life projects to the students. For 46% of them, the most important element in the selection of a project is the amount of content that it covers. However, 100% indicates that they seek interesting projects for students. In the time frame of a course, 43% of them prefer to assign several short projects instead of just one longer project. 69% of professors claim that the most important component of the project evaluation is that the programming works efficiently. However 93% of them consider the student's learning process as a component of the assessment. 79% of the professors give students feedback on their technical mistakes, and 43% of the professors express that students usually show little interest and commitment to solving projects.

c. *With regard to group work*: 100% of the professors prefer to work with small groups (maximum three students). 79% of the professors state that the working groups resolve conflicts that might arise by themselves.

d. *With regard to assessment*: only 7% of professors think that exams are the best way to evaluate student learning, and 79% uses self- and co-evaluation strategies to assess projects.

e. *With regard to motivation*: 86% of professors state that students need motivation to learn. 93% also believes that teaching strategies or pedagogical approaches can contribute to increase motivation and reduce failure and dropout rates. This point seems contradictory regarding the issue of not considering pedagogy as an important means to improve students' learning, which some professors expressed in the previous workshop.

The previous results show that there are many aspects where professors need to change their mindset in order to be ready to face an approach as POPP. They need to give students more autonomy and a high level of influence on the process of developing problems and projects. They also need to nurtue the research component of the learning process. These aspects may in turn contribute to increase student commitment. Professors also need to focus more on the learning process and provide feedback on this aspect and not only on the technical part and the content of projects.

Student Perspective

In order to learn the student perspective, a questionnaire composed of open and closed questions was designed. The goal was to assess students' preparation towards a curriculum organized under a POPP approach. The basic principles of the selected learning approach were taken into account when designing the questionnaire. The total population was 118 students (five groups of the EIF206 Programming III course), and the response rate was 58%. The main results are presented below:

a. Regarding problem solving: 76% of the students confirm that they recognize that the use of problems is a learning strategy in the curricula. 79% state that they like to solve problems or projects with known conditions, while only 57% say that they like the challenge of exploring unknown situations to them. As regard the extent of the authenticity of the problems only 55 students answered. Of these, 84% consider problems as good examples of real-life problems, 4% think they are completely fictitious, and 12% see them as authentic real problems. For design purposes, this suggests that we should provide students with experiences that foster a more positive attitude towards unknown situations that demand a more complex cognitive activity. The use of real-life situations closer to their future work and professional activity should also be reinforced.

b. With respect to the level of influence desired and exercised by students: Out of 52 students, 98% say that they would like to have an influence on the problems they solve. Additionally, only 58% state to have some level of influence on the problems posed by the professors, while 42% say they have no power in this regard. Furthermore, 75% feel able to decide which problems and projects can be solved. These data suggest that students are more ready to be autonomous compared to what the professors believe. This students' attitude is a key aspect that we need to foster, no matter they are or are not prepared. In this regard, we should not provide students with fully defined projects, but offer some level of infleunec on problem development, type of project, how to present the results, and so on.

c. With respect to experiences in real-life projects and the preparation obtained for approaching them: In the programming courses, students have to complete two to three projects a year. When asked whether they feel able to conduct real projects in a company or institution, 65% of the students express that they feel unable to deal with this type of work. They feel that they lack skills. In addition, they express that the kind of hypothetical projects carried-out in the classroom have not prepared them to face real ones. Whereas solving real-life situations is not only a motivating factor for students, but also trains them for future employment, it seems necessary to provide exemplary projects that enable them to exercise what will be demanded of them in their professional life.

d. With regard to group work: 72% of the students believe that teamwork is an appropriate learning strategy. However, 28% of them do not consider it suitable due to the conflicts that arise, such as inequality in task division and incompatibility of schedules and personalities. When conflicts arise, 58% of students say they are able to solve the conflicts by themselves, 36% require professor assistance, and 6% never solve the problems. Regarding supervision, 63% say they receive little or no professor supervision in the development of the project. The data suggest that it is important to keep group work as a strategy for knowledge sharing, but that students should be prepared to deal appropriately with conflicts that may arise, while professors need to be trained to provide the necessary and sufficient supervision and support.

e. *With regard to responsibility for the learning process*: 28% of students think that professors should take responsibility for the learning process, and just 41% believe that it is a shared responsibility. These data suggest that we should provide opportunities where students exercise greater control and learn to take responsibility of their learning process and to be more autonomous individuals.

In general, the above findings point to the relevance of moving the processes of teaching and learning towards a POPP approach, because it can offer students greater possibilities to make decisions when working with problem solving, and how to address the problem, and as consequence increase their motivation in the learning process and take responsibility for this process. Furthermore, the approach allows the integration of knowledge from diverse discipline areas and more contact with real-life problems. All of these are desired competences for computer graduates in order to contribute to the society development in an effective way.

Furthermore, the analysis reveals several key issues that are important for the success and contribution of PBL: a. Problems that are closely related to future work activities; b. Open problems that the students develop through the project work; c. Exemplary projects that allow students to exercise; d. Preparation of students to conflict-solving, and e. Shared responsibility between faculty and students for the learning process. All of these are desired skills for computer graduates in order to contribute to the Costa Rican development in an effective way.

Considerations of Programming Courses

The five courses in the area of programming are an essential part of the curriculum, in part because of the skills that students develop and the interest that programming generates. This is particularly true of the course Introduction to Programming, which is the first contact that students have with the disciplinary area. In turn, programming together with the mathematics courses are the courses with the highest failure and dropout rates.

According to data of the Informatics School, the average failure rate (including dropouts, because no individual records exist) of programming courses for the period between 2006 and 2011, can be seen in Table 2.

Table 2. Failure rates of programming courses

Programming course	Failure rate
Introduction to Programming	51,33 %
Programming I	35,93 %
Programming II	30,24 %
Programming III	20,35 %
Programming IV	16,72 %

As it can be seen from these results, the failure rate is higher at the initial and earlier stage of the education. The professors have made a similar observation concerning dropouts. This points to multiple explanations; one of them is that some of the students who start studying Computer Engineering discover after a while that they have made the wrong choice of study. Another explanation relates to the change of logic reasoning that is required for students to face the algorithmic resolution of problems. These indicators pose an additional challenge for the project. It is expected that the POPP approach can contribute to reduce failure and dropout rates, especially in the early courses.

The next section will try out the identified PBL principles: Problems related to future work activities, open problems, exemplary projects, conflict solving, and shared responsibility between faculty and students, and evaluated how they work.

Phase II: An Initial Design Solution

The initial phase of the project, proposes an educational intervention that takes into account two important aspects: (1) a process of faculty training and (2) the gradual introduction of some of the principles of the POPP in the programming courses through the definition and solution of problems. At this point, it is very important to clarify and explain that professors in the programming area have their own mindset about programming and teaching practices, and that the research project does not have any mandatory approach. It means that the professors are not required to make changes, but the project seeks to convince them to implement the proposed changes. As such, not all professors in a specific course adopt the approach in the same manner and to the same extent. This is a great challenges of the project.

Faculty Professional Development

In accordance with the results of the previous stage, it is clear that the curriculum innovation process needs to be linked to a strategy for faculty professional development that allows them to: (1) strengthen their skills in designing new learning environments, and (2) develop the necessary skills to manage a curriculum focused on problem solving and organized in projects.

This process of teacher training aims to strengthen the group of programming professors, and has a goal to establish gradually the basis for the formation of a community of practice as suggested by Wenger (1998). In this sense, teacher learning is conceptualized as result of a collaborative effort in which they receive support from their colleagues, external experts, researchers and administration (Rhodes & Beneicke, 2002; Schlager & Fusco, 2004). The pedagogical intervention aims for a process of collective reflection and continuous refinement in order to solve the challenges of teaching practice and enable the positive transfer of faculty learning into the classroom (Wing Lai, Pratt, Anderson, & Stigter, 2006).

The professional training involves formal and informal learning activities, where professors "learn by sharing". Short training processes each semester are suggested, with the goal of gradually developing skills that allow professors to design learning environments in accordance with the POPP principles, and provide them with opportunities to experiment in classroom. This opportunity of "experimenting" by introducing small changes in the classroom gives professor's the possibility to perceive the classroom as a research area.

Consequently, introducing the POPP principles in programming courses is a process adjusted to the needs and possibilities of professors, the students' maturity and the nature of each of the courses. This will be discussed in the next section.

Introducing the Principles of POPP

POPP incorporates a series of didactic principles as a basis for the design of learning environments (Dirckinck-Holmfeld, 2002; Graaff & Kolmos, 2003; Kolmos, 2004):

- Formulation and investigation of exemplary problems. In order to understand and solve a problem, the students have to go through systematic stages: preliminary investigation, formulation, theoretical and methodological considerations, and experimentation and reflection. The problem is thus considered the starting point and learning is organized around this.
- Participants control. The learning process is led by students in collaboration with the supervisor who guides and supports them in the process of defining and formulating the problem. The goal is to link the problem to their experiences and interests, hereby generating a higher motivation towards learning.
- Interdisciplinary learning. Problems may extend beyond the known disciplinary framework, which should be considered carefully by the professors when planning the teaching process.
- Joint learning and action projects. Learning is conceived as a social act that is carried out through dialogue, communication and collaboration in mixed groups. Often, the projects are carried out in collaboration with companies and public institutions.

For simplicity of understanding and application, the above principles are located in a continuum where the student is gradually gaining a higher level of decision-making and the professors are taking the role of facilitator (see table 3).

Table 3. Introduction levels of POPP in programming courses

Principles	Level 1	Level 2	Level 3
Problem solving	Emphasis on reproduction of methods Professor provides problem statement	Exemplary problems Professor provides problem statement	Exemplary and ill-structured problems Student identifies problems or need
Learner autonomy	Professor provides the specific knowledge and skills to learn	Professor identifies learning needs and learning objectives	Student identifies and establishes content acquisition and goals based on the defined need
Group work	Task divisions between students	Collaborative learning Strategies for conflict management	Collaborative learning Effective leadership

Principles	Level 1	Level 2	Level 3
Integration of theory / practice	Knowledge of theories and methods	Identification and selection of theories and methods	Research on theories and methods
Scaffolding and feedback	At the beginning and end of the project	At each stage of the project	Continuous and integrated in the classroom
Relationship with industry	Hypothetical problems based on real-life solutions	Contextualized industry real problems	Coordination with industry and its needs
Reflection	Minimal self-reflection on learning Reflection on final products	Learner reflection on theories and methods Self-reflection on learning process	Ongoing learner self-reflection Learner reflection on decisions, theories and methods, relationship with industry and the learning process
Evaluation	Professor defines assessments Students provide justification of solutions	Self-assessment, peer assessment Some flexibility in assessments based on student directions	Self-assessment on performance Peer assessment Internalization of feedback and achievement level

We have proposed the table above in response to the analysis of the context, which show evidences that students need to accept the responsibility of learning gradually, and that they also need to be trained in how to deal with learning and conflicts in group work. In a similar way, professors need to accept and learn how to effectively apply the POPP principles in their courses. Many of the courses in the programming area are currently at level 1, where disciplinary contents play a central role, and the professor almost has complete control of the learning process. In addition, reflection is not a common activity in programming courses, and learning is focused and evaluated by final products (programmed projects). At this level, the learning process is not an explicit goal. Thus, a strategy arises that allows to build and evaluate successful experiences in two years (Guskey, 2002), and in addition to move from the current level 1 towards the desired level 3 in the proposed courses.

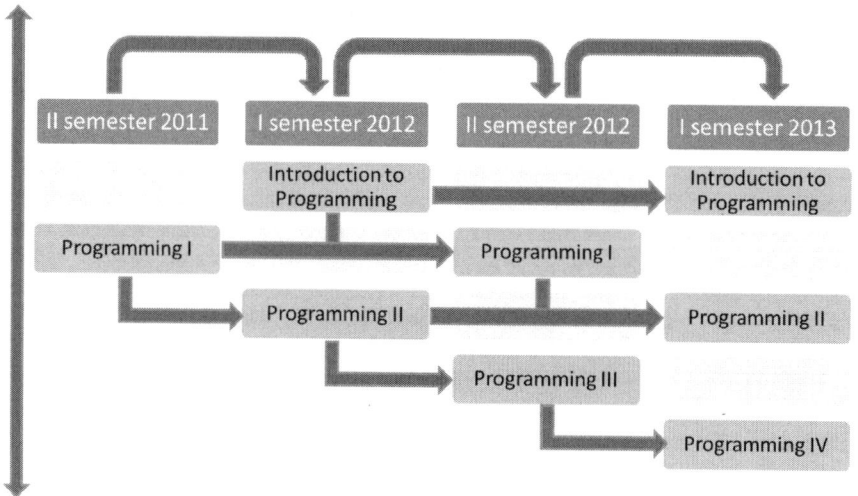

Figure 1. Gradual inclusion process of the POPP principles

Figure 1 schematizes the gradual process of incorporating the PBL principles in the programming courses. As can be seen in Figure 1, it is a continuous process of refinement where the results obtained at the level of a cycle have an impact on the next cycle, and these results have implications for the design carried out in the next course in the sequence. In this paper, we document the first two periods. In 2011, the intervention, in its exploratory approach, took place only in the Programming I course. In the first semester of 2012, the intervention was carried-out in the Introduction to Programming and Programming II courses.

The Problem: The Core of the Design

In inductive teaching, the problem serves as the stimulus for learning. It provides the context and the opportunity to learn, to investigate theories and concepts, and to apply them to real-life situations. In the case of computer engineering, and in particular in the area of programming, problem solving is operationalized through the formulation, implementation and presentation of a programming project, where the final product in most cases is a computer program that to some extent addresses the identified problems. In this way "a good problem" can articulate all the other principles of the POPP approach, and the project becomes the vehicle through which students seek viable solutions to solve them.

In this context, the design of this educational intervention focuses on generating, a new culture towards the resolution of problems, among students as well as professors. This is accomplished through working with the group of programming professors in the development and implementation of learning objectives, types of problems and disciplinary content.

- Learning objectives: The problem is a vehicle through which students gain knowledge and acquire the desired skills in the course (Prieto, 2006), and as such it should have a close relationship with the learning objectives of the programming courses and lead students to investigate and apply the desired knowledge about paradigms, languages, methods, programming best practices, and so on. According to the principle of interdisciplinary learning, the problem must include content from other courses pushing the students to explore links between different areas of computer engineering.

- Types of problems: Problems should be ill-structured, open, and complex; have ambiguous meaning and unknown elements; be open for various solutions; and integrate more than one discipline. Students ought to have the need to analyze and investigate. In this regard, the programming professors ought to move towards projects that involve problems with these characteristics, and thus promote the active construction of knowledge (Graaff & Kolmos, 2003). This leads to promoting a change in culture, for both professors and students, because under the current conditions, an "open project" can be perceived by students as lack of knowledge or effort from professors, and as such it might have a negative impact on the assessment of faculty performance.
- Content of the problems: Programming projects should formulate problems on real situations covering the topics of the courses and exercise what students have to do in their professional practice. This implies that problems should be exemplary and also reflect the level of knowledge and interests of students.
- Way of working: On programming projects, it is common that students divide the project work and at the end put all the parts together. Hence, it is necessary to design projects that create positive interdependencies between students, meaning that they must depend on each other to achieve the common goal. It requires a training process that allows students to develop the skills necessary for the group to function effectively, such as leadership, critical thinking and conflict resolution.

A key factor of the proposed intervention is the ability to develop or select problems with the above stated characteristics. Ideally this process should be a team effort that gives unity to the sequence of five programming courses and ensures incremental growth in the learning objectives. It is intended that as a group, professors can develop a set of projects for each of the courses, and students can select from a pool of these. This will ensure that the project meets the objectives and content of the courses and develops the desired skills of students. In addition, students will be more motivated because they may choose a problem that is meaningful for them. We also expect that this process of collaborative construction of projects among professors will contribute to group cohesion and will be the starting point for creating a community of practice.

In the next section, the preliminary results of two cycles of intervention are presented.

Phase III: Implementation, Evaluation and Refinement
The implementation, evaluation and refinement phase is an ongoing process

that began in July 2011 and is planned to finish in July 2013. Until now, two interventions have been carried out. The first one, that took place in the second semester of 2011, is considered as an exploratory intervention because at the same time professors were learning about the approach. In that sense, the obtained data helped us to refine the proposed design. The second intervention took place in the first semester 2012 and was carried out in two courses (Introduction to Programming and Programming II). The professional development of professors was a parallel and complementary activity. This section briefly reports on this process and on the first intervention, and focuses on the data obtained from the second intervention.

Faculty Professional Development

As part of faculty professional development, several formal and informal learning activities have been carried out with the purpose to prepare them to face a POPP approach. The main formal activity was an 8-week online course taught by Aalborg University. Throughout the course, the participant professors analyzed and discussed different approaches to curriculum design with emphasis on the AAU PBL approach. The experience was rich in ideas and reflections on personal and organizational barriers and challenges, but it also illustrated the scarce time that professors have for this kind of processes. In spite of the will to learn, only 8 out of 1 professors who began the process participated regularly in the learning activities.

In addition to the online course, two lectures were given by specialists from AAU, and a number of other activities such as workshops and meetings were organized. These activities aimed to create awareness among participants about the importance of incorporating into the curricula some of the principles of POPP. They were also an opportunity for professors to share their perspective on these principles and how to implement them in their courses. Moreover, they were vital to foster collaboration and build partnerships among the programming professors. From this respect, a group of enthusiastic and engaged professors participated in weekly sessions, where experienced professors presented disciplinary topics to be discussed, solved problems, discussed general teaching strategies, while novice professors improved their disciplinary knowledge in general. In addition, the novice professors shared their willingness to make changes in teaching practice with their experienced colleagues. So far, about 50% of the professors belonging to the programming professors are participating, but the goal is to increase this number, and gradually form a solid and stable community of practice.

The First Intervention

As shown in Figure 1, the first intervention took place in the Programming I course in the second period of 2011. It was carried out in 6 groups of students, for a total of 150 students and 5 professors. Because it is considered as an exploratory intervention, the changes were mainly focused on how to address the projects. In previous years, students were to develop two to three small projects, but it was considered that a single project consisting of three parts was a better alternative to integrate all of the course content and to facilitate student

learning. We found that:
- Students feel more comfortable developing a single project. They feel that it is easier for them to understand and acquire the skills needed in the course.
- Students argue that they do not receive timely feedback from faculty, because when they get the comments they no longer have enough time to correct their mistakes. In this sense, faculty also recognized the need to improve the feedback process. However, because the groups have about 25 students, and they are used to work in pairs, it takes long time to give feedback to 13-15 groups.
- When conflicts arise, students tend to dissolve the groups. They are not well prepared to resolve conflicts.

Based on these findings, on the next semester we encouraged faculty to make the following changes:
1. In order to improve the feedback process: (a) to split the project into smaller parts, thus students will have more frequent and timely comments; and (b) to increase the number of group members, thus in groups of four members, faculty will only attend between 5 to 6 groups instead of 13 to 15.
2. In order to promote autonomy: to present open and exemplary problems, that allows students to investigate and develop them through the project work.
3. In order to develop team work skills, increase the number of group members, thus students have more opportunities to learn how to share responsibilities and to solve conflicts.
4. In order to develop the shared responsibility in the learning process, to implement self-assessment and peer-assessment strategies in the group work.

The Second Intervention

The second intervention took place in the first semester of 2012. It was carried out in two courses: Introduction to Programming and Programming II, and about 350 students and 8 faculty members participated. The interventions in both courses are briefly described, and the results are presented below.

The course Introduction to Programming is the first course in the discipline (prior to the Programming I course). It introduces the principles of object-oriented programming with an emphasis on problem solving through the development of algorithms. In general, the course does not involve a project. The proposed change in this course was the introduction of a small project with an open definition to force students to do research and make decisions. In addition, students were asked to form groups of 4 to 5 members and to use self-assessment and peer-assessment strategies in order to promote collaborative work. The group also had to make an oral presentation of their solution in order to help them to develop oral communication skills.

Because the student's knowledge about programming was very limited at this stage, the faculty had defined the problem (about bacteria) as the basis of the project, which was to be modeled from the point of view of the object-oriented paradigm. In order to solve the problem, students had to choose one particular bacteria, research the behavior of it, , and model it under the paradigm. The students could decide themselves whether to implement the solution in a programming language.

The Programming II course is the third one in the sequence of programming courses. To some extent, this course is a prolongation of the Programming I course, and as such the proposed changes were related to the use of one single programming project in five smaller stages with one weekly feedback from faculty. To address the project, the students were formed in pairs. Even though we tried to convince the faculty to form larger groups, they continued to argue that the only way to check students' learning and ensure equal and fair task divisions, is by working in pairs. Also, in this course, the faculty decided to describe the project in a very detailed way, and it was related with a fictitious problem based on a real-life situation.

In order to evaluate and understand the experience, a focus group was conducted with the faculty members, and a questionnaire was designed and administered to the students. In the following we discuss the findings and results concerning how the implemented PBL principles worked in practice.

There were nine participants in the focus group, six (out of nine) from the Introduction to Programming course, and three (out of five) from the Programming II course. In both courses, faculty was satisfied with the changes and stated that the results exceeded their expectations.

In the case of the Introduction to Programming course, they claimed that students demonstrated an application of knowledge about the object-oriented paradigm in modeling the problem, and additionally investigated and managed to adequately justify its selection. This showed how students could apply theory to real-life problem-solving. With regard to group work, the students in some cases considered task divisions to be unbalanced, but overall the groups reached agreement on their performance. The self-assessment and peer-assessment strategies were an adequate tool to increase students' engagement with the group work.

In the case of the Programming II course, they expressed that overall the experience was positive, and that single projects allowed students to achieve the course learning objectives better. They reported an improvement in the course approval rate and in motivation of students. However, they expressed difficulties in giving continuous and timely feedback to group work, mainly due to the larger number of project stages. In addition, faculty claimed not to have sufficient time in class for feedback, forcing them to use a lot of extra-class time for this process. They also mentioned problems of coordination between the faculty who taught the course, which caused that not all groups achieved the learning objectives in the same way.

To understand the student perspective of the Introduction to Programming (IP) course, a questionnaire with 15 questions was developed and applied in six groups. We obtained 124 complete questionnaires out of 150 possible. For the Programming II (PII) course, the questionnaire comprised 19 questions, and was administered to five out of eight groups; 98 complete questionnaires were collected out of 125 possible. Both questionnaires were administered at the end of the semester. Both questionnaires were analyzed from the point of view of the PBL principles that the project aims to foster.

Table 4 presents these data. The percentage indicates the rate of students who agree with the statement. It is important to note that there is no intention to compare the course data in each of the aspects evaluated, because the modifications implemented in each of them were of a different nature, as well as were the learning objectives of each course. This also entails that in the course of Programming II more aspects were studied compared to the Introduction to Programming course.

TABLE 4. Data from the second intervention, 1st semester 2012

Principles	Introduction to Programming (IP) 124 students	Programming II (PII) 98 students
Project formulation		
The project is closely related to course learning objectives	88%	93%
The project managed to integrate theoretical knowledge with practice	85%	90%
The project description was sufficient	68%	76%
I prefer to make several shorter projects than a single large project	------	52%
To split the project in smaller stages is better for my learning process	------	86%
Preparation to face real-life problems and projects		
The project allows the integration of course content with real-life situations	85%	90%
Developing the project prepares me to face a real project in a company	------	85%
Professor feedback		
Professors give timely feedback at each stage	------	71%
The feedback given by professors allows to improve the project solution	------	73%
Level of influence		
I would like to have a higher level of decision-making on the type of problem to be solved in the project	58%	67%
Group work		

Principles	Introduction to Programming (IP) 124 students	Programming II (PII) 98 students
It is better to work in smaller groups (maximum 3) than in larger groups (4-5 people)	43%	79%
Group work is always contentious and difficult to manage	17%	35%
I like group work more than individual work	48%	------
Motivation		
Developing a project is an activity that motivates me	71&	88%
I like to work in projects in the courses	51%	63%
I prefer to work in projects rather than present exams	67%	71%
Assessment		
The criteria used to evaluate the project are adequate	75%	69%
The weight of the project within the course evaluation scheme is proportional to the time and effort I invested in it	56%	56%
Overall perspective		
The course met my learning expectations	81%	85%

From the above information, we can highlight some results:
1. Concerning the formulation of the project, the results show that students believe that both projects required integration of theoretical knowledge with practice, and that they were closely related to the objectives of course. Students from the IP course expressed they had to research more, and in a lower percentage they agree that the project description was enough. These data are consistent with the fact that they received an open problem in contrast with the project specification level in the PII course.
2. Regarding readiness and preparation to face real-life projects, a high percentage (85%) of PII students affirm that the development of the project is good training for them with regards to their future professional work. There was no intention to achieve this goal in the IP course, but it is interesting to compare this data with the data obtained in the questionnaire administered to students from the Programming III course (see Phase I: Analysis of the context). In that case, 65% of students expressed that they do not have the skills to face real projects in a company. One plausible explanation is that while the more "real" the problem that students face in the courses, the more prepared they feel for their future professional practice. This reaffirms the need to offer exemplary projects that enable the students

to exercise what they will be doing frequently in their professional life.
3. With respect to the feedback from faculty, data still show some problems in the way they address this process. As we have seen, faculty acknowledged this problem, but do not have the organizational structure and institutional support to spend more time on supporting group work.
4. With regard to the decision level, it seems that the more advanced the students are, the higher level of influence they want. Data from the questionnaire administered to students in the course of Programming III (see Phase I: Analysis of the context) support this assertion, where 98% of students said they would like to have more influence on the problems they solve. However, it is also important to note the high percentage of faculty who think students are not prepared for a higher level of decision-making. This is another challenge for this research project. It takes time and effort to convince faculty that they must gradually provide more autonomy to students.
5. With regard to group work, it is interesting to note the difference between the two courses. While just 43% of IP students prefer to work in smaller groups, this percentage is much higher in PII. An explanation could be that the IP students have had the opportunity to experience working in larger groups while those of PII have not. Moreover, although IP students worked in larger groups, these students reported less conflict in group work. This supports that working in large groups could be a productive way to balance group work and faculty staff efforts to attend the groups.
6. Regarding motivation, the values of the PII course are higher than those of the IP course. It needs to be considered that the first students have more experience working on projects. In addition, the problem that they solved in the course could be considered more interesting from a programming point of view than the problem assigned to IP students. With regard to assessment, is important to note than just 56% of students from both courses considered that the weight of the project within the course evaluation scheme is proportional to the time and effort they invested in it. This aspect is something that faculty have to reflect on.

Lessons Learned and Future Work

As it was mentioned before, after the exploratory phase in the second semester of 2011, the intervention took place in two courses during the first semester of 2012. From the preliminary results, the data show that in both courses, the failure rate was lower with respect to the average failure rate from 2006 to 2010 (see Table 2). In the case of the Introduction to Programming (IP) course the failure rate decreased from 51.33% to 46.9%; and, in the case of the Programming II (PI) course, it decreased from 30.24% to 17.8%. However, after just one cycle of intervention, it is not possible to assume that the positive result respond completely to the introduced changes. It is necessary to follow with the intervention during a longer period in order to have more clear results.

Regarding the research question 1, the study reveals several key issues that are important for the success and contribution of PBL to computer engineering

curricula, mainly in the programming area which is the focus of this study:
a. Problems to solve in the programming courses should be closely related to future professional work activities.
b. Problems should be exemplary and open in order to force students to formulate, investigate and develop them through the project work.
c. To work effectively in group work, students must be prepared to take and share responsibilities and to deal with conflicts.
d. The shared responsibility between faculty and students for the learning process needs to be promoted since the first courses.

All of these are desired skills for computer graduates in order to contribute to the Costa Rican development in an effective way.

In relation with the research question 2, the study revealed the following important key points concerning implementation and use of PBL:

Student perspective:
a. Clear integration of theory and practice, students should investigate about real-life situations and propose solutions to them using the skills acquired through the courses.
b. Student should lead the development of projects.
c. A close collaboration with and frequent supervision from faculty.
d. Autonomy should be gradually fostered.
e. Group size could be larger (than just pairs) to promote students skills in group work and to balance faculty effort in giving feedback.

Faculty perspective:
a. Importance of an iterative approach to curriculum development
b. Preparation of faculty to principles of PBL: Supervision and feedback, student autonomy, new learning strategies, and development and use of realistic problems
c. Group work among faculty members is important for the development of the programming area.

The results also show that the process of developing and implementing PBL teaching methodologies is very demanding, time consuming and sometimes frustrating. While most faculty participants expressed they are open to change, they still maintain control in classroom, and many of them are concerned about giving students more control over some aspects of their learning process. In addition, they still believe that covering a vast amount of content is paramount, and as such, the projects are often aimed at covering as much content as possible. This prevents them to propose more real-life projects. To some extent, students seem to be better prepared than faculty to cope with the changes; they ask for greater autonomy, want to work with real problems, and expect continuous and timely feedback from faculty.

As consequence of those results, we aim for the next cycles of the intervention, to continue moving programming courses from level 1 to 2 and 3 (Table 3). We will foster changes aligned with the PBL principles. In particular we aim to:

- Improve faculty' mechanism of feedback: it is necessary to find means of providing frequent and timely feedback, and also to provide more formative feedback.
- Promote students' autonomy: increasing the students' level of influence on assignments and activities. This may contribute to improve student motivation, self-confidence, responsibility for own decisions, and enthusiasm for learning.
- Focus on skills development and not only on content: faculty should be aware of learning strategies that promote deep learning, lifelong learning, and self-confident autonomous learners.
- Solving real problems: projects should focus on solving exemplary problems that allow students to do the work they will need to do in their professional practice.

It is also considered very important to the success of the project to continue fostering the formation of a community of practice among the faculty of the programming area. We envision that the community will encourage knowledge sharing, learning and change of teaching practices. This is an important issue, since Costa Rica is a small country. Many of the faculty at the School of Informatics works in other universities as well. Working as a community of practice, they will be able to create a common identity and engage with the PBL approach.

Conclusions

Costa Rica as developing country aspires to create the conditions to move towards a developed country, and one of the key elements to achieve this is the human resource. The long tradition of investment in education has produced valuable results. One indicator is the growing number of ICT companies that have established themselves in Costa Rica in the last 10 years. The ICT sector is increasing its impact on the development of the country. If Costa Rica decides to continue promoting policies to attract foreign direct investment, it is clear that universities are the ones that need to provide, at least partially, the needed qualified workforce.

The multinational and national companies in the Costa Rican ICT sector have specific needs, of which many are related to soft skills such analytical skills, reflection skills, and collaboration skills. All these skills are similar to the skills this research project aims to promote in students. In this sense, promoting these skills will contribute to making UNA's graduates better prepared to face industry demands, and in turn contribute to the development of the country.

This project, in spite of its local scope, can be considered a small step in the direction of providing more and better human resources in the Costa Rican ICT sector. In this respect, it is a contribution to the development of the country. The results obtained so far from the present study show that the change process and use of PBL principles is not straightforward. The current alignment of the curricula with deductive teaching methods is very strong, and inductive approaches require significant changes in the mindset of faculty and students. However, it is clear that universities can generate initiatives leading to promote changes, as is the case of the ICT graduates and their impact on the development of the ICT sector.

From the results of this study, we learned that PBL can contribute to develop student skills in real-life problem solving through key elements such as: a. Problems that are closely related to future work activities; b. Open problems that the students develop through the project work; c. Exemplary projects that allow students to exercise; d. Preparation of students to conflict-solving, and e. Shared responsibility between faculty and students for the learning process.

We also learned that the implementation of the approach has the potential to reducing failures rates, but it needs to consider students and faculty perspective. The approach has to clearly integrate theory and practice; to promote students contact with real-life situations and to promote autonomy in a gradual way. It also needs an iterative approach to curriculum development and has to prepare faculty to effectively integrate the PBL principles in the curricula. Only considering these elements the approach could contribute to develop in the computer engineering students the skills that the country requires.

References

ACM. (2011). *Computer Science Curricula 2013*. http://ai.stanford.edu/users/sahami/CS2013/.

Barge, S. (2010). *Principles of problem and project basic learning. The Aalborg PBL Model*. Aalborg: Aalborg University.

CINDE. (2011a). *CINDE Costa Rica*. http://www.cinde.org/

CINDE. (2011b). *CINDE Costa Rica*. http://www.cinde.org/en/services-sector/232-digital-technologies

CINDE. (2011c). *Education overview*. http://www.cinde.org/en/workforce.

Coto, M. (2010). *Designing for Change in University Teaching Practices. The case of UNAgora: A community of Practice Approach to Facilitate University Teacher Professional Development in ICT and Project Oriented Problem Pedagogy*. Aalborg Universitet, Institut for Kommunikation, Aalborg.

Coto, M., Mora, S. & Lykke, M. (2012). Design considerations for introducing PBL in computing engineering. In *Informatica (CLEI), 2012 XXXVIII Conferencia Latinamericana En*. 1-10.

Design-Based Research Collective. (2003). Design-Based Research: An Emerging Paradigm for Educational Inquiry. *Educational Researcher, 32*(1), 5-8.

Dirckinck-Holmfeld, L. (2002). Designing Virtual Learning Environments Based on Problem Oriented Project Pedagogy. In L. Dirckinck-Holmfeld, & B. Fibiger, *Learning in Virtual Environments* (págs. 31-54). Frederiksberg: Samfundslitteratur Press.

Dochy, F., Segres, M., Van den Bossche, P., & Gijbels, D. (2003). Effects of Problem-Based Learning: A Meta-Analysis. *Learning and Instruction, 3*, 533-568.

Graaff, E., & Kolmos, A. (2003). Characteristic of problem-based learning. *International Journal of Engineering Education, 19*(5).

Guskey, T. (2002). Professional Development and Teacher Change. *Teachers and Teaching: theory and practice, 8*(3/4), 381-391.

Hamalainen, W. (2004). Problem-based learning of theoretical computer science. *Proceedings of the 34th Annual Conference on Frontiers in Education, 3*, p. 20-23.

Hissey, T. W. (2000). Enhanced Skills for Engineers. *Proceedings of the IEEE, 88, 8*.

Kolmos. (2004). Estrategias para desarrollar currículos basados en la formulación de problemas y organizados en base a proyectos. *Educar, 33*, 77-96.

Mata, F., Matarrita, R., & Pinto, C. (2012). Assessing Computer Education in Costa Rica: Results of a Supply and Demand Study of ICT Human Resources. *CLEI Electronical Journal, 15*(1).

Mills, J., & Treagust, D. (2003). Engineering Education - Is Problem-Based or Project-Based Learning the Answer? *Australasian Journal of Engineering Education, 4.*

Monge, R., & González, C. (2007). *The role and impact of MNCs in Costa Rica on skills development and training: The case of Intel, Microsoft and Cisco.* CAATEC.

Nielsen, L. (2011). *Classifications of Countries Based on Their Level of Development: How it is Done and How it Could be Done.* International Monetary Fund.

Nuutila, E., Törmä, S., & Malmi, L. (2005). PBL and computer programming - the seven steps method with adaptations. *Computer Science Education, 15*(2), 123-142.

Prieto, L. (2006). Aprendizaje activo en el aula universitaria: el caso del aprendizaje basado en problemas. *Miscelánea Comillas: Revista de Ciencias Humanas y Sociales Vol.64. Núm.124. Págs. 173-196, 64*(124), 173-196.

Prince, M. (2004). Does Active Learning Work? A Review of the Research. *Journal of Engineering Education, 93*(3), 223-231.

Prince, M., & Felder, R. (2006). Inductive teaching and learning methods: Definitions, comparisons, and research bases. *Journal of Engineering Education, 95,* 123-138.

Prince, M., & Felder, R. (2007). The Many Faces of Inductive Teaching and Learning. *Journal of College Science Teaching, 36*(5).

Reeves, T. C. (2006). Design Research from a Technology Perspective. In J. Van den Akker, K. Gravemeijer, S. McKenney, & N. Nieveen, *Educational Design Research* (p. 52-66). London: Routledge.

Rhodes, C., & Beneicke, S. (2002). Coaching, mentoring and peer-networking: Challenges for the management of teacher professional development in schools. *Journal of In-Service Education, 28*(2), 297-310.

Schlager, M. S., & Fusco, J. (2004). Teacher professional development, technology, and communities of practice: Are we putting the cart before the horse? In S. Barab, R. Klin, & J. Gray, *Designing for Virtual Communities in the Service of Learning.* Cambridge MA: Cambridge University Press.

UNDP. (1990). *Human Development Report.* New York: Oxford University Press.

UNDP. (2011). *Human Development Report 2011. Costa Rica.* hdrstats.undp.org/images/explanations/CRI.pdf.

Universidad Nacional. (2007). *Modelo Pedagógico.* Heredia: Universidad Nacional.

Villalobos, V., & Monge-González, R. (2011). Costa Rican Efforts towards and Innovation-Driven Economy: The Role of the ICT Sector. *The Global Information Technology Report 2010-2011,* 119-126.

Wang, F., & Hannafin, M. J. (2005). Design-based research and technology-enhanced learning environments. *Educational Technology Research and Development, 53*(4), 5-23.

Wenger, E. (1998). *Communities of practice: learning, meaning, and identity.* Cambridge: Cambridge University Press.

Wing Lai, K., Pratt, K., Anderson, M., & Stigter, J. (2006). *Literature Review and Synthesis: Online Communities of Practice.* University of Otago, Faculty of Education, Dunedin, New Zealand.

Transformation of the Universities in Developing Countries to Support ICT for Development

Heilyn Camacho, Aalborg University, Denmark
and Universidad Nacional, Costa Rica
hcamacho@hum.aau.dk

Abstract

This chapter argues that Costa Rica is failing to leverage ICT to transform its economy and society. Therefore, it is the argument of the chapter that universities in Costa Rica can contribute tremendously to developing an approach to ICT for development within the triple helix model, which will support a move towards an innovation driven economy, as is the goal of the Costa Rica government. Using the experience of an action research project, the chapter presents a proposal describing how a particular university in Costa Rica could support the development of the SMEs sector through the use of ICT.

Introduction

ICT for development has been discussed quite extensively in literature, and the benefits and ways to use ICT for the improvement of different areas in developing countries have been demonstrated. Through the use of ICT, many developing nations aspire to achieving higher economic growth and the status of a developed nation. Yet, there is much discussion and research as to whether this is the best approach for developing countries to be successful in transforming their economies or moving to a higher development level.

Avgerou (2010) has identified four discourses about ICT and development based on two perspectives of the nature of the ICT innovation process: Transfer and diffusion, and socially embedded action. He also proffers on two perspectives of ICT-enabled development: progressive transformation and disruptive transformation.

The *transfer and diffusion perspective* takes the view that ICT innovation in developing countries is a process of diffusion of knowledge transferred from advanced economies, and that ICT innovation is adapted to the conditions of the developing countries. It can be transferred because material/cognitive entities that comprise information system technology and associated practices of organizing are independent from the social circumstances. While the *social embeddedness perspective* considers that the development and use of ICT in developing countries is concerned with the construction of new techno-organizational arrangements in the local context of the developing country, the innovation process is in situ and includes the cognitive, emotional, and political capacities of individuals. Furthermore, because innovation arises from local problems, it concerns what is locally meaningful, desirable, or controversial (Avgerou, 2010).

On the other hand, the progressive perspective considers ICT as an enabler of transformations in different domains of human existence. Furthermore, Avgerou stated that ICT-enabled developmental transformations are assumed to be achieved within the existing international and local social order. The *disruptive perspective* has a discourse of a political and controversial nature of development, it questions the benefit and intention of the ICT for development (Avgerou, 2010).

The four discourses are: a) ICT and development as socioeconomic improvements through the transfer and diffusion (transfer and diffusion plus progressive transformation perspectives), b) ICT and development as socioeconomic improvements through locally situated action (social embeddedness plus progressive transformation perspectives) c) ICT does not necessarily result in development for all: The transfer and diffusion of ICT leads to uneven development (transfer and diffusion + disruptive perspectives) and d) ICT does not necessarily result in development for all: it is subject to the power dynamics of IS innovation action (social embeddedness + disruptive perspectives) (Avgerou, 2010).

This chapter argues that Costa Rica should adress ICT and development as socioeconomic improvements through locally situated action. In that sense, the country will take a position that ICT has a potential to facilitate a socioeconomic transformation, seeing development as a change of socioeconomic conditions, rather than as economic growth (Avgerou, 2010).

Within this approach, ICT should be used for better lives for the poor, improved government services, enhanced internal economic activities, improved civil society, reduced bureaucracy and corruption, among others (Walsham, 2010). In this way, technology can bring improvement in the functioning and overall development of a society.

Furthermore, this chapter proposes that in order for Costa Rica to improve its level of preparedness to leverage ICT for competitiveness and well-being, work within the triple helix approach, where universities take a more active leader role in the development of the country, must be commenced. However, the universities must prepare themselves in order to to be able to play this role.

The central research question guiding this chapter is: 'How could universities in developing countries support the use of ICT from a more socioeconomic development perspective'?

This is a theoretical and conceptual chapter supported by empirical data of an action research project carried out in Costa Rica in 2008, which will be introduced later on.

The chapter is composed of five sections. In the first section, I introduce Costa Rica´s ICT development, while in the second one I develop a critique that development is not reaching all of society. In the third section, I explain the theoretical framework of triple helix, and continue with a discussion of the internal transformation that a Costa Rica University should make in order to work within triple helix. I conclude with an analysis of how informatics schools could be more proactive and act as leaders in the development and innovation of SMEs to improve the country's development and competitiveness.

Development of Costa Rica's ICT Sector

Costa Rica is the third smallest country in Central America. It has an area of 51,100 square kilometers and had a population of around 4,301,712 inhabitants in 2011. The country has one of the most stable democracies in Latin America. The country is a presidential democratic republic. Education is free for elementary and secondary school pupils, and the adult illiteracy rate is estimated at 4.4% (Estado-de-la-Nación, 2012).

Knowledge is considered a key element in economic development, and countries have been investing resources to enhance their research capacity in order to improve their competitiveness. Many of them have applied knowledge-based innovation strategies, and Costa Rica is no exception.

The Global Competitiveness Index, in line with the economic theory of stages of development, classifies the countries in three stages in order to measure their competitiveness: Factor driven economies, efficiency driven economies and innovation driven economies.

The factor driven economies are those countries which compete on the basis of their factors of endowments (unskilled labor and natural resources). Competitiveness at this stage means well-functioning public and private institutions, health and primary education, a stable macroeconomic enviroment, and well-developed infrastructure (WEF, 2012).

The efficiency driven economies are those countries that develop a more efficient production process and increase product quality. Competitiveness at this stage is driven by higher education and training, efficiency, good markets, well-functioning labor markets, developed financial markets, technological readiness and market size (WEF, 2012).

Finally, in those countries that are classified as innovation driven economies, competitiveness is driven by producing new and different goods, using a sophisticated production process and innovating new ones (WEF, 2012).

Costa Rica is classified as an efficiency driven economy. The country has had the ability to perform more efficiently than its neighboring countries, giving the country a comparative advantage. That efficiency together with a highly educated workforce, political stability, a policy to catch foreign direct investment, a peaceful culture and government policies that encourage innovation has made Costa Rica an option for many multinational corporations such as Hewlett Packard, IBM, Intel, Procter and Gamble and Western Union.

A new strategy to develop Costa Rica's comparative advantage in innovation was adopted in 2010 when the Presidential Council on Competitiveness and Innovation (PCCI) was created. The central element of the new initiative is the holistic approach to ensuring coordination of efforts needed to move from an efficiency driven to an innovation driven economy. This new strategy is focused on human capital and innovation, foreign trade and foreign direct investment (FDI), capital markets and financial reforms, infrastructure and regulatory reform red tape reduction areas (Villalobos & Monge-Gonzaléz, 2011)

Costa Rica has no doubt been successful in developing its ICT sector. The government has developed several strategies and policies to support the ICT sector, among them: Public investment in education, the reduction of internal taxes and trade barriers to technological products and FDI (Villalobos & Monge-Gonzaléz, 2011).

As a result of this effort, the country has been evaluated very well in a number of different international assessments of aspects related to ICT. The World Bank's Indicators 2010 ranked Costa Rica as the fourth largest exporter of technology per capita - worldwide (high-tech exports representing 39% of its total exports in 2008). The global information technology report 2010-2011 ranks Costa Rica in position 46, and this shows that the country went up 5 positions compared to the 2009-2010 report.

The general characteristics of the ICT sector in Costa Rica are: a) it is strong and well known in the region, b) Most of the companies are within the category of SMEs, c) The large companies are very well known, e.g. companies as Intel, Microsoft, Hewlett-Packard, Oracle, Skype, d) Its human resource is highly qualified, e) The sector has 805 companies in 2010, f) Between 2003 and 2008, the sector grew by 101%, g) It exports mainly to Central America, USA and to some extent to Europe, h) In 2008, the sector was 10.6% of the GNP, i) It represents the 3.4% of the labour force of Costa Rica (CAMTIC, 2011).

Inequality Development

The important achievements in the ICT sector are not enough to have a good performance as a whole country. Costa Rica is failing to leverage ICT to transform its economy and society. In order to achieve the goal of becoming an innovation driven economy, the most important issue is to transform information to knowledge, which requires a society better prepared to access, evaluate and apply information, and Costa Rica is not achieving this stage as a country.

As opposed to the improvement of Costa Rica in the ranking of the global information technology report 2011, the country went down five positions in the Global Competitiveness report 2012. Costa Rica is located below Panama, Mexico and Brazil, although in the report of 2009, Costa Rica was above them. Table 1 shows the rank of Costa Rica in the last years, where the decrement of the country is evident.

Table 1. Rank of Costa Rica in the Global Competitiveness Report from 2009-2012

GCI	Rank	Value
2011–2012	61 (out of 142)	4.3
2010–2011	56 (out of 139)	4.3
2009–2010	55 (out of 133)	4.2

In the Global Competitiveness Report 2011-2012, Costa Rica ranked well in terms of higher education and training, using indicators such as quality of the educational system, extent of the staff training and quality of management schools, but the country was rated much lower in technology readiness and innovation, using indicators like firm level technology adoption, availability of latest technologies, company spending on R&D and capacity for innovation.

In the same report, regarding the pillar institutions, Costa Rica ranks negative (below 3.6 in a scale of 1-7) in areas such as wastefulness of government spending, the burden of government regulation, the business cost of crime and violence, and public trust of politicians. There are three main issues affecting the competitiveness of the country: Security, corruption and bureaucracy.

The most problematic factor for doing business in Costa Rica is the "Inefficient government bureaucracy", according with the Global Competitiveness Report 2012. Bureaucracy is present in all public institutions, and it is these indicators that get the lowest rankings in the Report together with "days taken to create a company", which is related to the bureaucracy as well. The country is challenged to use the technology to improve the efficiency and transparency of government activities.

In another assessment, the Human Development Index, 2011, Costa Rica was ranked as 69th out of 187 countries, which is a composite index based on life expectancy, literacy and education levels, and economic standard of living.

Looking at internal research studies, we can get a better picture that Costa Rica is not developing in a holistic way. In the Estado de la Nación 2012, one of the most important and serious research studies in Costa Rica about the state of affairs of the country, points out that:

- There is an unequal income distribution. When there is economic growth, real income increases are not equitably distributed: The richest households concentrate benefits, while the poorest do not necessarily see their situation improved.
- In the last twenty years the country has not been able to achieve a reduction in poverty, and the consequence is an increase in the number of poor people. In 2011, a total of 287,367 households were living in total poverty and 85,557 in extreme poverty. This represents 4% of the Costa Rican population.
- Some policies have promoted economic development, with the result that today the country has a dynamic export sector and new services. However, this sector has few productive, social and taxes chains with the rest of the economy. Furthermore, large segments of the industry, the traditional agriculture and support services have low productivity and are not linked to the dynamic sector of the new economy, but they are the main generators of employment in the country. The presence of a dual economy and few links are creating a crucial weakness in sustainable human development.
- In recent years, the justice system has undergone a process of modernization that has led to, among other things, a tightening of sanctions and the streamlining of procedures to prosecute crime. However, sanctions and procedures under the legislation are still weak when it comes to corruption. This situation has resulted in a feeling among the citizens that when a crime (e.g. irregularities with public funds) involves high level government officials or private enterprises, impunity prevails.

Digging a little more in this lack of use of the ICT to develop the country as a whole, we can look to another national report, entitled the Cantonal Competitiveness Index, developed by The Development Observatory of the University of Costa Rica (OdD, 2012). In Costa Rica, we apply the name of canton to each municipality or local government.

The starting point of the conceptual and empirical Cantonal Competitiveness Index has been the Global Competitiveness Index. This study evaluates the productive potential and national competitiveness, based on an analysis of the reality of the cantons and their positions in relation to the seven pillars of competitiveness: Economy, government, infrastructure, business environment, work environment, capacity of innovation and quality of life. They measure 36 variables of these seven pillars.

The index studies the productive capacity of each canton, states the factors that promote or stop their growth, and describes the situation regarding the seven pillars. The Report also identifies opportunities for the entrepreneurship and investment that each canton offers. Moreover, it also shows the fields in which institutional or public policy interventions are required.

The report has identified five categories of competitiveness:

Table 2. Categories of cantonal competitiveness (OdD, 2012)

Category	Rate in the index
Very high	0.80 -1.0
High	0.60 – 0.79
Medium	0.40 – 0.59
Low	0.20 – 0.39
Very low	Below 0.20

Costa Rica has 81 cantons; 26% of them are within the category of very low, and 53% in the category of low. This means that 64 cantons out of 81 do not achieve the position of 'Medium' regarding competitiveness. Only two cantons are in the category of 'Very high' and four in the category of 'High', while 11 are in the category of Medium. Almost all the cantons classified as being Very high, High and Medium are from the main metropolitan area in Costa Rica, which, according to the Estado de la Nación Report 2012, has better conditions regarding to access to public services, quality of houses, and educational achievements, among others.

Furthermore, the report indicates that from 2006-2011, 62 cantons out of 81 stayed in the same category, there was no improvement, 12 progressed, and seven went down. Figure 1 shows this distribution in the map of Costa Rica, in which it is easy to see the inequality of the cantons.

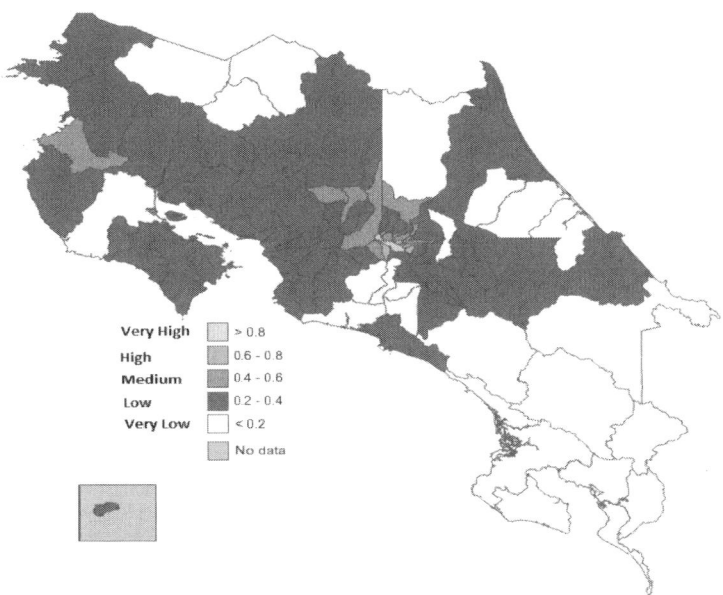

Figure 1: classification of the Costa Rican cantons regarding their levels of competitiveness (OdD, 2012)

The above situation may indicate that Costa Rica is facing warning signals about the need to close the gap of development between sectors and regions. To close this gap, it requires a holistic perspective and one element in this should be the use of ICT as a tool for access, assimilation and use information, education and research, which implies developing the capacity of the citizens to learn to learn and to collaborate. These are the main challenges to be faced in order to become a balanced knowledge society.

Theoretical Framework of Triple Helix

As many scholars have pointed out, there are three well known models about new ideas regarding the relationship between pure and applied research: Conceptualization of knowledge by modes 1 and 2 by Gibbons et al (1994), the triple helix model by (Leydesdorff & Etzkowitz, 1997) and the national innovation systems by Lundvall (2007). Although these models differ in focus, they all coincide in the need for industry/university interaction for country development.

This chapter takes triple helix as a theoretical framework for understanding the interaction of university, industry and government for the benefit of a country's development. Furthermore, it is important to clarify that scholars have proposed a fourth helix (Kwon et al, 2012) and N-tuple of helices (Leydesdorff, 2012), while others propose to conceptualize the Triple Helix as a dual set of helices or Triple Helix twins (Etzkowitz and Zhou, 2006). Leydesdorff and Sun (2009) discuss the addition of a fourth helix to the model in Japan´s case, because internationalization plays an important role; however this chapter will not discuss this literature and will focus on the triple helix model proposed by Etzkowitz and Leydesdorff in 1997.

Etzkowitz (2008) has stated that the path of the triple helix starts from two opposing standpoints, which are the statist model and the Laissez-faire model (where Costa Rica is, according with the author perspective). A summary of these three models is shown in figure 2.

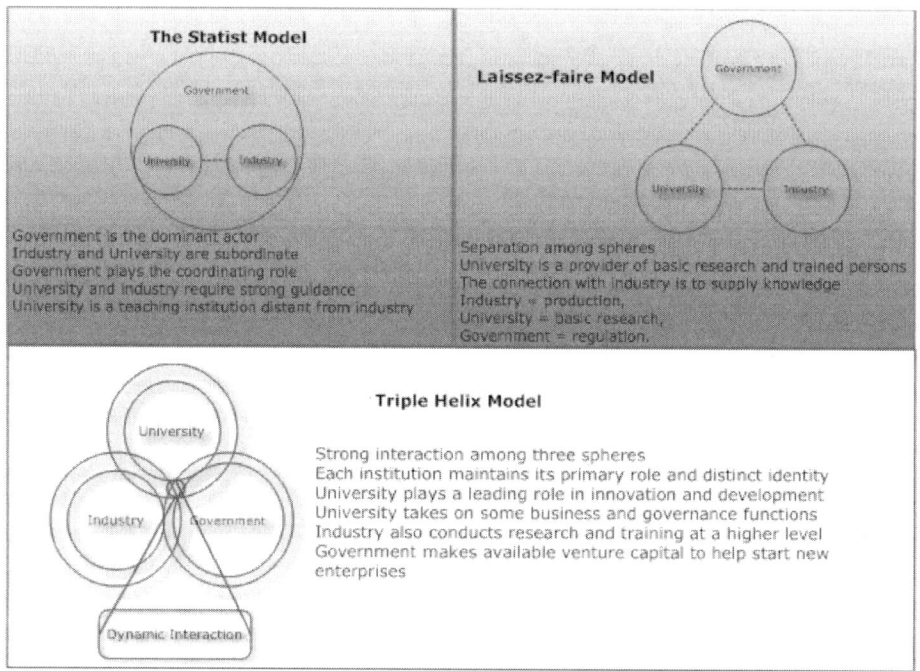

Figure 2: Path of Triple Helix based on (Etzkowitz, 2008)

This model aims to focus on creating mechanisms to substitute the weak or missing interaction between industry and university and between discovery and application, placing strong emphasis on interaction, linkages and collaboration (Dzisah & Etzkowitz, 2008).

The triple helix concept emphasizes the collaborative knowledge production process between university, industry and government. These three sectors work together, forming a relationship of mutual benefit, to achieve regional and/or national innovation and development, where "industry creates value directly, university provides knowledge resources, consultants or entrepreneurship initiatives. Government supports the framework for the creation and implementation of innovative activities in various ways" (Etzkowitz and Zhou, 2006, p. 4).

The first scope of the Triple Helix model is internal transformation in each of the participants. The second is the influence of one participant upon another. The third dimension is the change in the interaction and relationship among the participants creating new initiatives to support national development. The fourth dimension is the recurrent effect of this triple helix network (Etzkowitz, 2002).

'Triple Helix' denotes not only the relationship of university, industry and government, but also the internal transformation within each of these spheres. Universities and other knowledge production institutions play a new role in national development through educating students, conducting research and working to ensure that knowledge and human capital are effectively put in use. In this model, universities are central to a country's move to a knowledge society. They are actively involved in the national innovation (Etzkowitz, 2002; Etzkowitz and Zhou, 2006).

In other words, universities have the role of producing knowledge, being a motor of research and of applying this outside of academia. Furthermore, they are expected to provide entrepreneurial training, local and community development and to act as the leader in the development process. This last role is very relevant in developing countries.

On the other hand, the government is seen as a supplier of the appropriate regulatory framework to create environments of sustainable, dynamic and progressive growth; the government works in collaboration with regions and local authorities. Finally, companies are the actors generating new business opportunities (Dzisah & Etzkowitz, 2008; Etzkowitz, 2002).

The model encourages each sector to adopt activities from other partners. Under such a model, universities, for example, would be transformed into entrepreneurial universities playing the role of the business, while companies can assume an academic dimension and conduct their own research activities, and the government takes a more active role facilitating the relationship between research organizations and industry (Etzkowitz, 2002; 2008).

The principle of the model is that taking the role of the other does not necessarily mean a loss of a sphere's core identity. For example, the university can play the role of industry in assisting firm-formation and technology transfer, but the university does not become an enterprise. (Dzisah & Etzkowitz, 2008, Etzkowitz, 2008). On the other hand, it is very important for the collaboration that the participants are aware of and respectful of the core objectives of each participant (Konnerup & Dirckinck-Holmfeld, 2010).

Key elements of the success of this model are the circulation of personnel and information among the helices. Dzisah and Etzkowitz make the metaphor of triple helix circulation and the flow of the blood through the arteries. They argue that the circulation among university-industry and government is the generator of development, as the flow of blood dynamizes the circulatory system, which is the reason why they propose the enhancing of circulation of persons, ideas and innovation to overcome the underdevelopment. (Dzisah & Etzkowitz, 2008).

Sharing of experience and knowledge across institutions may lead to innovation, new ideas and an increase in their expansion speed. This process of sharing is the key element of the triple helix circulation. The circulation of people, which is the movement of people from one sphere to another within the university and industry ranges, allows the introduction of viable ideas from one sphere to another through the flow of people. This flow of people animates collaborative projects and fosters the understanding of institutions. This circulation may take place as 'unidirectional or permanent', 'double life' or 'alteration'. The first kind of circulation of people is when people move from the university to the industry or reversely. The second kind involves those who hold positions in both spheres, for example working half time in the industry and half time at the university. The third kind are those who spend a significant successive period in more than one sphere, for example somebody who works five year in an industry and another five years at the university (Dzisah & Etzkowitz, 2008).

The circulation of ideas explores the circulation of information through networks. Formal or informal, physical or virtual cross-institutional networks facilitate the communication and dissemination of a) government policies and funding resources, b) findings from university research and any other kinds of knowledge production organization, and c) the results and implications of the use and application of new technologies and activities in the industry (Dzisah & Etzkowitz, 2008).

Finally, the circulation of innovation deals with the production, dissemination and use of the knowledge on a larger scale to assist the knowledge-based development (Dzisah & Etzkowitz, 2008).

Furthermore, Dzisah & Etzkowitz link circulation with institutional change and state 3 steps to have triple helix circulation, which will differ in relation to the cultural and national contexts:

1. Bringing relevant actors together in a neutral environment to have a free and honest discussion of strengths and weaknesses of the triple helix actors and partners and blockages.
2. Carrying out precise studies to identify opportunities, limitations and barriers to overcome.
3. Formulating an action plan that may adapt organizational models or invent new ones that are particularly relevant to local circumstances (Dzisah & Etzkowitz, 2008, p.8-9).

In the setting of the triple helix, the networks developed may change the relevant fields of R&D, and new research agendas are constructed collaboratively for the benefit of the country's development. Furthermore,

> "Each of the helices develops internally, but they also interact in terms of exchanges of both goods and services, and in terms of their functions" (Leydesdorff and Meyer, 2003, p. 196).

Saad (2004) notes that the main barriers to successful implementation of the triple helix model are constituted by inadequate technology, inappropriate learning policies and learning approaches, and the lack of commitment and preparation of the participants. Furthermore, he has also listed the issues to overcome in the developing countries to obtain successful implementation of the triple helix:

- A strong culture of centralized economy and bureaucracy
- Reliance on state funding of innovation activities
- Lack of a close relationship between businesses and universities
- Lack of the commitment to the concepts of partnership, learning and

innovation
- Lack of strategic leadership
- Lack of a common purpose and transparent and mutually beneficial goals
- Resistance to the sharing of information, procedures and processes
- Inappropriate learning approaches

Some people may say that the aim of triple helix is not so much aligned with the perspective of ICT for development proposed in this chapter. Triple helix has been mainly focusing on production and economic growth. The chapter argues that the same benefit obtained from the interaction of U-I-G should be used in developing countries from a more socioeconomic angle. This is due to the fact that in developing countries there is a bigger gap in the social aspect than in developed countries. In developing countries, the interaction among UIG may support not only the economic growth, which is important, but also the concept of social innovation. It should be the task of the universities to give social embeddedness and the progressive transformation perspective orientation towards this interaction, due to its wider mission in society.

Internal Transformation of the Spheres: The Case of the University

In the following section it is my intention to exemplify how a university could work at the micro level of the triple helix and also support the leverage of ICT for the development of a country.

The data are taken from an action research project with the aim of supporting small and medium-sized enterprises (SMEs) to adopt ICT, the project taking as its point of departure that the interaction among university, industry and government in collaborative action learning projects (CALP) could be an efficient way to support the SMEs in their challenge to adopt ICT (Camacho, 2010).

In this context, an eight-month action research project was carried out in Costa Rica. 13 people participated in the project: One professor and five students from one university, six people from three SMEs and one representative of a governmental institution. The students, together with six representatives of the SMEs, formed the action learning set, with a supporting facilitator group constituted by one professor, the government representative, and two additional industry Helix people.

The project was designed under the principle of "doing" together, not just thinking and designing but also implementing together. In this sense, all the members of the project were committed to solving the companies' problems. During the project, the group participated in five workshops, five action learning meetings and one evaluation workshop.

The triple helix model suggests a high level of interaction among the sectors. It requires a culture of knowledge sharing, partnership, collaboration and other skills in the sectors, resulting in internal transformation in the parties, which are the key elements of its success.

Many of issues that can act as barriers against Triple Helix establishment factor are present in a Costa Rica reality and it is necessary to solve or overcome those challenges to be able to work in the triple helix framework or to become an innovation -driven economy.

Given the aim of this chapter, I focus in the transformation of a particular university in Costa Rica to be able to work within the triple helix framework and to be an enabler of development, namely the Universidad Nacional (UNA).

UNA was established in 1973 and is the second largest university and one of five public universities in Costa Rica. Its aim is to offer equal opportunities for accessing higher education to rural and disadvantaged populations.

This chapter takes the position that in developing countries, specifically in a country like Costa Rica, universities are called to be the leader in the triple helix model, therefore, the university should start this transformation process. This position is based on the fact that public universities in Costa Rica are autonomous institutions, which means that they decide their own pedagogies (outcomes, learning methodologies, selection of contents and assessment). Furthermore, they are not under the Ministry of Education or under any governmental institution, still they should follow the regulations of public institutions.

This "freedom" of the universities gives to the UNA a privileged position from which to contribute to the development of the country in different ways. However, university authorities should start on the internal transformation work within triple helix and foster the use of ICT for development, meaning here that ICT for development "is based on the belief that ICT has, potentially, the capacity to contribute to the improvement of various aspects of life, from alleviating poverty to strengthening the democratic polity" (Avgerou, 2010 p. 5). Thus it can support the country's vision of becoming an innovation-driven economy. Some steps for this internal transformation are described below, which are based on the experience of the empirical work from the action research project:

First, take seriously the responsibility of becoming an enabler of equal development of the country. Not until UNA takes a serious decision to support the national development, and changes its way to act, will there be change internally and externally. Once the decision is taken, academic staff and management teams should formulate a vision and they will become drivers for carrying out the change (Kolmos, 2010).

UNA professes to be the University for people with fewer possibilities, and its mission is to provide high-quality higher education to less privileged sectors, and becoming an active actor in the country's development will be very much in line with this mission.

Second, define a policy to be an entrepreneurial university (Gibb, 2005) or adopt another principle that allows the university to change its dynamic to support the national development. Part of this policy should be to become less bureaucratic, because the current bureaucratic rigidities make inter-institutional/inter-sectoral interaction and public-private partnerships difficult and costly.

Third, it is essential and urgent for the university to start working more with the industry. Important structural changes in university policies are required to be able to provide effective support to the productive sector, as well as to develop the right competences in the students.

There are several studies showing the benefit and the need of industry and university to work together (Orozco and Ruiz, 2009; Ruiz-Mejia 2006) but despite this enormous potential of benefit for both sectors and in general for the country, evidence suggests that linkages between universities and private companies are weak in Costa Rica. Universities need to work together with the industry, not only to know the kind of professionalism that the market needs but also to be the driver of innovation and development.

In a study carried out in Costa Rica, Nicholson and Sahay (2008) describe the factors that influence the weak relationship between university and industry. Among the factors are: Poor intellectual property laws, the inertia of the university structure in responding to the industry demands, lack of research and development culture, especially weak culture of applied research, no incentive from government to industry to support research, limited research budgets at the universities, lack of maturity in professors to learn and do research and lack of critical mass of researchers in computer science.

Continuing with this topics, Mario Pezzini, Director of OECD Development Center, said in an interview in a local newspaper:

> "Costa Rica has made a significant investment in education, but when you look at what it produces, today's higher education in the country is concentrated in disciplines of economics or social sciences, and what is needed are engineers or scientists. The gap means that what is needed in the productive sector does not match what universities produce" (La-Nacion, August 2012). (translated from Spanish to English).

Fourth, change the learning approach. The curriculum of the educational programmes is often disjointed from industry and its needs, and this produces professionals who are not well prepared to deal with labor contexts. This change in the learning approach would facilitate the collaborative work with the industry.

UNA must guarantee that students are good on the technical skills of their discipline as well as soft skills (creativity, problem solving, communication, teamwork, entrepreneurship, reflection and critical thinking) (ILO,2010), which are not only the skills that are demanded by the labor market but also the skills needed in a knowledge based economy.

Research shows that some pedagogical approaches are more successful in identifying and developing the new set of competences needed in nowadays' society, and, at the same time, they facilitate the collaboration between the productive sector and the universities. One of these pedagogical approaches is problem based learning (PBL).

Aalborg University in Denmark has developed an approach combining problem-based and project oriented learning; this model is called Problem Oriented Project Pedagogy (POPP). Dirckinck-Holmfeld et al (2009, p.157) define the POPP/ PBL as

> "a dynamic pedagogy where participants bring new problem areas to be studied. The problems to work with are not pre-defined by the curriculum or faculty, but brought in by the students and further

elaborated in discussions and negotiations between peers, faculty and external stakeholders. In most cases the problems to be investigated are related to students' work practices. It is especially problem formulation, in conjunction with problem solution that brings dynamics to the learning environment. Students are forced to critically rethink the problems to be studied: What is the problem? Who has the problem? When did the problem become a problem? Why is it a problem? How can the problem be solved?"

Kolmos et al (2007, p. 5) state that

"Implementing a PBL curriculum is demanding both in terms of resources and learner-teacher efforts and involves a gradual adaptation to regional and institutional conditions. Therefore, each institution must deal with its own and unique evolution, introducing specific ingredients to the characteristics of the PBL according to the surrounding circumstances".

Furthermore, Kolmos (2010) has listed seven premises for changing to PBL:
1. Governance and educational policy,
2. Educational research and political pragmatism,
3. Change at both the institutional and individual levels,
4. Motivation, leadership and visions,
5. Implementation strategy,
6. Trust in students' learning and global societies and
7. Regional and global communities as drivers.

UNA has had a long collaborative relationship with Aalborg University (around 15 years) and the authorities have been interested in implementing PBL at UNA, because in the organization culture and other areas, the transformation has started at a very slow pace. One initiative has been taken to convert to PBL, specifically at the Informatics School. This is not seen as a change at the system level, and as Kolmos (2010) points out this kind of changes will not endure because it is too dependent on individuals, which is the reason why all the organizational levels have to become involved to be successful, as well as a common vision at the level of leadership, which is missing in UNA´s project.

Furthermore, this initiative does not include the element of relationship with the industry, which is one of the components of the PBL approach. This lack of interaction between the university and the industry will hinder the disseminations of knowledge and mutual learning that may influence innovation, development and competitiveness.

Finally but not least, university should foster certain student values. Other changes that must be made internally at the university are related to the teaching of ethical and value-related issues. Costa Rica has been evaluated by international institutions as corrupt, and many of Costa Rica's problems are based on the lack of values such as honesty, respect, solidarity and trust.

The question is: Can ethics be taught? If ethics and values are not taught and strengthened in the education, this situation will cause a lack of integrity development in students and later on in professionals. The questions to reflect upon are: How can we ask the professionals to reflect on their values if they are not clear about values? How can we ask professionals for honesty, trust and collaboration if these values were not part of their professional education? A set of values and competences must be taught at the university.

UNA should foster values in the students and encourage them to pursue constant self-development, reflecting upon their decisions and actions in the frame of their values.

Furthermore, the university should prepare students for double-loop learning and avoid attitudes of becoming defensive, screening out criticism and putting blame on anyone and everyone but themselves, of hypocrisy, cynicism, scepticism and ridicule (Argyris, 1999) (Jones & Saad, 2003). This debilitates motivation and harms learning and innovation.

Universities as educational institutions have the responsibility to set up clear values according to the country's culture, history and society and expectations for the future. This establishment of the culture defines how people will meet and share in the future. In this sense, the university is called to preserve and enhance the values through its educational activities, teaching, research and dissemination and application of knowledge as has been highlighted by Zeleny (Zeleny, 2005).

Development of ICT Competences in SMEs Within the Triple Helix Framework

There is no doubt that SMEs play a significant role in countries' economy and development around the world. In almost all countries the SMEs constitute more than 90% of all the enterprises, and they employ around 50% of the workforce (European Union, 2008) which means that an efficient SME sector is a driver of rapid economic growth and national development (Kotelnikov, 2007). As a consequence, some government initiatives to improve SMEs' competitiveness and participation in the national and global markets have been developed, which are based on the adoption of ICT (Foong, 1999), clusters (Giraldo & Herrera, 2004), networks (Bessant & Francis, 1999), ecommerce programmes (Barry & Milner, 2002) and so on. This chapter presents a specific initiative to support the SMEs Costa Rican sector within the triple helix framework.

During the empirical work carried out in Costa Rica in 2008, I worked with students with one semester long internships. Even though the intervention had good results, the research showed that to maintain and continue progress in change and improvement requires a longer-term and stable relationship.

The first time of working together, the participants will spend energy to know each partner and to create group identity and establish a working method. Working in an isolated collaborative learning project, as was the case in this research, would not have the impact required to have a more significant transformation in the sectors, to have a sustainable model for improving efficiency and productivity of SMEs, and to have constant development of the university.

Furthermore, it is well-known that it is difficult for small enterprises to innovate on their own and also that these companies may benefit from using more

ICT as a part of their business. Therefore, the author considers that the role of an Informatics Schools may be essential and strategic to leverage the development of the companies through the use of ICT.

An Informatics School may work with high tech companies. However, as a way to promote equality development and ICT for development, the paper proposes that the Informatics School defines a clear strategic objective to support the SMEs sector to contribute to the development of the country. This does not mean that the School will not work with high teach companies, but that they will have a clear line to work with SMEs as well.

Jones and Saad (2003) present two types of partnering, one is called project specific partnering, and the other is called strategy partnering (figure 3). Therefore, the proposal is to create a strategic partnership among SME, the Informatics School at UNA, and an institution carrying out ICT project work to support SMEs.

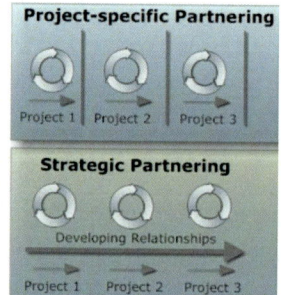

Figure 3: types of partnering. Modified from Jones & Saad (2003, p.205)

I have borrowed the definition of partnering from the construction sector. Even if it is from another field, it is applied for this context:

> "Partnering involves two or more organizations working together to improve performance through agreeing on mutual objectives, deriving a way of resolving any disputes and committing themselves to continuous improvement, measuring progress and sharing the gains". From Egan (1998) quoted by Jones & Saad (2003, p.193)

The Construction Industrial Institute defines this as

> "a long-term commitment between two or more organizations for the purpose of achieving specific business objectives by maximising the effectiveness of each participant's resources. The relationship based on trust, dedication to common goals, and an understanding of each other's individual expectations and values" (quoted by Jones & Saad, (2003, p.193)).

The proposal is that this collaboration among university, industry and government or other institutions, considers these definitions as principles for working together. The objective of this partnering is to accelerate the change in the organizations involved, improve management of the available resources and to help each other in the process of improving and learning. When working in this strategic partnership, the companies receive a longer support period that allows them to develop different ICT capabilities.

The Informatics School (hereafter "the school") has three different educational programmes: Software Engineering, Information Systems Engineering and Architecture and Telecommunication Engineering. This provides a variety of courses and specific areas of knowledge in which they can work together with the SMEs. Some of the courses can be used to develop ICT competences in the SMEs. This may create a sustainable strategy for supporting SMEs as well as a n added value to the formation of students.

At present the School has a combination of traditional and problem oriented learning approaches. Almost all the courses include the development of a project as a final assessment. It is important to clarify that only few courses follow the PBL approach explicitly.

Kotelnikov (2007) has determined four possible progression stages of adoption of ICT in SMEs. Basic communication (fixed line/mobile phone, fax), basic information technology (PC equipped with basic software and hardware, free open source, printer), advanced communications (email, internet, file sharing, website, ecommerce, VoIP) and advanced information technology (PC with advanced software, databases, ERP, IS).

He also notes that not all the SMEs need the same degree of ICT adoption. This, combined with the fact that the curriculum of the School also develops different levels of competences in the students and sophistication in the ICT, enables us to consider two development levels on which the Informatics School can support SMEs with basic and advanced ICT tools.

The overall strategy targets to support the SMEs for an extended period of time (not only in a one-semester project or in internships) by combining the education of the students of the Informatics School and the development of ICT competences in the companies while at the same time the School strengthens its teaching/learning and research. This strategic partnership may ensure the relevant adoption of ICT in the SMEs to improve their internal efficiency and productivity and as a consequence to support the national development. This will benefit students, because they work on real world problems developing academic and technical skills as well as personal and soft skills.

Development of Basic ICT Competences

There are many courses within the educational programmes where the students develop technical skills such as technical support, design of networks, development of websites, operating systems and so on. The students could work in SMEs and support them with the installation of networks in the company, the development of VoIP technologies, the development of their website, among other issues, thus reducing some costs in the company and at the same time putting into practice the knowledge acquired in their course.

Companies with a low ICT competence level may start adopting some communication technologies that do not require an analysis or transformation of their core business. When the company has developed more competences, it could develop more advanced information technology projects together with the School.

Development of Advanced ICT Competences

In the development of advanced ICT competences it is important that the company understands how to use ICT, the benefits and the transformation that the company could go through, and also understands that ICT may change their way to do business.

In the Information System programme, there are three courses called System Engineering 1, 2 and 3. Each course is one semester long. During these three courses, students develop an information system in a company. They start, in the System Engineering 1 course, with the basic steps and theoretical knowledge about how to develop an information system. Each semester, they will progress in knowledge and in the development of the system, finishing with the implementation of the information system in the company. The proposal is that students work with SMEs within these courses.

Aquiantaince with implementation of high-level technology, or a high degree of transformation in the company, may be ahcieved through the course called 'Project of applications in the organization' (PAO). It is a long semester course, and it is the period when the students develop their internship. This course could be used to implement advanced ICT in the company or as a deeper transformation process in the company.

In conclusion, the companies have the opportunity to work in three different types of projects: a) technical projects (developing basic ICT competences), b) information system projects and c) action learning ICT projects. The last two are projects oriented towards developing more advanced ICT solutions. These three project types may develop the three dimensions of IT competence proposed by Tippins and Sohi (2003), which are IT knowledge, IT operations and IT objects. These dimensions provide indicators of the ability of the company to understand and use IT.

The levels of ICT competences and knowledge are increasing, for both students and companies, as they move from one type of project to another. At the beginning of their careers, the students provide support of a more technical type, later on they will develop more advanced knowledge of ICT and other professional skills as well. The company may start using basic communication and information technologies and become better aware of the benefit of ICT for their business.

When the different participants enter into a collaborative project, they bring their own mindsets, which may be disclosed in experience, expertise, tacit knowledge, explicit knowledge, values, resources, beliefs, perspectives and so on. Inside of the project, they combine their individual mindsets, creating a temporary collective mindset according to which they carry out their actions and decisions for the project in question. Because these actions or decisions are based on collective knowledge, the action decided may be more effective or wiser than the action taken on the basis of the mindset of the individual.

In other words, the collaborative projects become like a "store" of information, knowledge and peers available for understanding complex situations, facilitating learning, development and growth, which is the objective of triple helix.

This relationship allows the flow of knowledge from university to the companies, the creation of new knowledge which is useful for the companies, the development of student skills and the encouragement of research in the university. So in this sense it is really in line with the objectives of the triple helix model. All partners gain from the collaboration, and at the same time, each partner also strengthens its own performance within its own sphere.

An important aspect of this proposal is the partnership interests. Students, teachers and companies should create a mutual learning relationship. If the only interest of the company is to develop a product without being interested niether in the learning process nor in the development of the students and the research, or if, on the other hand, the students only see the project as a requirement to pass a course, it will be difficult to create real learning conditions.

This proposal may have a wider impact if we take into consideration that UNA has six geographically distributed campuses. Each of these campuses is running the Information System programme. Therefore, each campus may support the development of the local SMEs. If we take the map of the cantonal competitiveness and mark the places where UNA has a campus, we can see that 4 of they are located in cantons classified as very low and low level in terms of competitiveness and that a serious and strategic decision of the University may make a difference in the use of ICT for the development of the less developed regions of the country.

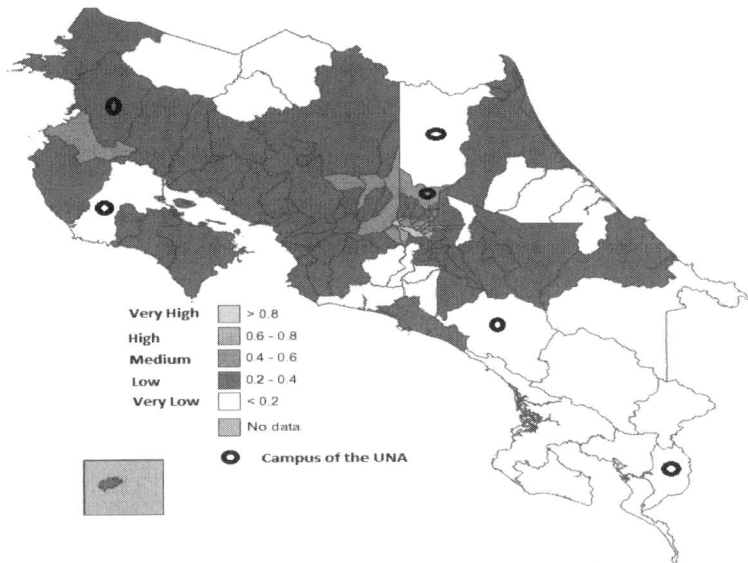

Figure 4: Campuses of the UNA, modified from (OdD, 2012)

Conclusions

The social embeddedness and the progressive transformation perspectives are not a framework or theory. However ,this provides a clear standpoint of how to use ICT in developing countries in order to contribute to life improvement, taking into account their cultures and local actors. Bearing this in mind, if the Informatics School decides to embark on a closer strategic partnership with the industry and with the objective to support the SMEs, they should comprehend the sector and determine the focus of the collaboration. There are several ways to go. The Informatics School might support a specific industrial sector, such as agriculture, or a more regionally oriented strategy, oriented towards the development of the SMEs in the area where the University is present.

Once they have selected the sector or region that they are going to support, it is a good idea to explore the specific barriers that this concrete sector is facing. They may also look at existing ICT-SMEs policies to align their strategy with the national strategy and also to create a network of possible partners to work with in the development of the SMEs sector.

In the specific issue about partnership to support SMEs, the objective of this partnering is to accelerate the use of ICT in the SMEs in Costa Rica so that they can become a more innovative and competitive sector, taking into account not only the economic growth but also the social impact that SMEs may have in the country.

On the part of the university, it is necessary that the UNA goes through a transformation process that changes its traditional learning approach to one that facilitates the development of competences required by the knowledge based society and also to work closer with the industry, to support ICT enabled development.

The challenge for Costa Rica is to build a collaborative culture among the university, industry and government; however, implementing some projects in this framework with the adequate learning approaches may develop the culture needed.

The main insight from the action research project regarding the triple helix model is the need to create small groups of practitioners from the three sectors that want to think and act together, that want to learn with and from each other, has a willingness to help each other, and that have the commitment to develop as persons, professionals and citizens. These small groups should identify individual and common objectives, share knowledge and experience, decide action upon their shared knowledge and experience, take action, reflect and learn from this and apply the good practices and the lessons learned in their individual professional practices. This interaction will facilitate the creation of a triple helix culture.

Finally, the experience gained in this research showed that the role of a person who serves as spark plug in the partnership's engine, activating and stimulating collaboration projects, is needed, which should be pointed out from the university authorities.

In the case of this research, I had this role. I took the risk and searched for the partnership and sold the idea to the partners. This does not mean that I was the owner of the project or that my work was more extensive or more important than that of others. It means that I was the person who moved the idea to a project, from the plan to the actions. Yet, whereas all the participants were willing to run the project once again in order to get better results, there was nobody who took the responsibility to be the leader of the project and organize all the things that I had organized to run the first project. This situation shows that it is true that some concrete initiatives may lead to good results; it is not going to be sustainable if it is not a decision from the top leadership of the university or at least from the head of the Informatics School. That would be only good intensions responding to individual objectives.

References

Avgerou C. (2010) Discourses on ICT and Development. Information Technologies & International Development. 6 (3), 1-18.

Argyris, C. (1999). On Organizational Learning (Second ed.). Oxford: Blackwell Publishers.

Barry, H., & Milner, B. (2002). SMEs and electronic commerce: a departure from the traditional prioritisation of training? Journal of European Industrial, 26(7), 316-326.

Bessant, J., & Francis, D. (1999). Using learning networks to help improve manufacturing competitiveness. Technovation, 19, 373-381.

Camacho, Heilyn (2010). Developing a Methodology Based on Action Learning to Facilitate the Adoption of ICT in Small and Medium-sized Companies in Costa Rica. Aalborg University.

Chamber of Information and Communication Technologies (CAMTIC) (2011). Costa Rica: Verde e Inteligente 2.0. San José, Costa Rica.

Dirckinck-Holmfeld, L., Jones, C., & Lindström, B. (Eds.) (2009). Analysing Networked Learning Practices in Higher Education and Continuing Professional Development, Rotterdam, The Netherlands: Sense Publishers.

Dzisah, J., & Etzkowitz, H. (2008). Triple Helix Circulation: The heart of innovation and development. International Journal of Technology Management and Sustainable Development, 7(2), 101–115.

Estado-de-la-Nación. (2012). Estado de la Nación (18). San José, Costa Rica.

Etzkowitz, H. (2002). The Triple Helix of University - Industry- Government. Implications for Police and Evaluation.

Etzkowitz, H. (2008). The triple Helix: University-Industry-Government Innovation in action. London: Routledge.

Etzkowitz H. & Zhou Ch. (2006). Triple Helix twins: innovation and sustainability. Science and Public Policy, 33 (1) 77–83.

Foong, S.-Y. (1999). Effect of End-user Personal and Systems Attributes on Computer-based Information System Success in Malaysian SMEs. Journal of Small Business Management, 37(3), 81-87.

Gibb, A.A. (2005) Towards the Entrepreneurial University. Entrepreneurship Education as a lever for change. NCGE Policy paper series.

Gibbons, M. & Limoges, C., Nowotny, H., Schwartzman, S., Scott, P. and Trow, M. (1994). The New Production of Knowledge, The Dynamics of Science and Research in Contemporary Societies, Sage, London.

Giraldo, O., & Herrera, A. (2004). An associative model with technological base for the competitiveness of PYMES: case Colombian florist. Journal of Information Systems and Technology Management, 1(1), 03-26.

International Labour Organization (ILO) (2010). A Skilled Workforce for Strong, Sustainable and Balanced Growth. Proposals to G20 Leaders for A TRAINING STRATEGY as per their request in Pittsburgh (September 2009).

Jones, M., & Saad, M. (2003). Managing Innovation in Construction. London: Thomas Telford Publishing.

Kotelnikov, V. (2007). Small and Medium Enterprises and ICT: United Nations Development Programme - Asian-Pacific Development Information Programme

Kolmos, A., Kuru, S., Hansen, H., Eskil, T., Podesta, L., Fink, F., de-Graaff, E., Wolff, J., & Soylu, A. (2007). Problem Based Learning. TREE-Teaching and Research in Engineering. Retrieved September, 2010, from the World Wide Web:http://www.unifi.it/tree/dl/oc/b5.pdf

Kolmos A (2010) Premises for Changing to PBL. International Journal for the Scholarship of Teaching and Learning, 4 (1)

Konnerup, U., & Dirckinck-Holmfeld, L. (2010, 3rd and 4th May). Community-centred Networks and Networking among Companies, Education and Cultural Institutions and Research. Paper presented at the Networking Learning Conference, Aalborg, Denmark.

Kwon, K. S., Park, H. W., So, M., & Leydesdorff, L. (2012). Has Globalization Strengthened South Korea's National Research System? National and International Dynamics of the Triple Helix of Scientific Co-Leydesdorff, L., & Etzkowitz, H. (1997). Emergence of a Triple Helix of University-Industry-Government Relations. Science and Public Policy, 23, 279–286.

La-Nación. (2012, 06 de August). Mario Pezzini : 'Universidades no procuden lo que necesita la producción'. La Nación, newspaper online.

Leydesdorff, L. (2012). The Triple Helix, Quadruple Helix, …, and an N-Tuple of Helices: Explanatory Models for Analyzing the Knowledge-Based Economy? Journal of the Knowledge Economy, 3 (1), 25-35.

Leydesdorff, L., & Etzkowitz, H. (1997). Emergence of a Triple Helix of University-Industry-Government Relations. Science and Public Policy, 23, 279-286.

Leydesdorff, L. & Meyer M. (2003) Gues Editorial : The Triple Helix of university–industry–government relations. Scientometrics, 58 (2), 191–203

Leydesdorff, L., & Sun, Y. (2009). National and international dimensions of the triple helix in Japan: University-industry-government versus international Co-authorship relations. Journal of the American Society for Information Science and Technology, 60(4), 778–788.

Lundvall, B.-Å. (2007). National Innovation Systems - Analytical Concept and Development Tool. Industry and Innovation, 14(1), 95-119.

Nicholson, B, & Sahay, S. 2008. Human resource development policy in the context of software exports: case evidence from Costa Rica. Progress in Development Studies 8, 2 (2008) pp. 163–76

Observatorio del Desarrollo (OdD) (2012). Índixe de Competitividad Cantonal. Universidad de Costa Rica, San José, Costa Rica.

Orozco, J., & Ruiz, K. (2009, October 6-8). Contributions of Universities and Public Research Centers to Innovation Processes in the industry: the Costa Rican case. Paper presented at the Global Network for the Economics of Learning, Innovation, and Competence Building Systems (Globelics), Dakar, Senegal.

Ruiz-Mejías, K. (2006). Costa Rica as a Learning Economy: An Exploratory Study of Competence-Building and the Significance of Labour relations and Labour Market Institutions., Aalborg University, Aalborg.

Saad, M. (2004). Issues and challenges arising from the application of innovation strategies based on the triple helix culture. International Journal of Technology Management and Sustainable Development, 3(1)

UNDP, (2011) Human Development Report 2011.

Villalobos, V & Monge-Gonzaléz, R. (2011). Costa Rica's Efforts Toward an Innovation-Driven Economy: The Role of the ICT Sector. En Soumitra Dutta & Irene Mia (Eds.), The Global Information Technology Report 2010–2011 Transformations 2.0.

Walsham, G. 2010. ICTs for the broader development of India: an analysis of the literature. The Electronic Journal on Information Systems in Developing Countries 41(4), 1-20

World Economic Forum (WEF, 2012. Global Information Technology Report. Geneva

World Economic Forum (WEF, 2011. Global Information Technology Report. Geneva

World Economic Forum (WEF, 2012. Global Competitiveness Report 2011-2012. Geneva

Zeleny, M. (2005). Human Systems Management: integrating knowledge, management and systems. Singapore: World Scientific Publishing.

Exporting a Scandinavian Learning Model to Egypt and Vietnam: Challenges and Implications

Sandra Safwat Youssef Fahmy, Aalborg University
ssafwat@hum.aau.dk

Ann Bygholm, Aalborg University
ann@hum.aau.dk

Kirsten Jæger, Aalborg University
kirstenj@cgs.aau.dk

Abstract

The recent advances in technology have made the process of exporting Western education more easy, and Blended Learning techniques is often the method of choice for exported educational programs. Although, in theory, this makes perfect sense, yet in practice, the export of education has encountered many challenges.

In this paper, we will present findings from an ethnographic study of the learning systems in higher education in Denmark, Egypt and Vietnam. The sample includes undergraduate level classes taught in Denmark, Egypt and Vietnam. The selected learning settings include an 'Academic Communication and Grammar' class in Denmark, a 'Financial Management' class in Vietnam and a 'Marketing Management' class in Egypt. To analyze the data collected, the researcher developed a model based on a constructivist understanding of learning processes.

Three detailed descriptions of observations made in the above mentioned classes by the researcher are offered in this paper. In the "Learning Situations" (LS) observed in Denmark, the interaction is interpreted as arranged in agreement with basic constructivist principles, whereas the interaction in Vietnam is predominantly student-teacher centered, and the LS observed in Egypt is predominantly student-materials centered.

Introduction

The export of education from Western countries in Europe, North America and Australia to other countries in the developing world has recently become very popular. This is due to the rising demand in these countries for Western education, which makes them an attractive market due to the obvious financial gains and also due to the aspiration of achieving global presence. A Western degree has become students' passports into the very competitive job market either globally or in their home countries. The result is that "There are 420,000 people outside the UK taking UK degrees through various arrangements in

100 countries." (UNESCO, 2011). This is both a challenge and an opportunity for educational institution exporting higher education programs because they may differ in context and in goals from the receiving country's educational system and practices.

The export of education is part of the larger framework which is "Internationalization of Education". Internationalization activities, according to Roger Bennett (Bennett and Kane 2009) include, but are not limited to international franchising, curriculum internationalization, exchange programs and the recruitment of foreign teaching staff. One aspect of the internationalization of education is the enrolment of international students in overseas universities in Western countries, which has increased significantly in numbers in recent years. For example, in the UK, the numbers of international students account for over 40% of UK postgraduate students and 50% of those studying in full-time research degree programs (UK council for international student affairs 2010). The direction of international student mobility is clear: from the global South to universities within the Western educational tradition, situated in the main Anglophone countries (Hughes, 2008, p. 5).The migration of students away from their countries of origin to Western countries may provide these students with a chance to receive quality education in the short run, but may eventually lead to a brain drain (the immigration of a large group of individuals with technical skills or knowledge) caused by an uneven distribution of the world's knowledge resources in the longer run. Thus, subsidiaries of Western universities may be able to play a positive role in the knowledge economy of developing countries if, on the one hand, they can provide more people with higher education and, on the other hand, enable talented people to stay in the developing countries instead of going abroad. With this vision and in an attempt to bring global educational standards to all nations, many institutions from Europe, North America and Australia export educational programs to other countries in Asia, Africa, the Middle East, Eastern Europe and Latin America.

Many factors contribute to the spread of exported educational programs from developed to developing countries. These factors include but are not limited to: the spread of web based learning, the enhancements in technology and the increased number of English speaking people in non-English speaking countries. In their book "The Impact of E-Learning Programs on the Internationalization of the University", Amirault and Visser argue that the spread of web based learning in recent years can lead to an increase of internationalization of education, but some issues must be taken into consideration such as the roles of faculty and students and the willingness of educators to take the role of facilitators in the online classrooms (Amirault and Visser, 2010). Caswell, Henson, Jensen, and Wiley (2008) refer to the impact of the reduced costs of reproduction of distance learning educational programs suggesting that the marked decrease in costs of online materials content has significant implications and allows distance educators to play an important role in the fulfillment of the promise of the right to universal education. At relatively little additional cost, universities can make their content available to millions. This content has the potential to substantially improve the quality of life of learners around the world (Caswell and Henson et al., 2008)

Remarks like these made by Amirault and Visser (2010) and Caswell et al. (2008) make it sound so easy to upload some course materials on a Learning Management System for students from different countries and couple this with some face-to-face sessions and turn it into a high quality Western education exported to developing countries. However, the problem with this fairly simple and cheap method of exporting education may be that students will not fully accept it as an alternative to the human interaction element in the learning process. Thus, the Blended Learning mode of delivery offers an ideal solution for exporting education as it provides the flexibility of online education, where students can study in their own time and without the obligation of geographical relocation to be in class, and the face-to-face part helps students not to feel isolated from their learning community. Blended Learning offers students the opportunity to interact with teachers and with other students in a physical world as well as interacting with them in the virtual learning environment.

Many researchers emphasize the great benefits of Blended learning (Woltering et al., 2009; Rossett, Douglis & Frazee, 2003; López-Pérez et al., 2011). In theory, it provides an attractive solution for exported education, yet in practice it encounters many challenges. Some of these challenges are the quality of education provided in the country of origin versus the quality of education provided in the countries to which the programs are exported (Bollag 2006) and teachers' acceptance and ability to use the e-learning component of the blended learning program (Ocak, 2011; Klein et al., 2004). The cross-cultural difficulties and challenges that educators as well as students may face when implementing this mode of education in cultures that may not be used to it or may even be resist it should not be overlooked. Nor should the technological infrastructure limitations be ignored. (Fahmy & Bygholm et al, 2012).

Danish Business School Experience as a Point of Departure for the Research

This research was triggered by the case of a Danish private business school "International Business School of Scandinavia" (IBSS) and its experience of exporting a Blended Learning MBA program designed in Denmark to countries in the Middle East and Asia and the challenges that it faced in doing so. IBSS started in the year 2000 with the belief that training and education could be optimized by the use of technology and has ever since worked on using blended learning as the platform for learning. Consequently, IBSS developed a blended learning MBA (Master of Business Administration) program aimed at developing applied skills of students within the business field.

IBSS uses a teaching philosophy derived from the social constructivist approach to teaching, which requires students to form new ideas and gain knowledge from experience and the sharing of experience and ideas. Modules are delivered as Blended Learning courses, which include classroom teaching and instruction, home and self study, and e-learning tutorials with text and streaming videos supported by online group activities which are either synchronous as online classes and webinars or asynchronous as online group forums.

For years, IBSS used blended learning when conducting different training programs for professionals in Denmark, and this was widely accepted by all attendees. But when "International Business School of Scandinavia" started exporting its MBA program to other regions such as Asia and the Middle East, students from these countries did not adopt the use of the e-learning component of the program and viewed it as an educational tool of lower quality than the conventional face-to-face teaching method. Furthermore, the constructivist teaching pedagogy adopted by IBSS, which uses simulations and activities to teach the students, was not appreciated nor adopted by students in countries like Egypt and Vietnam (Fahmy and Bygholm et al, 2012).

The problem which caused the Danish business school to instigate this research was the reaction of Vietnamese and Egyptian students to e-learning. Students from these countries did not engage in nor adopt the use of the e-learning component of the MBA program provided by IBSS. However, it seems that this reaction is only the tip of the iceberg of the much more fundamental problem (or set of problems) that we cannot address e-learning problems without understanding the underlying concepts of learning and teaching of the (e-) learner. The complexity of this problem is due to the differences between educational systems in different countries, which involve fundamentally different ways of conceiving of education and of what activities to expect within educational practices. In our opinion, learning in itself cannot be understood as an exclusively individual cognitive process but must be understood as embedded in social, cultural, economic and political contexts, which have a deep impact on the concepts of learning, or what is understood as learning by individuals and educational systems in different countries. This is particularly important when addressing learning in the context of 'exported education' since understanding these different learning processes and contexts in every country would help exporting institutions to adapt and customize their programs according to the varying needs of the students in each country.

Theoretical Framework: The Learning Situation Model

With the challenges faced in the export of blended learning educational programs as a core issue that drives this research, specifically the Danish Business School which is co-funding the research, the current study aims at shedding light on the differences in the learning practices of students in different countries. What we mean by learning practices is the planned activities and relations involved in creating some form of cognitive learning. Exploring and comparing the different educational systems and practices in different countries would help IBSS and other exporting educational institutions to understand how these differences in learning practices affect students' approach to learning and consequently their acceptance of new tools used for learning such as e-learning.

This study is an ethnographic study of teaching and learning practices within the higher education systems in Denmark, Egypt and Vietnam. The aim of the study is to understand the contexts in which higher education in these three countries takes place and what factors affect students' concepts of learning.

This will hopefully result in identifying the incongruence between e-learning tools and design and the actual sequence of events happening in the learning process in these countries. By observing the natural settings in which learning takes place and making descriptive analyses of selective learning situations in the three countries, we attempt to develop a better understanding of the different relations between the key players of learning in these countries. Coupling the non-participant observations with other methods of qualitative research such as in-depth interviews and focus groups will lead to better insight into the reality of how students and teachers (the key players in the learning process) understand and feel about learning, and how this can differ greatly from one culture to another.

The researcher chose an ethnographic research approach because of the long tradition of using ethnographic research methods to obtain a comprehensive understanding of the natural setting in which an activity (such as learning) occurs, with minimal disruption to this natural environment from the researcher. J. D. Brewer (2000, p. 10) defines ethnography as:

> "the study of people in naturally occurring settings or 'fields' by means of methods which capture their social meanings and ordinary activities, involving the researcher participating directly in the setting, if not also the activities, in order to collect data in a systematic manner but without meaning being imposed on them externally". (Brewer, 2000, p. 10).

Hence, using ethnographic research gives a broader understanding of the natural setting in which higher education takes place in these three countries, Denmark, Egypt and Vietnam, and by comparing learning practices in the countries, conclusions can be drawn about how to better design and adapt the exported educational programs to fit the natural understanding of education from the learners' perspective.

The sample studied included higher education students and teachers in public and private universities and colleges in the three countries: Denmark, Egypt and Vietnam. Denmark represents Northern Europe and Scandinavia while Egypt represents the Middle East and Vietnam represents developing countries in Asia. The study examines teaching setups in both public and private universities in Egypt and Vietnam, while in Denmark the focus was on public universities only as they represent the majority of education in the country.

The methods which were used by the researcher include:

1. Data collection by the researcher using non-participant observation and note taking, diary keeping, audio recordings and data reports for observing the activities and interaction taking place in the natural setting of higher education and identifying the detailed sequence of events involved in the routine performance of these activities.
2. Observation was coupled with focus group activities conducted in each of the three countries, using a semi-structured questions guide. The value of focus groups at this stage was that students from the three groups could

reveal aspects of experience and perspectives that would not be as accessible without group interaction. All focus groups were either video recorded or audio recorded.
3. Unstructured in-depth interviews were also conducted in all three countries with either students only or students and teachers to identify how teachers design and develop their courses and how students perceive the methods of teaching that are currently being adopted by teaching staff in the three countries and all interviews were audio recorded.
4. Documentary evidence from some of the materials used for teaching and studying in the three countries was obtained for analysis and comparison.

The researcher visited the three countries under study in this research project during the period from October 2011 to February 2012. The data collected in Denmark included two hours of recorded lecture, interviews with 5 students, non-participant observations of a two-hour lecture, as well as course materials. All this data was collected from one university: Aalborg University.

The data collected in Vietnam included visits to six different universities, and non-participant observations in three of them, which included total observations of fifteen hours of teaching (of which some was audio recorded), in addition to one hour of video-recorded focus group with eleven student participants and another hour of video-recorded focus group with four student participants and a total of ninety minutes of audio-recorded interviews with nine students and two teachers. Course materials, photos and timetables were also collected for analysis.

Data collected from Egypt include visits to five different universities and non-participant observations of a total of twelve hours of teaching at three of them. Most were audio-recorded. A focus group with four male students was video-recorded for fifteen minutes, and another focus group with twelve students was audio-recorded for twenty minutes (some female students who were in the focus group refused to be video-recorded), and an in-depth interview with two students was audio-recorded for forty minutes. Teaching materials, photos, student articles and timetables were also collected for analysis.

To analyze the data collected, the researcher developed a model inspired by the data collected as well as the constructivist approach to learning as opposed to the instructivist approach to learning. As most educational scholars agree, instructivism is based on the learners' passive reception and memorizing of didactically arranged information (Merrill 2008) and in accordance with this approach, exams are based on knowledge recall (Sweller, Kirschner et al. 2007). Constructivism understands learning as the learner's active construction of new knowledge based on the application of and to some extent also the alteration of existing cognitive structures (Bandura and McClelland 1977) and situated learning (Lave 1991). These two different approaches represent the opposing poles of the educational continuum that the "Learning Situation Model" is built on.

Our definition of a "Learning Situation" is an institutionally arranged situation in which the actors fulfill well-defined roles (as teachers and students) in order to accomplish student learning. The third element in the "Learning

Situation" model is the materials, like books, lecture notes, presentations-etc., which also play an important role in the learning process that takes place in these countries. Each "Learning Situation" is a formal teaching-learning episode which takes place within an institution and is normally scheduled in advance between students and teachers in the presence (or non-presence) of materials. This episode is intended to result in some form of cognitive learning by the students. In this research, students' accounts of "Learning Situations" were also included. Their feedback and feelings expressed towards the learning situations were analyzed as well.

The description and analysis of each "Learning Situation" (LS) categorizes it as either **(a)** predominantly student-teacher interaction, **(b)** predominantly student-materials interaction or **(c)** a mixed balance between student-teacher-material interaction (Figure 1). The model reflects a constructivist understanding of the learning process in that it identifies the learner's interaction with, on the one hand, learning materials and, on the other hand, the teacher(s) as producers of the inputs to the learner's construction of knowledge. This, of course, applies predominantly to formal learning settings within a classroom environment. If the main classroom activity takes place as interaction between students and teacher (a), it indicates that the learning situation may be controlled and dominated by the teacher. If the major part of the activities is organized as interaction between the individual student (or groups of students) and course material, this indicates that the class is organized as independent or self-managed learning (b) in which the teacher typically adopts the role of facilitator or supervisor instead of the role of instructor. Finally, if the class is organized as a combination of teacher-student interaction and student-material interaction, this indicates that the teacher is seeking to strike a balance between teacher-managed and self-managed learning (c) It is important to understand, however, that these categories are only initial, rather crude generalizations which require further refinement. For example, teacher-student interaction (a) may take place as student-centered dialogues in which students define the frames of the discussion and seek to elicit information from the teacher for purposes defined by the students themselves. Student interaction with learning materials may also be highly teacher-controlled if, for example, the students' options for action have been limited (e.g. in the case of a multiple choice test). Thus, the application of the model must be combined with qualitative studies of the actual interaction processes in the classroom.

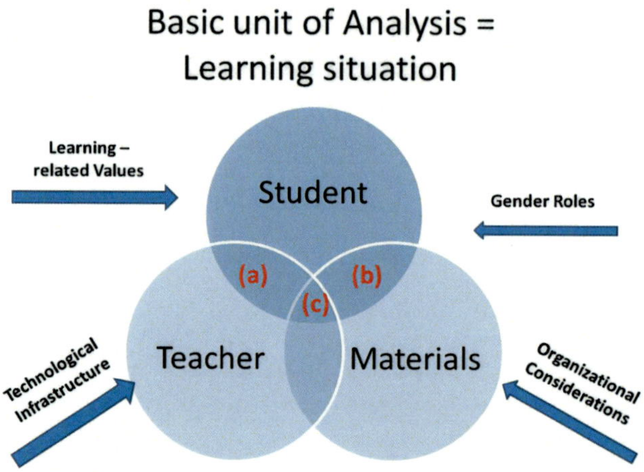

Figure 1: The unit of analysis in this study "the Learning Situation"

Although we are aware of the fact that learning is much deeper and broader than described in such simple relations, we find this model helpful in reaching the goal of this research. This model would help the Danish business school funding this project as well as other higher education exporting institutions in understanding the basic differences in learning practices among students from different countries and their approaches to learning. Understanding and appreciating these differences would help institutions to become more sensitive to students' needs and thus offer them the programs which truly cater to their cognitive practices, which would result in better results and better education.

An In-depth Descriptive Analysis of Three Different "Learning Situations" (LS) in Three Countries

In this paper, we present a part of the data which were collected from the three countries where the major players (students and teachers) share many similarities in terms of age, specialization and educational degree that they study. Before describing the "Learning Situations" which were analyzed in each country, some general data about higher education in Denmark, Egypt and Vietnam will be presented. Then, one observation of a "Learning Situation" in each of these three countries will be presented in an attempt to evaluate how similar or different the learning practices in these three learning situations may be.

Denmark

According to the statistics of the World Bank in 2008, the rate of enrollment of Danish students in tertiary education is 79% and out of these, only 2% are enrollments in private tertiary education. Higher education in Denmark is divided into three levels: short-cycle, medium-cycle and long-cycle. Short-cycle higher education is acquired at a non-university college and it includes programs in the commercial and technical fields mostly. The aim of these programs is to qualify students for practical and vocational jobs and to qualify graduates to find employment at specialist or middle-management level. Diplomas in short-cycle programs (business academy programs) or the Academy Profession Degree are awarded after two years of study (120 ECTS points). The medium-cycle programs prepare students for specific professions and include for instance Teacher training programs, programs in social work, journalism, nursing, engineering etc. Diplomas are awarded after a 3- to 4-year professionally oriented program at a level corresponding to a university Bachelor. The Professional Bachelor degrees are awarded on completion of programs which include research, practical training and development, and all of these programs also include compulsory periods of practical training. The long-cycle higher education in Denmark is conducted at university-level, and its main objective is to conduct research and offer research-based education at an international level.

There are four types of institutions offering higher education programs: first, the academies of professional higher education (offering short-cycle programs) and second, university colleges (offering medium-cycle programs) and third, universities (offering long-cycle programs), finally there are institutions which offer study programs in arts. All short-cycle higher education is concentrated on 10 business academies (academies of professional higher education), while most of the medium-cycle-education will be concentrated in eight University Colleges, and long-cycle higher education in concentrated in eight universities in Denmark. Five of these universities are multi-faculty universities, and the other three specialize in fields such as engineering (the Technical University of Denmark), information technology (The IT University) and business studies (Copenhagen Business School).

An observation study was conducted at Aalborg University (AAU) on 8 November 2011. We will provide a descriptive analysis of a "Learning Situation" of one of the lecture sessions of the first semester course "Academic Communication and Grammar". The session took place from 10:00am to noon.

The researcher entered the class at 9:45am and took a seat in the last row in the class to have a good view of all activities and interaction taking place during the session. The classroom was big enough for 100 students with around 50 students attending and chairs were arranged in the classroom style. The equipment used in this class were white boards, a screen, video projector and all classrooms in AAU are equipped with Wi-Fi connections, which means that each student gets a personal username and pass code for the university campus Wi-Fi. The teacher came into the classroom a few minutes ahead of the time scheduled for the beginning of the lecture, and the materials she used were power point presentations and the set book. The lecture started by the teacher asking the students to work in pairs to discuss a previous assignment, and then she presented a new idea for 20 minutes. The teacher then asked students to read from the course book and solve an activity in the book in groups and compare their answers to the answers at the end of the book. She finished the activity by a recap of the exercise. The lecture was generally interactive with questions from teacher to students and from students to teacher – students asked questions and the teacher answered patiently.

Some general observations were that few students had books but most had laptops. Students worked alone and in groups, and the teacher was moving around giving comments and motivating them. Students sometimes listened to the teacher, and sometimes they did other things, like listened to a fellow student or looked at their computers. The teacher seemed to be aware of each student's participation, or at least most of them – she walked around helping them with the exercise and asking those who seemed busy doing other things questions to make sure they were following the class. The general atmosphere was one of learning and mutual responsibility towards the learning process and although it was clear that students were engaged in the learning process and were participating, they also reverted to facebook every once in a while – this seemed to be out of habit. Apparently, all students were at the same level of understanding and learning – only two students seemed to be alone and not integrated in what was going on. One of them looked foreign.

The observations concerning interaction during class showed a high level of interaction between the students and the teacher and between students and their peers and also between students and the course materials. Technology seemed to be an important catalyst in all these levels of interaction, and the use of technology was an integral part of teaching, and class exercises included search on the internet. Students with laptops opened sites like Facebook – Youtube – some wrote notes – some googled words to answer teacher's questions. Students were allowed to eat and drink inside the classroom, and in a two-hours session, the teacher spoke for a total length of time of thirty minutes (fragmented).

During group work, students were all working and interacting together and learning, also discussing and having fun, some were playing games but overall it was clear that they were all keen to learn, and that they respected the session and the teacher. The same two detached students were not participating in group exercises, and each of them was doing something else on their laptops. The teacher came to each of them separately and talked with them – clearly asking if they were following the session or not. The session ended with homework being set (workshop after class), and this would link this class with the following class and motivate students to self learn.

In this observation, there was a high level of interaction at all three levels, student-teacher interface and student-student interface and also student-materials interface, which led to a high degree of interaction at the "(c)" level (as shown in the diagram). Based on the observation of this "Learning Situation" we can conclude that this class showed favorable interaction at all levels, and that the LS of this class is of level "(c)".

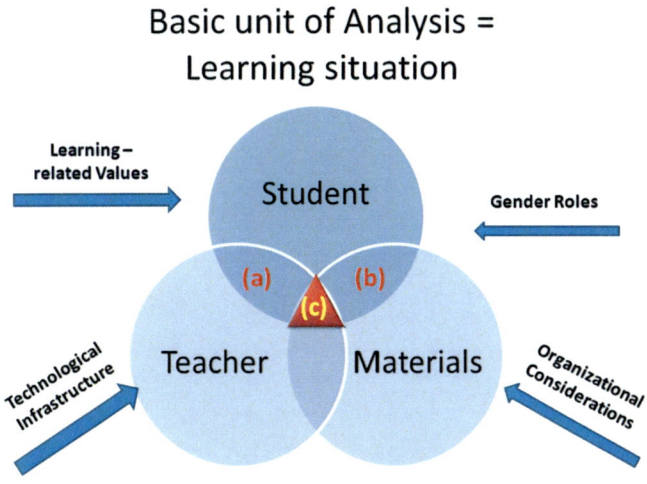

Figure 2: "Learning Situation" in Denmark

In the observation at AAU in Denmark, all the teacher's activities are student-centered and mutually interactive. The teacher respects the class and arrives on time and is always aware of everyone in her class, trying to motivate and help them. Students are equally responsible for their learning and participate proactively in all activities, while the teacher role is rather that of an orchestrator of the learning process, but the teacher is not the person responsible for it.

Vietnam

According to the statistics of the World Bank in 2008, the rate of enrollment of Vietnamese students in tertiary education is 18%. The current higher education (HE) system in Vietnam includes university (from 4 to 6 years, depending on the field of study), college (3 years), master (from 1 to 3 years after getting a university degree, depending on the field of education and the forms of study) and doctorate education (2 to 4 years after acquiring a master's degree). The total number of students in higher education in 2008-2009 was 1,719,499 and 87.3% of them went to public institutions (1,501,310 students) while 12.7% of them go to non-public universities and colleges (218,189 students). There are 295 universities and public colleges in Vietnam, while the number of non-public higher education institutions increased from 15 non-public universities in 1997 to 81 institutions by May 2009 (44 universities and 37 colleges).

An observation study was conducted in one of the private higher education colleges in Vietnam, Kent College, on 6 December 2011. A descriptive analysis of a "Learning Situation" of one of the lecture sessions of the course Financial Management which was held from 08:00 to 10:30 am, is presented.

This class was towards the end of the semester, and in the class students were presenting their assignments, which they had submitted a week before the presentations. There was no schedule for the whole course. Instead, students received a weekly schedule at the beginning of each week. There were

15 students at the start of the class in a classroom, which was big enough for 40 students. The number of students ended up being 24 as more students kept coming into the classroom 45 minutes after the session started. The number of females in this class was twice the number of males in the class. The class was air-conditioned, and the chairs were arranged in a theatre-like style. A note on the wall said "No food, drinks, chewing gum in class". The equipment used in this class was computer and video projectors. In this session, students presented their assignments in pairs. Students had sent their presentations to the teacher before the class in order to discuss them during the presentations. The teacher and the students were Vietnamese, but all interaction in class was in English.

The researcher observed that students had their laptops in class while the teacher was sitting at the end of the class watching the whole class and the presentations. The teacher asked other students to comment or ask questions but no one spoke up. Also, the teacher asked questions in an interrogating manner as illustrated in the following monologue produced as a comment on one of the student presentations:

> "I said this point in class before and other students too did the same mistake …We had a standardized format, why didn't you use that?" …"for sure follow the standardized format" …"didn't I ask everyone to use the standardized formats?"

One of the presenting students seemed embarrassed in front of other students and whispered to her partner, and they both laughed. The teacher asked the student to skip the introduction and go to the "income statements" (which was the topic of the assignments). Both students (two females) looked at each other and laughed. While the two students were presenting, the teacher did not pay attention but kept receiving assignments from other students and reading them. The teacher asked students to explain what they wrote in their presentations, and they found it hard to explain. The teacher seemed to be looking for "the right answer". Some students had their laptops in class, some looked at presentations on their computer screens, some opened facebook, and some were chatting. The teacher made fun of the students' presentations. Again, the students presenting seemed to be embarrassed and whispered to other students sitting in the first row. While students presented, none of their colleagues asked questions or gave feedback or comment. The teacher commented by saying "Really?" and "Are you sure" and "Oh, Gee". When presenting, one of the students put her hand over her mouth, and the other student locked her hands behind her back. The teacher commented that only two students wrote references in their assignments. During all of the students' presentations, the teacher did not listen to students but kept receiving the assignments. The teacher was sitting right behind one of the students, who was on facebook, and asked her to explain what was going on, and when she could not answer, the teacher commented "when you did your presentation they listened but when it is their turn you don't listen to what they say". The teacher asked this student to walk out of the classroom because she was not paying attention and was on facebook and chatting. Some other students sneaked out of the class, and they all stood outside next to the stairs chatting with her. She was allowed by the teacher to enter the class again after fifteen minutes. Again, she went to her laptop and opened facebook while the teacher was sitting behind her in class and could see what she was doing on her computer.

The teacher made a wrong comment in class, then apologized for it and corrected it. Some students looked at each other and laughed. All students were embarrassed and looked ashamed when they presented in class, and the teacher talked about exams and mentioned again the importance of using the standardized formats and templates.

During the session, students kept their mobiles on, and they made calls and took calls during the class. Students called the teacher "TEACHER", and they submitted assignments to the teacher using both hands while bowing down a little (as is the custom of Asians as a sign of respect and humility).

The analysis of this "Learning Situation" is that all interaction is in the "student-teacher interface" (which we refer to as the ("a") section as shown in the figure). One-way communication from teacher to students is the dominant form of communication, and the relationship between the teacher and students is very formal. The teacher is the source of all information in class, and both students and teacher act on this basis. Students accept this distance and may even see it as justified and essential to their learning process (as was clear from students' comments in the interviews). This is coherent with the Vietnamese belief system, which is very much affected by Chinese culture, due to the long history of colonization of Vietnam by China, a fact mentioned by one of the students in the focus group interview. The Vietnamese –just like the Chinese – are affected by the teachings of Confucius, and an important virtue in Chinese culture is what is called "filial piety", which means holding the highest level of awe and respect to one's parents and ancestors, and this respect extends to teachers and elders in general (Yao 2000). This concept is reflected to a great extent in this "Learning Situation", where the students hold a lot of respect for the teacher's opinions and for the teacher himself, while the teacher, at the same time, treats the students as less competent and assumes that they should follow his instructions without arguing. Thus, we can conclude that the learning process in this case is mainly centered on the relations and interaction between the students and the teacher.

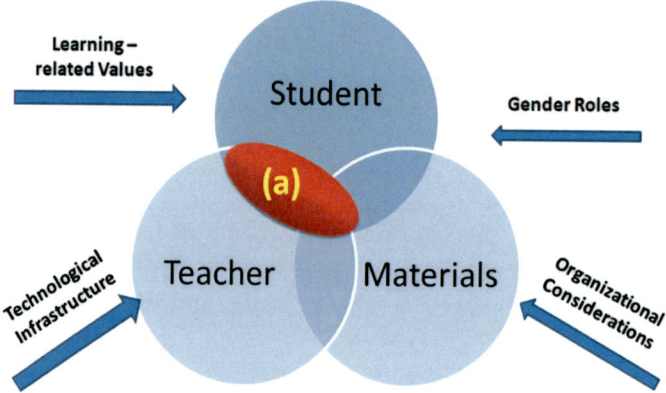

Figure 3: "Learning Situation" in Vietnam

In the Vietnam observation, the teacher's role is that of a "Guru" rather than a facilitator of learning. He has all the knowledge and he passes this knowledge on to students and expects them to keep this knowledge locked in their heads and use it as it is in evaluations such as assignments and exams. This is made clear in the teacher's comments, for example "I said this point in class before". The teacher provides standard concepts and puts them in templates that the students are expected to use without making alterations, which we can see from comments like "didn't I ask everyone to use the standardized formats?" When the students do not follow the exact instructions of the teacher and use the "standardized formats", the teacher is not satisfied with their work and starts to punish them by making harsh comments, and he ridicules them in front of other students in class by uttering comments like "Really?" and "Are you sure?" and "Oh, Gee". At such moments, students are clearly embarrassed. There is also a controversy in the students' attitude towards the teacher where, although they respect him and call him "Teacher" and bow down a little when they hand in their assignments, they arrive late in class and keep their mobiles on during the session, answer calls in class and do other things on their computers in class rather than concentrating on the session. This is also clear from the incident of the student who was chatting on her computer in class, and the teacher asked her to leave class for some time (as a punishment). Instead of complying with the punishment, her friends went out to keep her company. When she was allowed to come back in class, she started chatting on her computer again as if rebelling against the control of the teacher in class. The teacher is the center of the learning process, and students are followers and passive participants in the learning process. The teacher is not obliged to give them his undivided attention in class because he represents the "core" of their learning, and thus students do not take any responsibility for their own learning.

Egypt

According to the statistics by the World Bank in 2008, the rate of enrollment of Egyptian students in tertiary education is 31% and the number of students in tertiary education per 100,000 is 3328. There are two education systems in Egypt, the secular and the religious (Al-Azhar) system. We will focus only on the tertiary education level in the secular system, which consists of all post-secondary education institutions including universities and 2- or 4-year degrees offered by non-university higher education institutions. The higher education system in Egypt is composed of public universities (dominant and large), public non-university institutions (small and limited), a number of small private universities, and a large number of private non-university institutions. In 2008, the system was composed of: eighteen public universities and sixteen private universities and thirteen public non-university institutions. The public non-university institutions are subdivided into eight technical colleges and five higher technical institutes, which provide four to five years of higher technical education. There are also 96 institutions, 88 of which offer four-year education programs. Out of these, eight institutes offer two-year middle technical programs, and four offer both two and four-year programs. There are another eleven non-university institutions established by entities other than the "Ministry of Higher Education" or under special agreements and two private foreign institutions: the American University in Cairo (AUC) established 1919, and the Arab Academy for Science and Technology and Maritime Transport (AAST-MT) established in 1972.

An observation study was conducted in one of the biggest higher education universities in Egypt, Cairo University, on 14 February 2012 and we will present a descriptive analysis of a "Learning Situation" of one of the lecture sessions of the course "Marketing Management", which was held from 10:00 to 11:00am.

The lecture was held in an auditorium big enough for 500 students, and 300 students attended. Female students were almost four times the number of male students in the auditorium, where the genders were segregated from each other, so that females were sitting together and males sitting together. The auditorium had broken windows and no air conditioners, and there were fans hanging from the ceiling. None of the students had a laptop or hand-held devices in the class, only mobile phones. The equipment used in class was an over-head projector and a video projector.

The teacher dictated the lecture to the students, and they wrote down what she dictated. She read from her notes and explained to the students and then continued to dictate to them. Students studied by memorizing the lecture notes that the teacher dictated. In the exam, the students wrote down what they memorized. The teacher wrote down on transparencies (on an old over head projector) while explaining to students and dictating them slowly so that they could write what she said. Some of the words she wrote in English were spelled incorrectly. She kept dictating to them, and they wrote what she said. She stopped every once in a while to explain a certain concept and give examples to illustrate it. During the lecture, all students were silent and wrote down every word the teacher said. Some students made their own notes, which contained the contents of the lecture but rewritten in good handwriting or typed, and they would distribute them to their fellow students who did not attend the lecture. Students kept coming in class after the start of the lecture, and the teacher let them in. The teacher asked questions to test students' knowledge, and some students answered her. One student asked a question about an example which the teacher had used to illustrate a point, and another student gave an example of an incident that happened to him to confirm a point that the teacher was explaining and the teacher listened attentively and commented on the student's example.

The analysis of this "Learning Situation" is that all interaction is in the "student-material interface" (which we refer to as the ("b") section as shown in the figure. Students learn by memorizing information written in books or notes which the teacher obliges them to study, and the students' relationship with their teachers is based on the teachers' giving the students the "materials" and explaining (or not) explaining to them the contents of the materials.

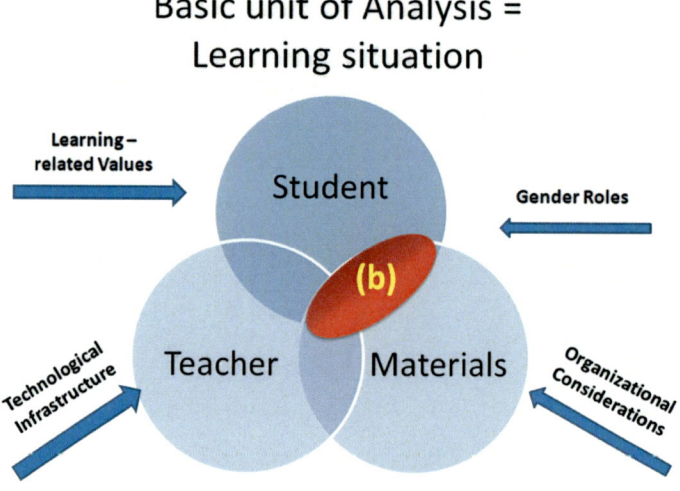

Figure 4: "Learning Situation" in Egypt

The case of Egypt is not so different from the Vietnamese case, as the students are also not in the center of teaching activities and are not viewed as active players in their own learning. In this observation, the materials prescribed by the higher education council in Egypt are in the center of teaching activities. The teacher is only a "representative" of these materials and tries, to some extent, to help students make sense of the information presented to them and relate this to their previous knowledge. There is minimal direct interaction between the teacher and the students, and the teacher can very easily be replaced by a tape recorder or printed materials, and this would not have affected the teaching process taking place in this class observation. The "instructivist" nature of this learning situation is very obvious, and students are viewed as passive reservoirs of information into which the teacher pumps the information from approved materials. They are expected to keep this information inside their heads until the exams and simply pour it out of their heads into the exam papers. This is how they would pass the exams in Egypt.

Discussion and Concluding Remarks

The analysis of the three "Learning Situations" show major differences in the learning practices followed in the three countries, Denmark, Egypt and Vietnam. In the following, only the differences pertaining to the problem of Western export of education in the form of Blended Learning programs will be discussed.

Obviously, Denmark has a much higher enrollment rate of students in tertiary education. Almost all students study in public education institutions. In Vietnam and Egypt, the overall rate of students' enrollment in higher education is lower, but the rate of students' enrollment in non-public education is higher than in Denmark.

The low enrollment rates in Vietnam and Egypt compared to Denmark and the social and economic factors determining these rates must be seen as the backdrop against which the described learning practices are understood and discussed. Despite the determining influence of such macro-level factors, institutional everyday practices and the ensuing conceptualizations of teaching and learning have to be taken into account when planning curricula and programs. Thus, this study includes ethnographic observations in different learning settings in three different countries. Among these observations, three learning situations were selected and described in depth in this paper.

When comparing the learning situations, profoundly different concepts of teaching and learning and of the roles played by teachers, learners and materials emerge. In the Danish case, the student is constituted as the agent of the learning process, and the teacher is responsible for creating a resourceful learning environment through a careful arrangement of learning materials, collaborative learning forms and her own presence as a provider of help and encouragement. Learning is assumed to result from the student's active involvement and participation in planned activities. Within certain boundaries, learning activities are self-managed. Contrary to the high levels of learner responsibility and agency found in the Danish setting, self-managed learning is discouraged in the Vietnamese and the Egyptian learning settings. In the Vietnamese case, students are expected to present acquired knowledge on their own but are through reprimands and corrections combined with constant reminders of upcoming exams made aware of the teacher's and the institution's authority. The available laptops allow for diversion of the students' attention from the teacher-controlled interaction. Such diversions are considered to have adverse effects on learning and are punished. Thus, classroom practices reinforce the notion that learning takes place in the interaction between teacher and students, and that the teacher (not information found on the internet) is the only source of relevant knowledge. The absence of elements of self-managed learning processes is even more striking in the Egyptian context. Apparently, student behavior is fully controlled by the teacher's instructions. However, as it turns out, both student and teacher behaviors are controlled by an external authority. Thus, the real authority of the learning situation is the *text* transmitted by the teacher (presenter) and received and repeated in a written form by the students.

An important lesson to be learnt from this study is that ethnographic studies of teaching and learning practices represent a necessary supplement to quantitative studies and statistic data. The observations show how the availability of technology can coexist with authoritative notions of teaching and learning and with classroom practices discouraging, and even punishing students' independent use of technology. They also reveal that students' engagement with study materials does not necessarily involve such processes as independent information retrieval, creative thinking or (self) reflection. In none of the learning settings outside of Denmark is the student perceived as a self-motivated, self-regulating individual capable of pursuing knowledge on his/her own.

However, this is the type of learner that many blended learning programs take as their point of departure, especially programs designed in contexts in which such learners constitute the majority of higher education students. The observation of the Danish EFL class demonstrates how students are encouraged to adopt the role of the self-managed learner, who is driven by intrinsic motivation, i.e. his/her own interest in learning and uses the learning environment to obtain his/her goal. When starting a university education, Danish students are well trained in collaborative and independent learning forms such as those applied in the observed learning situation, and the observed students perform more or less as expected. However, when learning forms demanding high degrees of individual agency, self-motivation, independent, technology-enhanced information retrieval and collaboration with peers are introduced as parts of blended learning programs, students socialized in settings similar to the Vietnamese or the Egyptian classes described above have no prior experience that might help them make sense of these learning forms. On the contrary, as the observations show, some types of conduct demanded from the students in blended learning programs are directly discouraged in these settings.

An important question is how exporting educational institutions may approach these different modes and concepts of learning? Should they enforce their own methods and just expect everyone to follow them? Or should they modify their teaching methods to meet the different needs of each group of students? And if they take this approach, what impact will this have on their profitability? In continuation of this study, two strategies towards a more satisfying study experience for non-Western students enrolled in 'exported' education are suggested. First of all, more research on concrete learning practices in higher education institutions in developing countries is needed. Importantly, research should acknowledge the fact that learning practices are varied and diverse as a consequence of the different types of higher education institutions. Secondly, the task of adjusting blended learning programs to specific ethnic and cultural groups may exceed the capacity of the individual provider of blended learning programs. However, this study demonstrates that it is very important for blended learning providers to explicate in great detail and in a language accessible to future learners the expectations regarding the levels of student motivation, activity, and agency demanded in such programs. In a similar vein, research results as those presented in this study must be communicated to blended learning providers in order to help them make realistic assessments of the resources needed when offering education in culturally, socially, and economically unfamiliar settings. Without the necessary investments in training, materials, technology, and not least human resources, it might not be worth the effort to enter the educational market of developing countries.

References

Amirault, R. J. & Visser, Y. L. (2010). The Impact of E-Learning Programs on the Internationalization of the University. Nova Science Publishers.

Bandura, A. & McClelland, D. C. (1977). Social learning theory. Englewood Cliffs: Prentice Hall.

Bennett, R. & Kane, S. (2011). Internationalization of UK University Business Schools: A Survey of Current Practice. Journal of Studies in International Education,15(4), 351-373.

Bollag, B. America's Hot New Export: Higher Education. Chronicle of Higher Education. 2/17/2006, Vol. 52 Issue 24, pA44-A47.

Brewer, J. D. (2000). Ethnography. Buckingham: Open University Press.

Caswell, T., Henson, S., Jensen, M. & Wiley, D. (2008). Open Content and Open Educational Resources: Enabling universal education. The International Review of Research in Open and Distance Learning, 9(1). Retrieved from http://www.irrodl.org/index.php/irrodl/article/view/469/1001.

Fahmy, S. S., Bygholm, A. & Jæger, K. (2012). Issues in Internationalization of education: The case of a Danish Business School exporting a blended learning MBA program to developing countries. In V. Hodgson, C. Jones, M. De Laat, D. McConell, T. Ryberg & P. B. Sloep (Eds.) Proceedings of the Eighth International Conference on Networked Learning 2012, April 2-4. Maastricht.

Klein, J. D., Spector, J. M., Grabowski, B., & Teja, N. (2004). Instructor competencies: Standards for face-to-face, online and blended settings. Greenwich, Connecticut: Information Age Publishing.

Lave, J. (1991). Situating learning in communities of practice. In L. B Resnick, J. M. Levine, & S. D. Teasley (Eds.), Perspectives on socially shared cognition, (pp. 63-82). Washington DC: American Psychological Association.

López-Pérez, M. V., Pérez-López, M. C. & Rodríguez-Ariza, L. (2011). Blended learning in higher education: Students' perceptions and their relation to outcomes. Computers & Education, 56 (3), 818-826.

Merrill, M. D. (2008). Why basic principles of instruction must be present in the learning landscape, whatever form it takes, for learning to be effective, efficient and engaging. Learners in a changing learning landscape. Lifelong Learning Book Series (Vol. 12), 267-275.

Ocak, M. A. (2011). Why are faculty members not teaching blended courses? Insights from faculty members. Computers & Education, 56(3), 689-699.

Rossett, A., Douglis, F.& Frazee, R. (2003). Strategies for building blended learning. Learning circuits, 4(7).

Sweller, J.,. Kirschner, P. A & Clark, R. E. (2007). Why minimally guided teaching techniques do not work: A reply to commentaries. Educational Psychologist, 42(2), 115-121.

Woltering, V., Herrler, A., Spitzler, K., & Spreckelsen, C. (2009). Blended learning positively affects students' satisfaction and the role of the tutor in the problem-based learning process: results of a mixed-method evaluation. Advances in Health Sciences Education, 14(5), 725-738.

Yao, X. (2000). An introduction to Confucianism. Cambridge: Cambridge University Press.

Part II

Approaches to Development

Application of PLA Methods in Educational Technology Research: A Rural Bangladeshi Case

Md. Saifuddin Khalid, Aalborg University
khalid@hum.aau.dk

Tom Nyvang, Aalborg University
Nyvang@hum.aau.dk

Abstract

This chapter examines barriers and methods to identify barriers to educational technology in a rural technical vocational education and training institute in Bangladesh. It also examines how the application of participatory learning and action methods can provide information for barrier research and stakeholders in and around the school to pave the way for change by building awareness of both educational technology and the complexity of barriers. In this case study, school stakeholders are involved in the research and awareness-building process through three different data-production methods: cultural transect, problem-tree analysis and focus-group discussion. The paper concludes by categorizing the barriers identified at different levels: micro (roughly the individual level at which the lack of knowledge and motivation are significant barriers), meso (roughly the school level at which the lack of teachers and computers are significant barriers) and macro (roughly the national level at which the lack of government planning and the lack of training of teachers are significant barriers). Finally, the paper also concludes that applied participatory learning and action-oriented techniques showed potential to provide researchers and local practitioners with situated insights that could not just have been lifted out of existing research literature.

Preamble

The integration of information and communication technology (ICT) in education and the adoption of educational technology have been subject to research for at least thirty years (Lowther, Inan, Strahl, & Ross, 2008). A simple search on this issue returned 80,500 articles from the Educational Resources Information Center (ERIC) database. A large part of this literature, in the context of educational institutes, has explored the barriers, grouped them into categories, identified relationships and suggested approaches to eliminate or circumvent barriers (see for example, Balanskat, Blamire, & Kefala, 2006; Chan, 2011; Ertmer, 2005; Ertmer et al, 2012; Hew & Brush, 2006; Pelgrum, 2001). However, previous literature lacks advice on methodological approaches to explore barriers of a situated context and lacks a theoretical foundation for categorization. Thus, the current chapter addresses these issues through three interrelated questions. Firstly, which methodological approach and which methods would enable participants to extract and present the interdependent barriers in a specific context? Secondly, in a situated case, how are these barriers related? Thirdly, do the barriers in the situated case indicate any pattern for theoretical contribution?

Methodologically, the current chapter takes its point of departure in Hew and Brush's (2006) findings, arguments and directions for further research on educational technology integration and adoption barriers. They analyzed 48 empirical studies from 1995 to 2006 and found that previous literature appeared to have one or more of the following four main limitations: (a) incomplete description of methodology (i.e., research duration, number of participants involved and interobserver and intraobserver reliability), (b) sole reliance on participants' self-reported data (i.e., interviews or surveys), (c) short-term in duration (i.e., five days to less than two years), (d) primary focus on the teacher and what went on in the classroom (i.e., not on the decisions and policies at school and district/national level). They suggested that future technology integration research should be based on the principles of mixed methods. This is defined as "the class of research techniques, methods, approaches, concepts or language in a single study" (Johnson & Onwuegbuzie, 2004, p. 17). Mixed- methods research frequently results in superior research because of its key- defining feature — methodological pluralism (Johnson & Onwuegbuzie, 2004, p. 17). Hew and Brush (2006) specified that future mixed-methods-based educational technology research should underpin the following principles: (a) thorough description of methodology (including length of the study, number of participants, interobserver and intraobserver agreement reliability), (b) observation of actual practice and no reporting of self-reported data, (c) longitudinal research, (d) examination of other decision-making stakeholders (i.e., school administrators, leadership, decision-makers in a broader context). Current literature attempts to overcome the identified methodological limitations through the application of participatory learning and action (PLA) methods, previously known as participatory rural appraisal (PRA) (Robert Chambers, 1994a, 1994b; Narayanasamy, 2009). With a strong foundation in methodological pluralism principles, PRA and PLA have a long history in the development research fields of agriculture, health, and education (Robert Chambers, 2008; Narayanasamy, 2009) (Robert Chambers, 2007; Narayanasamy, 2009), but to the knowledge of the authors, PLA has not been applied in the context of educational technology.

For situating the case, Bangladesh was purposefully selected, as Khan (Khan, Hasan, & Clement, 2012) reviewed the barriers in a Bangladeshi context and stated in his concluding statement:

> "as ICT is a relatively new field in Bangladeshi education systems, more in-depth research should be conducted related to the integration of ICT into classroom situations".

Thus, considering the situated-single-case qualitative research in Bangladesh for the integration and adoption of ICT in education, a second tier research question is: how do the stakeholders of rural Bangladeshi educational institutes experience educational technology integration and adoption barriers?

This chapter is organized into four sections. The first section deals with the application context of PLA. In the next section, the context-appropriated methodology and selected methods of PLA will be elaborated. In section three, the initial phase of case experience, data collection, and analysis will be reported, and in the fourth section, based on the evident pattern of relationships, the barriers will be categorized and mapped in a macro-meso-micro model of the education system.

The Context of the Case Study ICT in Education and TVET Education in Bangladesh

In the developing countries of the Asia Pacific region, there is an increasing emphasis on ICT in education (Akhtar & Arinto, 2009). Notably, the "Vision 2021: Digital Bangladesh" declared that improving the education sector through the use of ICT in education is a strategic priority of the nation (A2I: PMO, 2009; BOI: PMO, 2009). The country's Access to Information (A2I) project hosted by the Prime Minister's Office (PMO) plays the central role in all the public initiatives related to this vision. The current research project was inspired by an A2I presentation titled "Strategic Priorities of Digital Bangladesh: Improving Education Sector", which mentioned six focus areas for improving teaching and learning through the use of ICT: general and TVET education systems, ICT literacy for students, professional development of teachers using ICT, education-related citizen services, ICT in education administration, ICT infrastructure and delivery channels (A2I: PMO, 2009). The presentation also put explicit "focus on subject-based use of ICTs rather than ONLY ICT literacy" (A2I: PMO, 2009), which referred to educational technology integration and adoption. Moreover, it called for special emphasis on TVET (A2I: PMO, 2009). It envisioned "ICT literacy as a market-driven trade in TVET" (A2I: PMO, 2009). In addition, the education and research objectives of the Bangladeshi government's national ICT Policy-2009 (MoICT, 2009) and its strategic themes and action plans guided the scope of current research. Furthermore, the country's strategic approach to develop a knowledge economy is commensurate with the scientific course: "ICT in education as a resource for better teaching and learning and as a preparation of citizens for the Knowledge Society" (Khakhar et al, 2007).

Bangladesh has three different parallel education systems, i.e., General, Madrassa (Islamic) and TVET. Among these, to get accredited by the education board, only TVET institutes are required to have at least one computer lab and a computer teacher. Until 2011, at the K-12 education levels, only the TVET curriculum had a compulsory computer course from the ninth grade and above. In addition, for the populous rural area of Bangladesh, TVET is a prospective system for human resource development, poverty alleviation, rural development and education for all achievement (Basu & Majumdar, 2009). Emphasizing these areas, the European Commission (EC) provided financial support for the "TVET reform project" (Mia, 2009) and researchers identified TVET curriculum reform requirements (Ahmed, 2010). Moreover, the period 2005-2014 is the United Nations Decade of Education for Sustainable Development, and

TVET has been nominated as one of the key areas for a collective UNESCO effort (Hollander & Mar, 2009). Thus, the current research case was propelled by the international and national agenda for TVET and ICT in education.

Significance of Rural and Private Institutes in Bangladesh

Most of the populations of developing countries and their educational institutes are rural disadvantaged and therefore require great attention. Almost 70% of the world's poor live in rural areas (World Bank, 2012). Similarly, Bangladesh has a population of about 142 million (BBS, 2011) and 72% of the citizens live in rural areas (World Bank, 2012). At the secondary level of General education (i.e., junior secondary school, secondary school and school and college), 80% of the institutes/schools (i.e., 15285 out of 19083) are located in rural areas (BANBEIS, 2010). Among these schools, more than 98% (18766 out of 19083) are private schools, and among the private schools more than 81% (15257 out of 18766) are located in rural areas (BANBEIS, 2010). On the contrary, less than 9% (28 of 317) of the public schools are located in rural areas. In the TVET sector, more than 91% of the institutes/schools (2597 out of 2848) are private schools (BANBEIS, 2011). Moreover, schools in developing countries lack school facilities, which affect academic achievements (Okoza, Aluede, & Akpaida, 2012; Sabitu, Babatunde, & Oluwole, 2012; Vandiver, 2011). In addition, ICT in TVET necessitates more school facilities, which is a great challenge for the low-capital private school founders and in the rural context. Thus, educational development initiatives in Bangladesh could very well be centred in rural areas and focused on private institutes/schools.

Methodology

Transformative researchers "believe that inquiry needs to be intertwined with politics and a political agenda"(Creswell, 2003, p. 9) and should include an action plan for change "that may change the lives of the participants, the institutions in which individuals work or live, and the researcher's life" (Creswell, 2003, pp. 9 10). This paradigm argues for participatory methodology and mixed-method approaches for the development of "more complete and full portraits of our social world through the use of multiple perspectives and lenses" (Somekh & Lewin, 2005, p. 275) to gain an understanding of "greater diversity of values, stances and positions"(Somekh & Lewin, 2005, p. 275). The transformative paradigm does not generally begin with a theory but "generate or inductively develop a theory or pattern of meanings" (Creswell, 2003, p. 9) during the research process. However, unlike other paradigms, transformative research emphasizes social justice and marginalized people (Creswell, 2003, p. 9). So guided by the transformative paradigm, the current research project brings voices from the rural marginalized people and looks for patterns of barriers in the integration of educational technology.

This section presents the case and methods as recommended by Hew and Brush (2006), which was discussed in the 'preamble' section.

The Case: Rural Bangladeshi Private TVET Institute

This chapter's first author was this research project's change agent (CA) (Rogers, 1995) in the field. The current chapter uses the acronym and the term to indicate the first author.

A typical private rural TVET institute in Bangladesh, named Tofail Ali Technical School and College (TTSC), was purposefully selected. The CA had acquaintances with the TTSC founding members and had been facilitating ICT adoption at the institute during the period mid-2009 to mid-2010, i.e., before the current project was initiated. Thus, within the duration of the current research project, TTSC was the only institute in a rural context that would allow sufficient mixed-method-based understanding gained for a period of two years or more. The intention was to overcome the limitation "short-term in duration (i.e., five days to less than two years)" (Hew & Brush, 2006) of qualitative studies on educational technology. Therefore, in December 2010, as part of the current project, TTSC administrative authorities approved continued research by the CA and approved to take on the role of consultant to enable change at the institute. The CA conducted two field studies within the current project: from August 2011 to January 2012 and from August 20, 2012 to September 29, 2012. The CA played the role of a CA for the diffusion of ICT in the learning activities in formal (both curricular and extra-curricular activities), non-formal and informal contexts. In addition, the CA facilitated the adoption of ICT in the academic administration and the overcoming of overall ICT adoption barriers. This chapter is based on the mixed-method application experience conducted during the first field study.

The authors arranged a sponsorship of USD 3000 for the TTSC (CLP, 2010) and partnered with an NGO-initiated three-year public-private-partnership pilot program called "Computer Literacy Program" (CLP, 2012). In 2010, the program called for a sponsorship to pay part of the cost for establishing one smart classroom (SCR) and one computer literacy center (CLC) at the sponsored school (CLP, 2011a, 2011b). The project partners include: an NGO named Development Research Network (D.Net), a Volunteers Association for Bangladesh, New Jersey, USA (VAB-NJ) and the Bangladesh Computer Council (BCC) under the Ministry of Information and Communication Technology, Bangladesh. At the TTSC, the SCR was established in June 2011. The CLP provided one laptop, one 32-inch LCD TV, 200-watt hybrid solar system, one audio cable, one VGA cable, a one-year maintenance contract and four trained teachers (CLP, 2011a). The CLC was established in June 2011, equipped with four laptops, one laser printer, one EDGE modem, one flash drive and two trained teachers. The initial goal of the SCR was to bring change to teaching and learning activities in relation to English, mathematics, science and geography for 6th to 10th grade students. The goal of the CLC was to provide computer literacy to an 8-student batch per month, giving BDT 500 (corresponding to USD 6.15) as incentive to a teacher for the additional effort of 40 hours and a BDT 200 as incentive to a student assistant (corresponding to USD 2.46) for the same duration. The pilot project provided no further explicit information about the operations and maintenance costs and services, integration or adoption strategies.

The TTSC had been imparting education to IX-XII/9th to 12th grade students since its inception in 2000. The Bangladesh Technical Education Board (BTEB) approved the TTSC for teaching seven trade disciplines in Secondary School Certificate vocational (SSC voc), two trade disciplines in Higher Secondary Certificate in Business Management (HSC BM) and seven short-duration vocational certificate courses. In addition, the TTSC Junior School (TTSC-JS 6th-8th grade) and the Tofail Ali Kindergarten (TTKG; pre-school to primary) were established later on to ensure quality and quantity of students for the TTSC. These three institutes situated in close vicinity of each other were founded by the same person. The TTKG and the TTSC-JS were founded to become feeder institutes/schools to the TTSC, because, if a neighbouring school's students want to be admitted to the TTSC, the host institute does not approve the transfer. Despite being two separate institutes operationally, the TTSC and the TTSC-JS (combined 322 students in December 2011) had been sharing teaching loads and institutional resources. During December 2011, the TTSC's SSC VOC/voc had 16 (out of 23) vacant teaching and staff positions and the HSC BM's vacancy count was 3 (out of 11) positions. The founder is a retired public official who used to work in many administrative and academic positions in the Bangladeshi TVET system. The chairman of the school board is a high-ranking administrative officer of the Bangladeshi government. The top-tier administrative positions include the founder, chairman and the principal.

Methods – Participatory Rural Appraisal (PRA)

PRA, also termed participatory learning and action (PLA) (Chambers, 1994), is established and defined as an umbrella of methods, techniques and principles. The current research project applies this mixed-method approach in a single-case educational technology research study. The CA began the first field study with this question — which PRA/PLA methods are suitable for participatory collection and analysis of barriers to educational technology integration and adoption?

The PRA methods have been adapted and contributed through this research project in some ways: application in a new intervention discipline (i.e., ICT in education), the participants (i.e., stakeholders in education) and the facility locations (i.e., schools or academic institutions). The research project experienced academic institution-centered PRA method adaption. Through these methods, data were collected from students and teachers in the form of text and narratives. The CA and some teachers facilitated large groups of participants. This PRA application also used academic institution members as a hub of community, who analyzed the rural context. Identifying the most suitable method was very much situation dependent, experience guided and participant supported. For instance, the CA wanted to gain a quick overview of the situation at the beginning of the field work and applied his own experience of using PRA in other contexts. Thus, the problem-tree analysis was selected as the central method, while other methods were used for 'triangulation' – to verify and validate. The methods used will be discussed in the following.

Problem-tree analysis (PTA) is one of the flow diagramming techniques (Narayanasamy, 2009). Practically, a flow diagram makes it possible to assess the causes and effects of a defined problem or issue, determine the baseline and impact of development interventions and to study the flow of resources. In particular, the problem tree or the problem-tree analysis discovers the negative aspects of a situation and represents 'cause-and-effect' relationships between the problems that exist. The procedure preceded a focus-group discussion which identified and defined a problem. In view of the problem, the exercise will result in a visual presentation in the form of a 'problem tree' or 'directed graph' to establish 'cause-and-effect' relationships. The two following alternatives are at hand: Firstly, Gubbels & Koss (Gubbels & Koss, 2000) demonstrated a simple 'problem tree' presentation with a hierarchy of causes and effects. Secondly, Narayanasamy (Narayanasamy, 2009) showed a problem tree in the form of a 'directed graph', which he termed 'hierarchy of problems'. During this research project, both presentations were exercised/applied. Each group iterated the exercise twice. In the first exercise, the 'problem tree' was used, and in a second exercise, the 'directed graph' was diagrammed.

The focus-group discussion (FGD) method was found the most effective one by the participants from academic institutes. It identified the problem to be addressed with facilitation from the CA. This action research applied FGD as a two-way communication between the CA and the participants. As David L. Morgan (Morgan, Krueger, & King, 1998) mentions, a three-part process of communication is seen in an FGD: (i) the research-team member decides what he needs to hear from the participants; (ii) the focus groups create a conversation among the participants about these chosen topics; and (iii) members of the research team summarize what they have learned from the participants. Furthermore, to facilitate the group discussion, Chamber's (1992) recommendations were followed — "relaxing not rushing, showing respect, 'handing over the stick' and being self-critically aware". Thus, FGD was used as a vehicle for a two-way 'diffusion communication' (Rogers, 1995). The probable roles of the 'change agent' (Rogers, 1995) in relation to ICT integration and adoption were also discussed. Consequently, the participants were facilitated to define a problem which can be addressed with support from the CA.

Semi-structured interviews (SSI) were conducted to clarify and further analyze the cause-and-effect relationships of the problem-tree analysis, because some of the terms were context sensitive and more analyses from the local analysts (students and teachers) were required. Theoretically, in PRA, the SSI technique is used extensively as a "guided interview where only primary questions are predetermined" (Narayanasamy, 2009). During these research interviews, the participant groups' problem trees were used as a flexible 'checklist or guide' (Mikkelsen, 2005). Five teachers and seven students voluntarily participated in SSIs, which in the case of students turned out to be FGDs of three and four members. During the SSIs, barrier relationships were verified individually and in groups, and each relationship was validated by means of specific examples.

Cultural transect enabled the researcher(s) "to traverse through the 'life' of a person, a subset of the village, or the village itself over a period of time (it may be a day, or a week, or more)" (Mascarenhas, 1992). The CA attached himself to a lecturer and the principal, grouped with sports-enthusiast students, lived with a family and actively engaged in ICT integration and adoption activities, observed others' experiences and discussed how to discover patterns of the academic life of students and teachers in rural settings — why they are what they are. Thus, cultural transect includes all the live-in-field experiences of being part of a rural family during the entire stay, being associated with three academic institutes, students, parents, teachers, often providing the administrative support, teaching, fund raising, facilitating official meetings, conducting in-house training, student counseling, winter cloth distribution for charity, etc., - all inseparable parts of being 'a member of the institute'. In other words, the daily logs, notes, images, videos, face-to-face interactions and activities and unplanned observations constitute the cultural transect data.

Participant observation and non-participant observation were conducted during the study. By definition, participant observation is a method according to which the observer is a part of the phenomenon or group which is being observed and he/she acts both as an observer and as a participant (Robert Chambers, 1994b). In case of 'non-participant observation', the observer does not participate in the phenomenon being observed. In this research project, both methods were applied as part of the cultural transect. A checklist including the causes and the effects identified in the problem-tree analyses was the basis when looking for evidence. The CA kept notes of the events, incidents, conversations and discussions related to the qualitative insights gained about the checklist or additional issues that were not discussed in the PTA.

Combinations and Sequences of Methods

This section shows an at-a-glance presentation of the application sequence of the PRA methods, because one of the greatest strengths of these methods is their combinations and sequences (Shah, Bharadwaj, & Ambastha, 1991) (Robert Chambers, 1994b). Through this methodical non-linear sequence, the intention was to facilitate the participants to select a problem, identify the causes, analyze the cause-and-effect relationships and identify the issues which could be handled with immediate facilitation. The selection and application process of this method was situation experienced rather than based on pre-knowledge planning. Thus, the four stages in Table 1 attempt to summarize the application of PRA with the purpose to answer: Firstly, which methodological approach and which methods would enable participants to extract and present the interdependent barriers? Secondly, in a situated case, how are these barriers related?

Table 1. Stage-Outcome-Method-Participants
Sequence of PRA for Problem Formulation

Stage	Method(s)	Outcome	Participants
Commonly agreed problem selection and definition	2 FGDs	Problem statement	19 12th graders 7 teachers
Cause-and-effect relationships with the problem	2 problem-tree analyses	Cause-and-effect analysis	19 12th graders 7 teachers

Stage	Method(s)	Outcome	Participants
Context-dependent clarifications about cause and effects	FGDs and SSIs	Explicit examples to represent causes and effects, context appropriation for translating local terms	5 12th graders 5 teachers
Causes – why do these barriers exist? Who causes barriers in which way? Do relationships and/or patterns appear evident?	Cultural transect	Outsiders become 'participant observer': change agent live-in-field experiences from daily practices and events	Change agent, students, teachers, admin roles, parents

Triangulation — The Validation Process

Triangulation (Grandstaff, Grandstaff, & Lovelace, 1987) is an essential PRA principle. It is a validation process of progressively learning, cross checking and approximating through progressive plural investigation. The process involves various ways of "assessing and comparing findings from several methods - often three: type of item or set of conditions, points in a range or distribution, individuals or groups of analysts, places, times, disciplines, investigators or inquirers and combinations of these" (Robert Chambers, 1994b). There are many types of triangulation; Mikkelsen (2005) suggested five types and their sub-types: data triangulation, investigator triangulation, discipline triangulation, theoretical triangulation and methodological triangulation. Furthermore, data triangulation is further divided into three types: personal triangulation, space triangulation and time triangulation. Within the third-level categorization, personal triangulation is defined as the process of considering the reactions at three levels of analysis: (i) individual, (ii) groups and (iii) collective. Regarding methodological triangulation, two types exist: the within-method and the between-method. If the same method is used for different topics, it is called within-method triangulation. Between-method triangulation includes a blend of two or more different methods in the analysis of the same topic.

The current research project conducted data triangulation at each of the three personal triangulation levels in the form of SSIs with individuals, groups' FGDs and problem-tree analyses, and collective cross-checking and summarization using cultural transect experience of the change agent. Therefore, the current research project involved data triangulation of the personal triangulation type conducted at the same space or in the same situation and during the same time interval, i.e., FGDs, problem-tree analyses and two SSIs were conducted on the current topic, during three afternoons within a period of nine days in September 2011. In addition, this research project applied between-method triangulation by applying all the methods on a single topic. Therefore, validity was addressed in a two-fold triangulation 'process: by means of three sources and three methods (see Figure 1.).

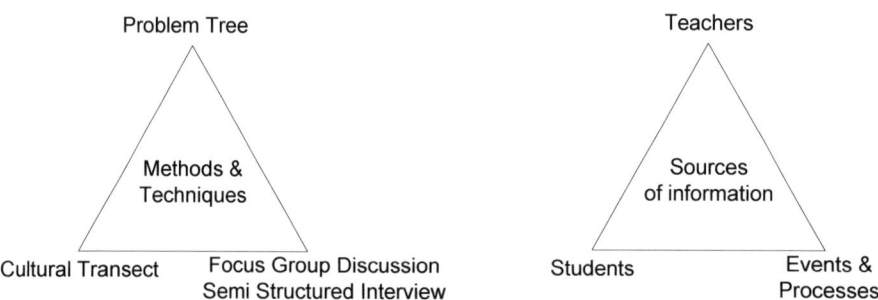

Fig 1a. Between-method triangulation   Fig 1b. Personal triangulation

The application of these methods preceded a 'rapport building' (Robert Chambers, 1994b) phase of about seven days. During a period of approx. six months, fieldwork in Bangladesh, FGD, PTA, and SSI were applied within the first two weeks of an overall four-month stay in the village. However, validation by cultural transect may have been covered by some insights gained from second-field studies and subsequent communication over the telecom and internet media.

Facilitation of PRA Methods

In the current research project, it was mainly the 12th grade students and the teachers of the TTSC who participated in the PRA methods (i.e., FGD, PTA, and SSI). In addition, daily interactions and conversations with the students from ninth, tenth and eleventh grade significantly contributed to the validation through cultural transect experiences. The facilitator role was conducted by the CA and he was often assisted by one lecturer of the TTSC. The lecturer is very popular with the students of the institutes and was recommended by teachers to take on the role of facilitator. In some cases, the principal is in charge of the facilitator role, thus providing an increased opportunity for the participants to be heard by an administrative person. Hence, an institution-based PRA application might be easier compared to other contexts in which an agreed-upon popular leadership or positively-accepted administrator is not at hand during the facilitation process.

Two workshops were conducted for the problem-tree analyses, each of which began and ended with a focus group discussion. Each workshop took about three hours during two afternoons. In the first workshop, the participants comprised 19 12th grade students who split into three groups. In the second workshop, seven teachers participated. Their designations were principal, lecturer (accounting), lecturer (management), computer demonstrator, trade instructor (general electrical works), assistant teacher (language) and assistant teacher (mathematics). During the two workshops, one group of teachers and three groups of students created four problem trees. Similarly, immediately after the exercise, each group conducted a rigorous analysis while creating a dependency relationship of causes and effects. Both groups' workshops ended with a focus group discussion of approx. half and hour on how to solve the problem. In particular, the discussion took a turn towards identifying who would be responsible for the desired change and for addressing barriers to the change.

The field activities were recorded in the form of plans, actual activities, problems faced, discussions, analyses, decisions and various incidents. These were recorded on paper, smart-phone, and computer – in the form of text, images, audio and video recordings. The participants' workshop activities were conducted on large sheets of papers using multi-color pens, sign pens and pencils.

Dealing with Local Dialect and Translation

All the methods were conducted in Bengali, the native language of the participants and the CA. Furthermore, since most of the participants used to speak the local dialect of Brahmanbaria, the facilitators (particularly the CA) tried to use the local accent. This attempt often eased the communication and enabled stronger rapport building.

Strong emphasis was put on the translation process to ensure context-appropriate translation. Firstly, the CA together with the English language teacher of the TTSC translated the problem-tree diagrams from Bengali into English. The teacher is a permanent resident of a neighboring village, which made it possible to deal with the contextual meanings. Thus, the translation exercise contributed in the form of a semi-structured interview. Secondly, the translations were verified with/by an urban-school English language teacher, who had affinity with rural education. Thirdly, the translations were verified with/by a Bangladeshi researcher.

The PRA Application Experience and Data Analyses

Setting the Scene – How the Application Process Began

The PRA implementation process began with the village mapping method. This method resulted in geographical, demographical and additional information about the study village, which is the host/hometown of most students and teachers. Approx. all the 12th graders and four alumni of the TTSC participated in the village mapping workshops. During the last workshop, in the presence of two lecturers, the principal initiated an unstructured group discussion regarding "educational ICT skills and adoption - what can be done next to take advantage of our brother [CA]?" After minutes of motivational words from both the teachers and the CA, the students began to respond. The participants decided on one common issue: "we have not acquired enough/any idea on how or why to use computer and Internet for a real-life purpose although we have and had compulsory computer subject(s)". The teachers supported the students' grievances by saying,

> "we never had such a skilled teacher, we always lack a computer teacher, we are not subject experts, and we have too many problems......we feel that there is a need....but we cannot say what that is".

Eventually, the facilitation to form a problem statement looked like this:

> "students are not acquiring computer and Internet-related vocational and practical skills from the institute".

Driven by the jointly identified problem and previous PRA application experience, the CA felt that it might be appropriate to use the problem-tree method. The CA tested it with a few students and a teacher before deciding to do so.

Data Analyses and Discussions

These analyses include the participants' analyses and the researchers' analyses of the problem statement: "students are not acquiring computer and Internet-related vocational and practical skills from the institute". Through the PTA method, the participants identified the barriers (as causes), the relationship within the barriers, the effect of the barriers (as effects) and the relationships of the effects. The CA merged the four tree diagrams into one — for gaining further insights from the relationship of the barriers. While the first phase of the PTA was based on the participants' analyses, the merging process involved the CA's analyses. With this backdrop, the process of merging the PTAs and the process of validation using FGD, SSI and cultural transect will be discussed in this section.

During the field study, the first four problem-tree analyses were central to exploring the problem landscape. The causes and effects of the PTA have been summarized in the following two tables. Table 1 and 2 show the causes and effects, respectively. Against each cause or effect, each group is represented by a letter: the teachers' group by a T, the students' group one by an A, group two by a B and group three by a C. The student workshop identified and analyzed 25 causes and the teacher workshop discussed their 32 causes. The three student groups A, B, and C contributed 18, 14 and 13 causes, respectively. Table 1 shows the accumulated 43 causes analyzed by both teachers and students. Among these, 18 causes were only mentioned by teachers, 11 causes were only mentioned by students, and 14 causes were mentioned by both teachers and students. The participants confirmed that the 14 causes mentioned by both groups are the most frequently discussed issues and these might be the urgent ones. In addition, the participants discussed/agreed that these barriers cannot be addressed one at a time; each cause is related to several other causes. Furthermore, the teachers explained that the acquisition and maintenance of technology resources involve many issues that are related to the institution's initiatives, rural infrastructure and cultural attitudes.

Table 1. Summary of Causes of the Problem

Causes	Groups			
Long delayed acquisition and repair of equipments	T	-	-	-
Low teacher quality	T	-	-	-
Lack of teacher training	T	-	-	-

Causes	Groups			
Negative attitudes of surrounding social environment	T	A	B	-
Insufficient number of computers	T	A	B	C
Lack of computer accessories (printer, memory card, Internet Modem, Card Reader)	T	A	B	C
Unreliable network (both mobile and Internet)	T	-	B	-
Lack of technical support for maintenance (caused by, 1) the lack of facility in close vicinity, 2) the lack of facility at the school)	T	-	-	-
Lack of parents' awareness	T	-	-	-
Lack of (vocational trade) teachers due to the government's teacher registration examination	T	-	B	-
Students' irregular attendance	T	-	-	-
Infrastructure problems	T	-	-	-
Unreliable electricity	T	A	B	C
Higher student population than available resources	T	-	-	-
Lack of well-groomed students as former educational attainment quality is lower than essential	T	-	-	-
Insufficient number of laboratories	T	A	B	C
Low teacher retention (troubles students and reduces attendance rate)	T	-	-	-
Troublesome commuting system and facility	T	A	B	C
Lack of (technically) skilled teachers	T	A	-	C
Due to financial insolvency, teachers lack concentration in delivering lessons	T	-	-	-
Students' weakness in English	T	A	B	C
Insufficient classrooms	T	A	-	C
Unavailability of (computer) teachers despite repeated employment notices in the newspapers	T	-	-	-
Lack of computers in working condition	T	-	-	-
Directorate of Technical Education (DTE) and Bangladesh Technical Education Board (BTEB) lack sufficient manpower for proper administration	T	-	-	-
Cannot give appropriate honorarium to part-time teachers	T	-	-	-
Institute's financial insolvency	T	A		C

Causes	Groups			
Lack of government's planning and patronizing	T	-	-	-
Financial insolvency of a students' family	T	-	-	-
Teachers lack application skills (despite passing from polytechnic institute)	T	-	-	-
Lack of facilities for industrial attachment	T	A	-	-
Lack of directions from teachers	-	A	-	-
Lack of general knowledge	-	A	-	-
Lack of library to try (new) applications	-	A	-	C
Lab classes are not held regularly	-	A	-	-
Lab class exercises lack computer use appropriation for practical needs	-	A	-	-
Local managing committee lacks sapient members	-	A	-	-
Lack of teachers	T	A	-	C
Lack of books on computer and Internet applications	-	-	B	C
Students lack motivation	-	-	B	C
No scope of access outside school	-	-	B	-
Family cannot afford computer, etc.	-	-	B	-
(Students and Teachers) fear of computer usage/causing malfunction	-	-	B	-
Number of effects mentioned in each problem tree	32	18	14	13

Stating causes was much easier than reflecting on the effects, and the active participation of the CA was facilitating. Both the teachers and the students had difficulties in visualizing the benefits of the skills. The significance of the challenge may be realized by a teacher's reflection, who is a graduate from a polytechnic institute. The teacher stated, "last year I had accumulated savings of 70,000 taka with a plan to buy a computer and an Internet connection. I could not finally decide on buying those. I could not see much benefit because I did not have the required knowledge, confidence and skills. But, now that you [CA] are here, I shall buy soon and learn from you". The participants confirmed that the discussions and activities with the CA, the feeling of living together in the same environment and the active participation in the activities had enabled them to realize the effect. Otherwise, reflecting on the effects might have been much harder. As part of the effects analyses, the teachers discussed their nine effects and students discussed their 19 accumulated factors identified by the three groups. Student groups A, B and C wrote twelve, six and seven effects, respectively. Table 2 shows the merged list of 27 effects. Among these, seven effects were mentioned by the teacher group only, and 18 effects were mentioned by the students only. The participants expressed that these effects could only be realized through the activities and discussion with the CA. On behalf of the group, one teacher summarized that

> "if we can learn to apply these technologies, we shall benefit from getting access to the new public services on the Internet, we can look for better job opportunities, and it will benefit our teaching and learning activities"

Thus, it is evident from this statement that the current barriers could hinder the desired change in ICT for education, livelihood and public services.

Table 2. Summary of Effects of the Problem

Effects	Groups			
Cannot sustain in the competitive technology job market	T	-	-	-
Cannot apply TVET education in job	T	-	-	-
Cannot communicate for higher education	T	-	B	C
Limiting scope of pursuing higher education through the computer	T	-	-	-
Not being able to use for practical needs of life (educational and other information and news)	T	-	B	-
The goals of TVET are not being achieved	T	-	-	-
Increasing rate of unemployment	T	-	-	-
Job opportunities exist but the unskilled cannot be employed	T	-	-	-
Ending with general education despite studying in technical educational institute, resulting in losing interest in technical education	T	-	-	-
Cannot/shall not get a suitable job	-	-	-	C
Cannot create self employment	-	A	B	-
Cannot print various documents	-	A	-	-
(Due to a lack of English proficiency) cannot communicate with non-Bangla speakers	-	A	-	C
Cannot access online results	-	A	-	-
(Without Internet) necessary travel and communication for possible online activities increase cost	-	A	-	-
(Without Internet) cannot access (all public services and academic) forms	-	A	-	-
Collecting entertaining media from distant market(s) or place(s) costs more time	-	A	-	-

Effects	Groups			
(Without Internet) academic communication takes more time	-	A	-	-
Cannot search for jobs (online)	-	A	-	-
Cannot communicate (online) with relatives staying abroad	-	A	-	-
Cannot read online newspapers	-	A	B	-
(I or family) cannot decide on the purchase of a computer and Internet access	-	A	-	C
Cannot share (spread) technology knowledge among others	-	-	-	C
Not getting a good job due to weakness in computer skills and English	-	-	-	C
Cannot access various news and general knowledge about the world	-	-	-	C
Cannon play computer games for entertainment	-	-	B	C
Cannon access educational information available online	-	-	B	
Number of effects mentioned in each problem tree	9	12	6	7

All causes and effects were validated by all the participants and noted by the CA through the events. Focus was only on the causes (i.e., barriers), which were the focus of this study. The validation process involved FGDs, SSIs and cultural transect (i.e., observed evidence and group reflections). In this process, FGDs after the PTAs validated the causes and the effects. In addition, a high degree of the validation was completed in the students' PTA discussion. The after-PTA exercise, i.e., the FGD with teachers, involved the validation of the students' PTAs. Subsequently, the CA looked for specific evidence through SSIs and cultural transect to further understand the context and thus contribute to the validation process. During the events of participant observation, the CA conducted SSIs and noted the events to validate the causes, effects and the underlying relationships. The FGD-PTA-FGD sequence, the SSIs and cultural transect applied between-method triangulation through each of the workshops. In addition, the merging process from three different groups involved within-PTA-method triangulation. Furthermore, data sources from students, teachers and other events in which the CA participated applied personal (more specifically, group) triangulation.

Through this methodology, as opposed to participants' own collection methods and techniques to identify agreement or disagreement, each of the methods intended to come to a common understanding and shared viewpoints. This also allowed the CA to reflect on the observations and take the opportunity of "diffusion communication" (Rogers, 1995) on ICT in education. The CA used the checklist for validation and verification during the translation process with the teacher of the institute, through formal and informal discussions with the students and the teachers, in conducting curricular and co-curricular activities, at the time of visiting the houses of students and teachers, while participating in administrative activities, during the observation of classes and while experiencing the life in the village. For instance, the fact that the institute's financial insolvency cause was mentioned by the three groups satisfied the verification part in itself and the validation was done by the principal, a member of the local managing committee (i.e., the parents' representative), the chairman of the management and the founder. Similarly, with respect to students' irregular attendance, it was observed that on most days only half of the 11th grade students were present, as indicated by the attendance record book and students' response in a face-to-face interaction.

In the quest for overcoming educational technology barriers, the researchers' analyses include the reconstruction of the problem tree, categorization of causes and the selection of three research directions for analyses.

The authors re-constructed the problem tree (as in Figure 1) from the merged list and the four problem-tree diagrams. Based on the relationships of the participants' problem trees, the authors categorized the causes as: teachers' deficiencies, students' challenges, academic institute's inabilities, rural disadvantaged context and national issues and central administrative barriers. These cause categories appeared to be grouped according to their association with roles or organizations. During the problem-tree reconstruction, the authors experienced that some of the dependent causes are related to several preceding causes. The tree diagram only allows a one-to-many relationship, but representing the reality requires a many-to-many relationship. For instance, most of the students and teachers do not have access to computer or Internet in their informal life due to the rural disadvantaged condition. Thus, in the diagram this could only be associated with the students' challenges and not the rural condition.

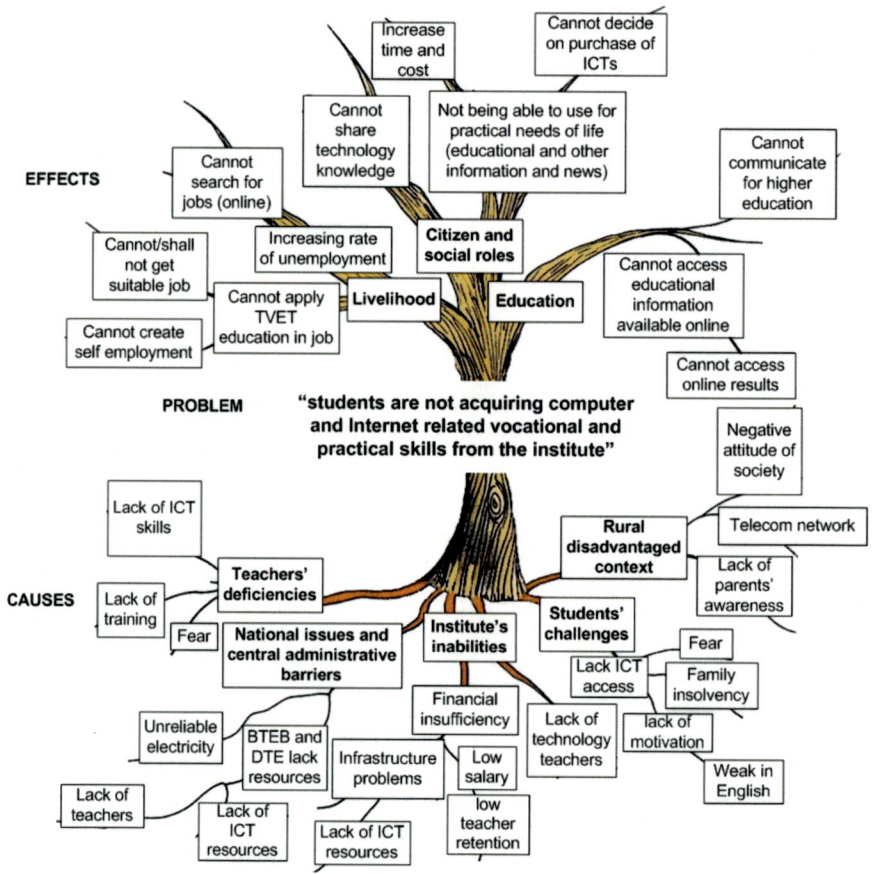

Figure 1. Partial View of Problem-Tree Analysis of Teachers and Students of Rural Vocational Institute

The natural many-to-many relationship among the barriers showed the complex nature of these barriers. In addition, the one-to-many dependency relationship of the problem-tree analysis might be an approach for simplification and a scope for a systematic solution approach. Furthermore, this representation provides greater insights among the relationships, addresses the situative contexts and overcomes limitations of previous barrier categories. For instance, Hew and Brush's (2006) categorization and relationship among direct and indirect barriers might be further contributed by this approach; a directed graph method could also be used instead of a tree diagram.

Beyond PRA: Mapping Barriers into Macro, Meso, and Micro Levels of the Education System

The transformative researchers of the current chapter posed the question, "do the barriers in the situated case indicate any pattern for theoretical contribution?" The authors conducted a review of the existing categorization of educational technology barriers, to identify a possible match between barrier categories in previous literature and barrier categories and relationships of the current case. A representative number of previous studies have either built on or fall into the pattern of the following categories: extrinsic or first-order and intrinsic or second-order (Albirini, 2006; Ertmer, 1999; Snoeyink and Peggy A. Ertmer, 2001) material and non-material barriers (Pelgrum, 2001), teacher-level barriers (confidence, competence, and resistance to change and negative attitude) and school-level barriers (time, training, accessibility, technical support) (Bingimlas, 2009), resources, knowledge and skills, institution, attitudes and beliefs, assessment and subject culture (Hew & Brush, 2006), direct and indirect (Hew & Brush, 2006), teacher level, school level and system level (Balanskat et al., 2006), and micro level (individual or classroom), meso level (educational institute) and macro level (national organizations related to educational role) (Balanskat et al., 2006; Chan, 2011; Looi, So, Toh, & Chen, 2011; Pelgrum, 2001). Within these categories, the authors looked for and could find a trace of an evident pattern in the relationships and general categories of the causes of the merged problem tree. The cause categories can be related as micro-level or stakeholders' barriers (i.e., teachers' deficiencies and students' challenges), meso-level or institute's barriers (i.e., institute's inabilities), macro-level or national-level educational entities' barriers (e.g. national administrative barriers) and external disadvantages (e.g. rural disadvantaged context). Figure 2 shows this concept of categorization.

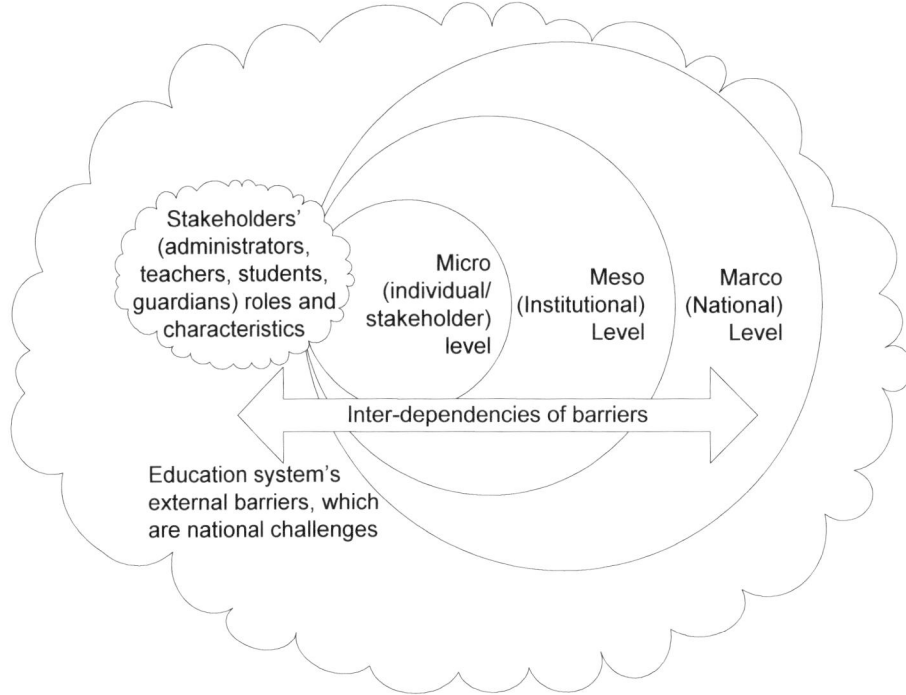

Figure 2. Framework of Barriers in Educational Technology Integration and Adoption

The authors applied this framework and reported the causes of two barriers in Table 3. This mapping reflects the participants' viewpoints on the education system and the causes of barriers.

Table 3. Mapping Barriers into Macro-Meso-Micro Levels

Barrier	Long delayed acquisition and repair of equipment	Lab classes are not held regularly
Macro	Lack of government's planning and patronizing,	Lack of (vocational trade) teachers, low rate of persons passing the government's teacher registration examination, lack of (technology) skilled teachers.
Meso	Financial insolvency, no separate IT budget, principal requires approval from managing committee, lack of tech-support in school, lack of technically skilled teachers	Insufficient number of (working) computers, lack of computer accessories, lack of tech-support, insufficient number of laboratories, high student-computer ratio, low teacher retention, lack of teachers, unavailability of (computer) teachers despite repeated employment notices in the newspaper, lack of funds for teachers' honourium.
Micro	Lack of knowledge about – quality of equipment, quality of markets; lack of confidence.	Students lack motivation, students' irregular and low attendance, overworked teachers give priorities to other classes and tasks
External	Poor transport system infrastructure, lack of tech-support in close vicinity, lack of confidence in ICT seller and service provider, security vulnerabilities, access to required information for purchase decision, etc.	Unreliable electricity, lack of tech-support, troublesome commuting system.

Taking a step further from the above framework (Figure 2) and mapping (Table 3), the cause categories indicate change processes at organizational and individual levels. Roger's theory of diffusion of innovations established that innovation adoption involves changes at individual levels (i.e., stakeholders) and the organizational (i.e., education and other) levels (Rogers, 1995). Furthermore, the application of PRA methods contributed as a diffusion communication strategy, both at individual level and at the organizational level.

Conclusion and Future Scope

In the preamble to this chapter the authors identified three interrelated questions: Firstly, which methodological approach and which methods would enable participants to extract and present the interdependent barriers to educational technology in a specific context? Secondly, in a situated case, how are these barriers related? Thirdly, do the barriers in the situated case indicate any pattern for theoretical contribution?

With regard to the first question, the authors have tried out participatory learning and action (PLA) methods in practice in an educational institute in rural Bangladesh. By applying techniques grounded in the PLA methods, the authors found that actors in and around the school increased their awareness by identifying a core problem in the school: students are not acquiring computer and internet-related vocational and practical skills. In this respect, it is important to stress that the problem or barriers leading to it are not surprising per se, as they are at the abstract level more or less in line with research from other parts of the world. The new thing is that the authors have verified the barriers and arrived at a thick description of the barriers in a rural Bangladeshi context and that local actors were heavily involved in the process of identifying and understanding these barriers. The local involvement in the identification and verification of the barriers also developed local awareness by making stakeholders talk and exchange viewpoints and experience. This prepared the change agent who was to integrate educational technology in the institute in order to deal with the barriers. The authors also expect that it has prepared the school for change. Considering the data analysed in this chapter, it is, however, not possible to sustain that the process did in fact prepare the school for change. For a solid answer, more research into the longer-term effect of participatory learning and action methods is needed.

With regard to the second question, the barriers are weaved together in a web of causes and effects. Categories of causes that appear in the research data include teachers' deficiencies, national issues, institute's inabilities, students' challenges and the rural disadvantaged context. Categories of effects include livelihood, education and citizen and social roles. These categories of problem causes and effects also indicate that they can meaningfully be categorized at different levels: the individual stakeholder micro level, the national political and administrative macro level and in-between them a school and local management meso level.

With regard to the third question, it is still difficult to theorize about the relation between problems, barriers and methods to integrate educational technology in rural contexts in developing countries. The authors attempt to start theory-building with a focus on the way barriers are connected across the micro, meso and macro levels because they appear to be so, but more research is needed to further develop and confirm this theory. The current research project has therefore primarily viewed the meso and macro levels from the micro level – i.e., through the experience and expression of teachers and students, but other levels may view the problems and causes differently and may develop our impression of the way barriers travel across the levels.

References

A2I: PMO. (2009). Strategic Priorities of Digital Bangladesh: Improving Education Sector. Access to Information, Prime Minister's Office, Bangladesh. Government of Bangladesh. http://www.digitalbangladesh.gov.bd/documents/Education.pdf

Ahmed, M. F. (2010). Technical and Vocational Education and Training– Curricula Reform Demand in Bangladesh. Qualification Requirements, Qualification Deficits and Reform Perspectives. Universität Stuttgart. University. http://elib.uni-stuttgart.de/opus/volltexte/2011/5912/pdf/DissertationFaruqueAhmed.pdf

Akhtar, S., & Arinto, P. (Eds.). (2009). Digital Review of Asia Pacific, 2009-2010. Delhi: SAGE Publications.

Albirini, A. (2006). Teachers' attitudes toward information and communication technologies: the case of Syrian EFL teachers. Computers & Education, 47(4), p. 373–398.

Balanskat, A., Blamire, R., & Kefala, S. (2006). The ICT impact report. European Schoolnet. http://www.lopstechnology.com/fotos/editor2/relatorios/ict_impact_report_1_.pdf

BANBEIS. (2010). No. of school, teacher and student by area status ,management and gender,2010. Bangladesh Bureau of Educational Information and Statistics. Government of Bangladesh. http://www.banbeis.gov.bd/webnew/index.php?option=com_content&view=article&id=178:no-of-school-teacher-and-student-by-area-status-management-and-gender2010&catid=39:se-basic-tables&Itemid=144

BANBEIS. (2011, August 27). Number of Vocational Institution, Teacher and Enrolment by type, management and sex - 2010. Bangladesh Bureau of Educational Information and Statistics. Government of Bangladesh. http://www.banbeis.gov.bd/webnew/index.php?option=com_content&view=article&id=451:number-of-institution-teacher-and-enrolment-by-type-management-and-sex2010&catid=77:technical-and-vocational-education-2010&Itemid=185

Basu, C. K., & Majumdar, S. (2009). The Role of ICTs and TVET in Rural Development and Poverty Alleviation. In R. Maclean & D. Wilson (Eds.), International Handbook of Education for the Changing World of Work (pp. 1923–1934). Dordrecht: Springer.

BBS. (2011, July). 2011 Population & Housing Census: Preliminary Results. Bangladesh Bureau of Statistics. Government Official. http://www.bbs.gov.bd/WebTestApplication/userfiles/Image/Census2011/Bangladesh_glance.pdf

Bingimlas, K. A. (2009). Barriers to the Successful Integration of ICT in Teaching and Learning Environments: A Review of the Literature. Eurasia Journal of Mathematics, Science & Technology Education, 5(3), p. 235–245.

BOI: PMO. (2009). Government Vision 2021. Board of Investment, Prime Minster's Office, Bangladesh. Government of Bangladesh. http://boi.gov.bd/about-bangladesh/government-and-policies/government-vision-2021

Chambers, R. (1992). Rural appraisal: Rapid, relaxed and participatory. London: Sussex Univ. Brighton (GB). Inst. of Development Studies.

Chambers, R. (1994a). The origins and practice of participatory rural appraisal. World Development, 22(7), p. 953–969.

Chambers, R. (1994b). Participatory rural appraisal (PRA): Analysis of experience. World Development, 22(9), p. 1253–1268.

Chambers, R. (2007). From PRA to PLA and Pluralism: Practice and Theory (No. Working Paper 286). Brighton, UK: Institute of Development Studies, University of Sussex. http://www.dfid.gov.uk/r4d/PDF/Outputs/CentreOnCitizenship/gaventawp264.pdf

Chambers, R. (2008). PRA, PLA and Pluralism: Practice and Theory. In P. Reason & H. Bradbury (eds.), The SAGE handbook of action research: participative inquiry and practice. London: SAGE.

Chan, C. K. K. (2011). Bridging research and practice: Implementing and sustaining knowledge building in Hong Kong classrooms. International Journal of Computer-Supported Collaborative Learning, 6(2), p. 147–186.

CLP. (2010). CLC & SCR Online Pledge Form « Computer Literacy Program. Computer Literacy Program, Bangladesh. NGO. http://www.clp.net.bd/clc-scr-online-pledge-form

CLP. (2011a). Smart Class Room of Tofail Ali Technical School and College. Computer Literacy Program, Bangladesh. NGO. http://www.clp.net.bd/blog/2737/tofail-ali-technical-school-and-college

CLP. (2011b). Computer Literacy Center of Tofail Ali Technical School and College, B.Baria. Computer Literacy Program, Bangladesh. NGO. http://www.clp.net.bd/blog/2484/tofail-ali-technical-school-and-college-b-baria

CLP. (2012). Computer Literacy Program, Bangladesh. Computer Literacy Program, Bangladesh. http://www.clp.net.bd/

Creswell, J. W. (2003). Research design: Qualitative, quantitative, and mixed methods approaches. (2nd ed.). Thousand Oaks: SAGE publications.

Ertmer, P. A. (1999). Addressing first- and second-order barriers to change: Strategies for technology integration. Educational Technology Research and Development, 47(4), p. 47–61. doi:10.1007/BF02299597

Ertmer, P. A. (2005). Teacher pedagogical beliefs: The final frontier in our quest for technology integration? Educational Technology Research and Development, 53(4), 25–39. doi:10.1007/BF02504683

Ertmer, P. A., Ottenbreit-Leftwich, A. T., Sadik, O., Sendurur, E., & Sendurur, P. (2012). Teacher beliefs and technology integration practices: A critical relationship. Computers & Education, 59(2), p. 423–435. doi:10.1016/j.compedu.2012.02.001

Grandstaff, S. W., Grandstaff, T. B., & Lovelace, G. W. (1987). Summary Report. In Proceedings of the 1985 International Conference on Rapid Rural Appraisal (pp. 3–30). Presented at the Systems Research and Farming Systems Research Projects, Khon Kaen, Thailand, University of Khon Kaen, 1987.

Gubbels, P., & Koss, C. (2000). From the roots up : strengthening organizational capacity through guided self-assessment. Oklahoma City: World Neighbors.

Hew, K. F., & Brush, T. (2006). Integrating technology into K-12 teaching and learning: current knowledge gaps and recommendations for future research. Educational Technology Research and Development, 55(3), p. 223–252. doi:10.1007/s11423-006-9022-5

Hollander, A., & Mar, N. Y. (2009). Towards Achieving TVET for All: The Role of the UNESCO-UNEVOC International Centre for Technical and Vocational Education and Training. In R. Maclean & D. Wilson (Eds.), International Handbook of Education for the Changing World of Work (pp. 41–57). Dordrecht: Springer Netherlands. Retrieved from http://www.springerlink.com/index/10.1007/978-1-4020-5281-1_3

Johnson, R. B., & Onwuegbuzie, A. J. (2004). Mixed Methods Research: A Research Paradigm Whose Time Has Come. Educational Researcher, 33(7), p. 14–26. doi:10.3102/0013189X033007014

Khakhar, D., Cornu, B., Wibe, J., & Brunello, P. (2007). ICT and Development. In W. Shrum, K. R. Benson, W. E. Bijker, & K. Brunnstein (Eds.), Past, Present and Future of Research in the Information Society (p. 63–73). Boston, MA: Springer US. Retrieved from http://www.springerlink.com/index/10.1007/978-0-387-47650-6_5

Khan, M. S. H., Hasan, M., & Clement, C. K. (2012). Barriers to the Introduction of ICT into Education in Developing Countries: The Example of Bangladesh. International Journal of Instruction, 5(2), p. 61–80.

Looi, C.-K., So, H.-J., Toh, Y., & Chen, W. (2011). The Singapore experience: Synergy of national policy, classroom practice and design research. International Journal of Computer-Supported Collaborative Learning, 6(1), p. 9–37.

Lowther, D. L., Inan, F. A., Strahl, D. J., & Ross, S. M. (2008). Does technology integration "work" when key barriers are removed? Educational Media International, 45(3), p. 195–213.

Mascarenhas, J. (1992). Transects in PRA. MYRADA, PRA-PALM Series, Paper 4E. http://myrada.org/myrada/pra4e

Mia, A. (2009). Qualifications Frameworks: Implementation and Impact Background case study on Bangladesh. Skills and Employability Department, ILO. http://www.ilo.org/wcmsp5/groups/public/@ed_emp/@ifp_skills/documents/genericdocument/wcms_126590.pdf

Mikkelsen, B. (2005). Methods for development work and research: a new guide for practitioners. Thousand Oaks: SAGE Publications.

MoICT. (2009). Bangladesh National ICT Policy 2009. Ministry of ICT, Bangladesh. http://www.ictd.gov.bd/administrator/components/com_filecabinet/uploads/National_ICT-Policy-2009-Bangla.pdf

Morgan, D. L., Krueger, R. A., & King, J. A. (1998). The focus group guidebook. Thousand Oaks: SAGE Publications.

Narayanasamy, N. (2009). Participatory rural appraisal: principles, methods and application. Los Angeles: SAGE Publications.

Okoza, J., Aluede, O., & Akpaida, J. E. A. (2012). Secondary School Students' Perception of Environmental Variables Influencing Academic Performance in Edo State, Nigeria. Bangladesh e-Journal of Sociology, 9(2), 84–94.

Pelgrum, W. . (2001). Obstacles to the integration of ICT in education: results from a worldwide educational assessment. Computers & Education, 37(2), 163–178.

Rogers, E. M. (1995). Diffusion of innovations (4th Edition.). New York: Free Press.

Sabitu, A. O., Babatunde, E. G., & Oluwole, A. F. (2012). School Types, Facilities and Academic Performance of Students in Senior Secondary Schools in Ondo State, Nigeria. International Education Studies, 5(3).

Shah, P., Bharadwaj, G., & Ambastha, R. (1991). Farmers as analysts and facilitators in participatory rural appraisal and planning. RRA Notes, 13, 84–94.

Snoeyink & Ertmer, R. (2001). Thrust into Technology: How Veteran Teachers Respond. Journal of Educational Technology Systems, 30(1), 85–111.

Somekh, B., & Lewin, C. (2005). Research methods in the social sciences. London: SAGE Publications.

Vandiver, B. (2011). The Impact of School Facilities on the Learning Environment. Ph.D. Dissertation, Capella University.

World Bank. (2012). Agriculture & Rural Development Data. http://data.worldbank.org/topic/agriculture-and-rural-development

An ICT Implementation Strategy for Primary Schools in Fiji

Dr Vinesh Chandra, Queensland University of Technology,
v.chandra@qut.edu.au

Ramila Chandra, Bremer Institute of TAFE,
Ramila.Chandra@tafe.qld.edu.au

Abstract

While in the developed countries most citizens have access to one or many of the devices which utilize ICT, in developing countries this "luxury" can only be afforded by a privileged few. The use of these technologies in primary schools in developing countries is low. Quality primary education and global development partnerships are two of the eight Millennium Development Goals (MDG) of the United Nations. This chapter discusses how greater collaboration between stakeholders in developing and developed countries may be established, in order to attain the MDGs. How do stakeholders from developed countries engage with partners in developing countries to deliver meaningful and relevant outcomes for primary school students using ICT? This chapter investigates in particular how ICT can be implemented in primary schools in Fiji. It proposes a three-layered approach which focuses on: (1) the community, school leadership, and teachers; (2) content, pedagogy, and technology, and (3) sustainability.

The Rationale for ICT Integration

ICT is re-shaping the economies of many developed countries. Developing countries see this as a great strategy for their own advancement. The assumption here is that the economies of these countries can also grow if ICT is embedded in their development strategies (Hudson, 2001). Schools are good places where students can be nurtured and educated about the new technologies. Therefore, the integration of ICT within education systems should not be viewed as a burden. On the contrary, it should be seen as a vehicle towards the economic prosperity of these nations. More importantly technologies are here to stay (Mishra & Koehler, 2006).

There is evidence to suggest how good ICT integration strategies have impacted on some developed countries. For example, Hietanen (2006) believes that in Finland, ICT driven changes occurred in three phases. In the first phase, the sale of technology products such as mobile phones had a positive impact on the economy. In the second phase, wealth was generated through the use of these technologies. This involved creating content and services. In the third phase, effective use of social media technologies is generating wealth. Macroeconomic factors such as effective monetary policies fueled the growth of the ICT sector and as a consequence some companies have benefitted from them

(Kiander, 2004).

The points raised by Hietanen (2006) and Kiander (2004) support the widely acknowledged claim that ICT can enable developing countries to become wealthier and as a consequence narrow the gap with their developed country counterparts. The participation of ordinary people in e-businesses facilitated by online market places such as *eBay* is one example of how this transformation can occur. However, this may not always be the case. In a study conducted in Nigeria, it was found that such an opportunity existed only for those who had the knowledge and access to using these technologies (Toluyemi & Mejabi, 2011). The findings of Toluyemi and Mejabi reaffirm Hudson's (2001) suggestion that ICT integration within education systems should be viewed as a vehicle to prosperity. Giving children in developing countries opportunities to develop their knowledge and understanding on how these technologies work can be the catalyst to this prosperity.

Understanding the Context

A range of independent and inter-related complex factors often determines a country's prosperity and future outlook. Understanding some of these factors is the key to initiating support driven projects. A good starting point is the Human Development Index (HDI) which is published by the United Nations on a regular basis. This measure is considered to be far more meaningful than other measures such as the Gross Domestic Product (GDP). The magnitude of this index is dependent upon three factors: (a) life expectancy; (b) education, and (c) standard of living (Human Development Reports, 2010). On the basis of their ranks, countries are grouped into four quartiles - very high, high, medium, and low HDI. In the most recent Human Development Report (2011) Fiji was ranked at 100 out of 187 countries. It falls in the medium HDI category. Collectively, the countries in this category represent more than half of the world's population. With a HDI of 0.688, statistically it is almost at the median of this measure. While no statistical measure can absolutely generate a country's standing against others, it is a good starting point to understand the level of development in countries around the world. For example, it makes sense why in the Oceania Region, Australia and New Zealand have a higher HDI and are in a different category when compared to countries like Fiji, Samoa, and Papua New Guinea.

Fiji comprises of more than 300 islands with a population of approximately 900,000. Almost half of the people (52.3%) live in urban centres (Human Development Report, 2011). The GDP per capita is $4,526 (expressed in purchasing power parity –international dollar terms). Public expenditure on education is 3.4% of GDP. Some of the neighboring countries (with similar GDPs) in the medium human development category allocated a higher percentage of their budget to education (e.g. Tonga, Samoa, Federated States of Micronesia). The gross enrolment ratio at primary, secondary and tertiary levels was 94.2, 80.9 and 15.4 respectively (Human Development Report, 2011). In primary schools, the pupil to teacher ratio was 26:1 which compared very well with a number of countries ranked higher in this report. Almost 97% of the teachers were qualified in their roles (Human Development Report, 2011). On average, the citizens of Fiji have 10.7 years of schooling. In addition more than 85% of both males and females (ages 25 years or older) had at least some secondary education. In this statistical measure, Fiji excelled and this figure was well above a number of countries with higher HDI (e.g. Singapore, Denmark, Switzerland) and on par with countries like Netherlands and Sweden.

The data presented thus far paints the picture of Fiji as a country where most children are: (i) enrolled in primary schools (does not necessarily equate to school attendance); (ii) taught by trained teachers, and (iii) from families with reasonable levels of education. However, 31% of the population lives below the poverty line and this has been on the rise for some time (Human Development Report, 2011; Rahiman & Naz, 2006). With a low GDP (when compared to most countries with a "very high" and "high" human development), affordability of digital technology based commodities by families is an issue. It is therefore reasonable to assume that most homes would not have computers. In 2004, a study commissioned by International Telecommunication Union (ITU) predicted that about 10% of the homes in Fiji had computers (International Telecommunication Union, 2004). Therefore, the school is possibly one of the few places where children can have access to these technologies. However, investment in public education systems is low and this is probably related to the country's low Gross National Income (GNI). The ITU report pointed to the fact that there was "no precise data on the number of schools with PCs and Internet access" (p. 16) and it predicted that less than 3% of the schools (especially secondary) provided their students with this access.

However, in line with how the world is moving in terms of ICT acquisition, the vision of the Fiji government is no different. As part of their strategy for the future, it is stated that: "100% of all primary and secondary schools shall have broadband access by 2016" (Government of the Republic of Fiji, 2011, p. 16). For schools to take advantage of such technology, schools need to become broadband ready. This can only occur if schools have access to computers.

Designing a Workable Framework

On the basis of the statistical data presented above, it is reasonable to assume that assistance from the governments, institutions and citizens of more developed countries can help schools in Fiji to step into the information age. But computers and the Internet are merely tools. They do not make a difference on their own. Therefore it is imperative that a strategy needs to be developed on how to integrate these technologies. The identified strategies should not only be theoretically workable but also be realistic. Drawing on their study in Uganda, Mutonyi and Norton (2007) pointed out that there was a need for a concerted effort to identify what is already there (ICT ressources) and how accessible it is to the users. This should be a pre-requisite to developing any ICT integration strategies.

Several ICT integration strategies have been proposed but there is no one-size fits all approach. For example, Arias and Clark (2004) expanded on the contextual analysis model proposed by Tessmer and Richey (1997) to suggest that for ICT integration to succeed - social, cultural, environmental, and institutional factors need to be considered. In their report on ICT in developing countries, Hepp et al. (2004) pointed out that there were "no universal truths" about ICT integration in Education. The rationale of its deployment and integration varied from country to country. Much of it depends on a "country's reality, priorities and long–term budgetary prospects and commitment" (p. IV). Five years ago, more than 800,000 OLPC laptops were deployed to schools in Peru at a cost of US $200 million (Cristia et al., 2012; Jamaica Observer, 2012). The effectiveness of this initiative has been in "serious doubt" and questions are being asked about whether this "ambitious" effort to "lever digital technology in the fight against poverty" was the best solution. Software bugs, issues with Internet connectivity, and the unavailability of electricity in some areas had serious impact on the initiative. Perhaps the most significant of all was that the program was rolled out "without preparing the teachers" (para. 4). The report in Jamaica Observer (2012) went on to point out that:

> "The magical thinking that mere technology is enough to spur change, to improve learning, is what this study categorically disproves," co-author Eugenio Severin of Chile told The Associated Press. The study found no increased math or language skills, no improvement in classroom instruction quality, no boost in time spent on homework, no improvement in reading habits" (para. 15, para. 16).

This Peruvian experience supports Hepp et al.'s (2004) suggestions about setting realistic goals and expectations. Research evidence into ICT integration in schools can provide rich data on the "do's" and "don'ts" and as a consequence provide insight into how such initiatives are implemented. In a review of 244 peer reviewed and grey literature on ICT, LeBaron, and McDonough (2009) proposed that for ICT integration to succeed, five key areas needed to be focused on:

a. Effective and ongoing training of school leadership teams including principals.
b. Research driven ICT integration initiatives to inform practices in both pre-service and in-service teacher education.
c. Development of teachers' networks to facilitate effective role-modeling and mentorship.
d. Collaborative planning at all levels.
e. Co-ordination of leadership at all levels.
f. Provision of resources to support all participants.

But in learning environments where ICT has never been implemented and is not fully understood, a strategy with some overlap with the ideas proposed by LeBaron and McDonough is needed. Given the nature of the Fijian context, a three-layered approach could work to support ICT integration (Figure 1). The first layer focuses on educating the movers and shakers within education systems – community leaders, principals and teachers. The second layer is directed towards the three key pillars of ICT integration – content, technology and pedagogy as proposed by Mishra and Koehler (2006). The third layer is focused on sustainability.

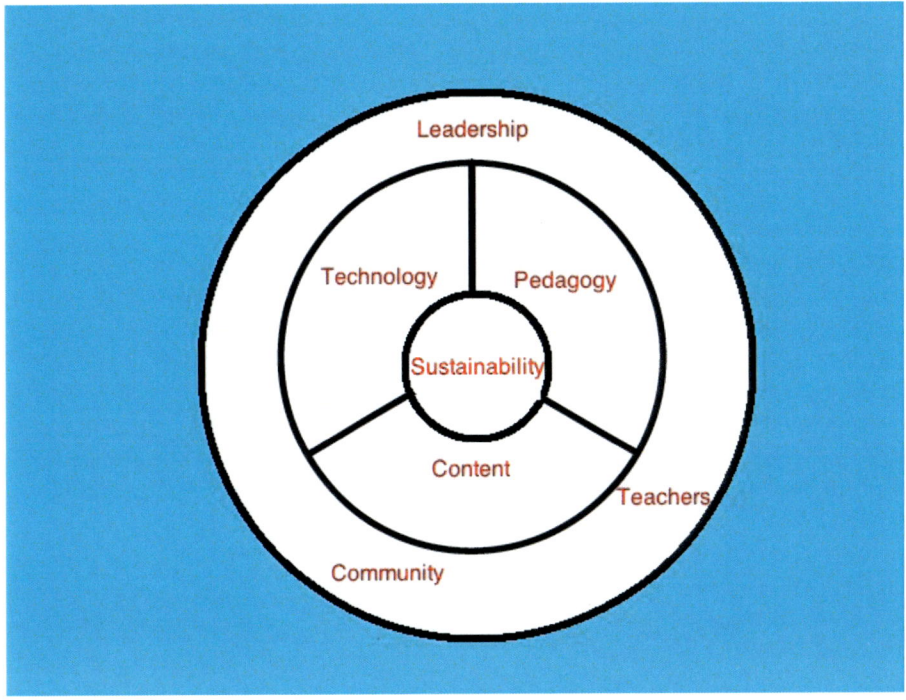

Figure 1 – A three-layered approach to ICT integration

Layer 1 – The Community, Administration and Teachers
Community
Just over 2% of the schools in Fiji are government run and managed by the Ministry of Education. The government pays most of the teachers. In addition, the government also sets the curriculum and assessment requirements. Religious and community-based organizations own and operate the schools. Local communities elect school committees and they have the responsibility for managing the majority of the 900 plus schools throughout the country. For this reason, when working in a school which is managed by a non-government organization, explaining the intent of initiatives needs to be clearly spelt out to the school committee. Research evidence suggests that the knowledge and understanding about ICT is generally quite low amongst people at the village level in Fiji (Rahiman & Naz, 2006). Therefore, the explanation needs to be quite simple, free of jargon and where possible presented in their native language. In many cases, the school head-master (principal in western schools) can act as a go-between. Emphasizing on the importance of community relations in their clinical trials on Malaria, Nyika et al. (2010) proposed the following:

> "Sponsors and researchers should…make efforts to enhance two-way communication with communities to discuss issues that may be of concern to the researched communities. Such communication could

go a long way in fostering partnerships between researchers and communities based on mutual trust and a sense of collective ownership of the research. Partnerships could minimize risks of potential misunderstandings that could be fuelled by various factors such as rumours circulating in the communities, incorrect media reports that may crop up, and inadequate information and explanations given to participants" (p. 3).

School Leadership

New initiatives like ICT integration should be treated similarly. Good partnerships with the community can also pave the way to the sustainability of the initiative in the long term. The role of the head master (principal) is equally important. As in schools throughout the world, the head master can be the enabler of innovative changes. Under the leadership of effective chief executive officers, businesses embrace innovative practices and prosper. Likewise, good head-teachers too can initiate curriculum reform and make a positive contribution to student learning (Mitchell & Sackney, 2000). In an OECD (n.d.) report which investigated ICT and organizational change in 22 countries, the role of school principals in driving this change was significant. The participants in the OECD case study comprised principals, teachers, students, and parents. Participating countries identified the schools – a key criterion for their section was effective school wide integration of ICT. In these schools, "major" investments led to "major innovations". But without effective principals this may have not eventuated.

For head teachers to embrace ICT driven reforms, they need to have an understanding of how it can impact on the classroom landscape. It is only through this understanding, that teachers can be influenced. In the OECD report (n.d.), the principals had a vision about this change. For example, in Hungary "a highly motivated principal saw ICT as an important skill for the future" (p. 4), in Greece a principal pointed out that through the computer learners' "knowledge is extended". It is such vision that head-teachers need to be excited about themselves before they can invite their teachers to become partners in the educational reform (Fullan, 1991). It becomes a daunting task for head-teachers to convince their staff if they themselves do not believe in ICT integration.

However, they do not need to be experts in the field, they can deliver innovative outcomes just by being effective facilitators as these examples from the OECD (n.d.) study showed:

> "A Mexican primary school attributed the introduction of ICT to a principal who did not have technical expertise herself but, despite this and unsupportive district officials, she identified ICT as a priority, built up the infrastructure, and encouraged staff to adopt it (MX04, p. 3). Similarly, a Canadian school suggested that a clear vision was more important than extensive infrastructure. The ICT coordinator in Spencer school argued "if the school leadership has a vision for the use of technology, and can get staff to share that vision, the innovation can be carried out with available technology." (p. 18)

Acknowledging and supporting teachers' efforts, taking note of students work output in ICT driven activities could be good starting points. Of equal importance is knowing the ICT capabilities and responding accordingly with appropriate support. In the OECD (n.d.) report, a Vice Principal at a Canadian school pointed out that they realized that there were "many people on the staff that may have never touched a computer... so we had low-level training" (p. 16). While this teacher attribute is universal, what is also important here is that Canada is a developed country (Human Development Report, 2011). If some teachers in such countries (where ICT is more readily accessible) are facing these challenges than the difficulties faced by teachers in developing countries is quite understandable.

In a study focused on the investigation of the role of school principals in school reforms in Nigeria, Ifeoma (2010) gathered data from 80 principals and 1678 secondary school teachers. Lack of principals' support and interest had a rippling effect on school reform initiatives:

> "... this study found that Anambra State (one of the schools in the study) principals do not discuss with teachers on how inventive creativity should be made an explicit goal of teaching and learning nor work jointly with staff and expert consultants to implement ICT use (computers, internet, e-mail) in schools. ICT use was almost zero! ... Where principals do not discuss with teachers on how inventive creativity should be made an explicit goal of teaching and learning, the possibility of the teachers implementing inventive curriculum strategies requirements is in doubt. And without ICT implementation in schools, the schools are not being led in a way to position staff and students for curricular reforms". (p. 89)

In-Service Teachers

The importance of head-teachers working with their teachers to facilitate ICT implementation cannot be over-emphasized. The "hole in the wall" experiment conducted in under privileged environments in India and elsewhere showed that without any expert supervision, children develop their own ICT skills "irrespective of who or where they are" (Mitra, 2005, p. 71). But schools are quite different, curriculum requirements have to be met and students cannot be left on their own to explore new technologies thorough unstructured activities. If time were not a constraint, then such exploration could be quite significant to students' learning and knowledge construction though their own discoveries. Therefore, teachers' positive attitudes as the frontline agents for the delivery of learning outcomes using ICT are critical. In a study done with Turkish science teachers (Cavas, Cavas, Karaoglan, & Kisla, 2009), the researchers found that while teachers had positive attitudes towards ICT, these attitudes were found to be influenced by age, access to computers outside school and level of computer expertise. Teachers' positive beliefs about using the technologies have been reported to be more important than their level of technological expertise (Kim & Rissel, 2008). However, there is a positive correlation between beliefs and attitudes about ICT use and actual use (Williams, Coles, Wilson, Richardson, & Tuson, 2000). Thus, an understanding of teachers' beliefs and attitudes towards ICT is important. If teachers' attitudes and beliefs towards ICT is negative, appropriate strategies need to be applied before the technology is handed to them.

Gathering data about teachers' attitudes, beliefs, and their familiarity with ICT is an important first step. Positioning teachers on the UNESCO advocated five-step ICT model of adoption: 1. Yet to begin, 2. Emerging, 3. Applying, 4. Infusing, and 5. Transforming gives a good idea about teachers ICT competence (Anderson, 2010). From this data, professional development strategies can be formulated. While ICT expertise and confidence cannot be built in teachers overnight, an effective strategy would be to direct efforts to supporting ICT champions initially (OECD, n.d.). These teachers lead and drive innovative approaches in schools. The OECD (n.d) report explained their influence in schools as follows:

> "In some of the schools, much of the development was attributed to the energy and drive of one particular staff member, often a keen ICT enthusiast and a supporter of colleagues to the extent of providing direct training for them. In Park Garden primary school (CA03, p7), for example, the technology teacher provided much of the school's professional development during lunch hour and after school. In St Sheila's School, Ireland, a strong ICT enthusiast on the staff provided both training and technical support for colleagues (IE02). In other cases, the ICT champion provided a model of ICT use and did the preparatory work, such as in Aurora School, Finland" (p. 18)

In the Fijian context, the five step "innovation model" proposed by Rogers can work effectively with teachers who are identified as ICT champions (Rogers, 1995). In the first step "knowledge" - the teacher champions develop an understanding of the rationale of the innovation. The second step - "persuasion" is aligned with motivation. If teaches are already motivated and have positive attitudes, then little persuasion may be needed. The third step of "decision" will also fall in to place because for such teachers they want to use ICT and as a consequence, they will either learn by themselves (e.g. online help tutorials) or others (e.g. ICT communities). When professional learning opportunities arise, the ICT champions are likely to participate in them without hesitation. ICT champions are intrinsically motivated – as a consequence they will willingly "implement" their new learnt knowledge in the classroom (step four). For such teachers, they are always looking for new ways to renew their pedagogical and technical knowledge. As a consequence – step five follows with ease.

When these champions start using ICT in their classrooms, they are more likely to share their knowledge with other teachers. But at the same time, other teachers can also see how ICT can be embedded in classrooms. With such evidence – other teachers are more likely to dabble with technologies for their own classrooms. It is also economical because supporting small groups of teachers is more feasible and effective than *en masse* workshops. The small group strategy can be affordable in countries like Fiji where large scale workshops can be constrained by financial resources. Of equal importance is that through such an approach, technology is not imposed on all the teachers. Those who are "yet to begin" can adopt the technologies when they are ready (Anderson, 2010). In their investigation of ICT integration in South African schools - Slay, Sieborger, and Hodgkinson-Williams (2008) proposed that not imposing the integration on all teachers can be a workable strategy. By not mandating the use of ICT in every classroom, teachers are given time to evolve in terms of what they think about such an approach. A number of researchers have suggested that the traditional approach of ICT training of all teachers does not produce deep understanding and as a consequence their knowledge of technology and pedagogy remains limited (Mishra & Koehler, 2006). As a consequence integration of ICT occurs at a minimal level. Therefore – supporting the ICT champions initially may be the way to go.

Pre-service Teachers
Like other countries, in Fiji pre-service teachers are trained by universities and teaching colleges. The goal of teacher education should be to "not indoctrinate or train teachers to behave in prescribed ways but to educate their teachers to reason soundly about their teaching as well as to perform skillfully" (Shulman, 1987, p. 13). When a country embraces the idea of technology driven innovations in schools, the pre-service courses should also designed to meet the goals. It is a lot easier and far more cost-effective to design, develop, and implement an ICT subject/unit as part of teacher training than to offer a similar unit to teachers once they are already in the service. Getting in-service teachers to engage in such professional learning can be more expensive – they have to be released from their schools to attend. Other costs associated with travelling and accommodation need to be factored in. In a place like Fiji, teachers have to travel to towns and cities to participate and in some cases may require hours and days of travelling. Online training is not an option, because of the hardware and connectivity issues. Therefore, quality training of pre-service teachers sets a strong foundation. With good training in ICT practices, they can bring specialist knowledge and skills to schools upon their appointment. For this to occur the universities and colleges have to develop appropriate ICT rich learning environments. The International Telecommunications Union (2004) reported that there were "no concrete plans to integrate ICT training in the teachers' education program" (p. 17). In 2012, anecdotal evidence suggested that there were plans to introduce an ICT course in the primary pre-service course.

A computer lab on its own does not deliver a high quality of teachers. The quality of delivery is dependent upon the knowledge and confidence of the relevant lecturers in tertiary institutions. In a study conducted across three universities in Zimbabwe with 21 participating lecturers, researchers Chitiyo and Harmon (2009) identified a number of issues associated with pre-service teacher education. They reported that lecturer' competency and proficiency in using the digital technologies was at a basic level. Many were at the early stages of technology adoption. Poor access and availability of appropriate digital resources to both staff and students, lack of professional development opportunities and institutional policies were some of the other barriers, which prevented the delivery of high-quality programs.

Chitiyo and Harmon's investigation suggests that the challenges faced in embedding ICT in classrooms in schools is no different to the challenges that may be faced in higher education and other technology-rich learning environments. Staff who teaches pre-service teachers should not only have access to digital technologies but also be motivated with positive attitudes in their classrooms. Such initiatives can enable the staff to showcase how ICT can be used in classrooms. Good practices such as this can have a positive influence on pre-service teachers and as a consequence they may embrace some of the strategies for own classrooms in future.

Layer 2 – Content, Technology and Pedagogy

Integrating ICT technologies in a formal learning environment is challenging. Simply having the technology in schools does not guarantee integration. In their study on ICT integration across a number of schools in South Africa and Zimbabwe, Cawthera (2002) reported that computers were not used to their full potential. Where computing facilities existed, their use was estimated to be around 20 to 30%. As a number of researchers (including Cawthera) have suggested, many teachers do not use these technologies in their classrooms because of their inability to marry content, technology and pedagogy in their classrooms. This probably explains why computers are not used more regularly. The success of ICT in classrooms is very much dependent on the teacher. Mishra and Koehler (2006) argue that the "thoughtful pedagogical uses of technology require the development of a complex, situated form of knowledge" (p. 1017). They called it the Technological Pedagogical Content Knowledge (TPCK) Framework. Teachers need to develop this knowledge if integration of ICT is to succeed in their classrooms (Figure 2).

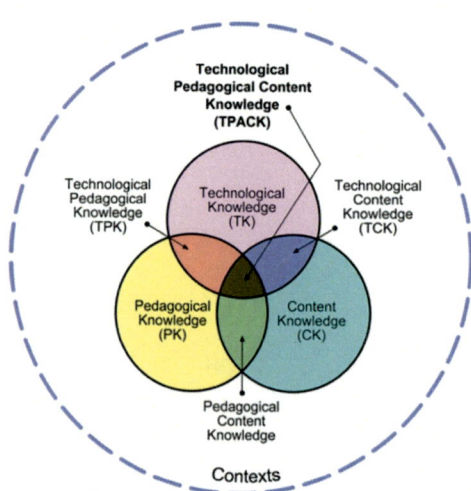

Figure 2: The TPCK framework (Source: http://tpack.org/)

The TPCK framework above can be interpreted as follows. All teachers should know their content (C) and they should be able to deliver this through appropriate pedagogies (P). In many instances, this delivery may require tools

(T). Traditionally, teachers have used a range of tools. These included chalk, blackboard, books, charts, and so on. Some of these tools have been used for so long that they have become "a part of the furniture". Teachers embrace them unequivocally and without question (Bruce & Hogan, 1998). But each time a new tool emerges for classrooms, a level of anxiety develops amongst teachers – some will embrace it quickly while others may take more time. This is also the case with ICT. For teachers to embrace this new tool, they need to not only understand the technology (T), but they also need to have a good understanding of how the content fits in with the technology (TCK). They also need to develop an understanding of how pedagogies fit with the technology (TPK). It is only when these pieces of the "jigsaw puzzle" are put together confidently that teachers become proficient in demonstrating their Technological Pedagogical Content Knowledge (TPCK). Through this understanding they can "develop appropriate, context-specific strategies and representations" (Mishra & Koehler, 2006, p. 1029)

In developing countries like Fiji, the integration of ICT in primary schools is just beginning. As pointed out previously, 97% of the teachers have been professionally trained (Human Development Report, 2011). As part of their training and their own in class experiences, teachers would have developed their strategies for delivering the content. However, when ICT emerges in their classroom, they would need to rethink how this new tool would fit into their teaching practice. In the Fijian context, no formal courses in the primary teacher training program add another layer of challenge. As Anderson (2010) proposed, once ICT becomes more pervasive, teachers will go through the five stages of adoption namely: (1). Yet to begin, (2). Emerging, (3). Applying, (4). Infusing, and (5). Transforming. However, there is a possibly a "just looking" stage as well which precedes the five proposed by Anderson (Figure 3).

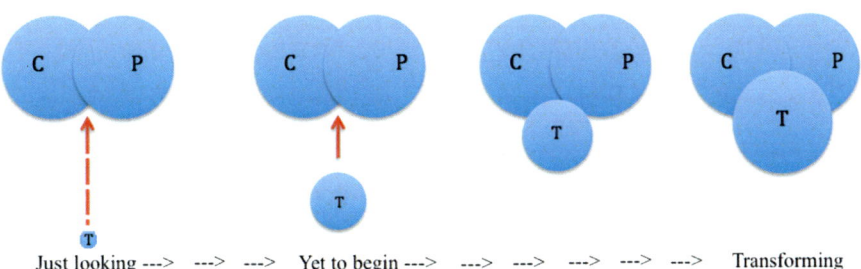

Figure 3: TPCK in a developing country context

In the early stages when ICT emerges on the scene, teachers are "just looking". This is a critical stage because it can make or break such initiative. How the Technology (T) fits in with the existing content (C) and pedagogy (P) needs to be clear, user-friendly, and convincing. The fact that technologies are here to stay should be elaborated to the teachers in these early stages (Mishra & Koehler, 2006). A well thought strategy during the "just looking" stage could act as a hook to convince teachers to embrace ICT. The hook should be such that teachers can see how the technology adds value to their classrooms. It should also be user-friendly and easy to implement. A poorly thought out strategy can have the opposite effect and as consequence discourage teachers from embracing the initiative altogether. But for this to occur, three important aspects that overarch the technology domain need to be dealt with (Figure 4).

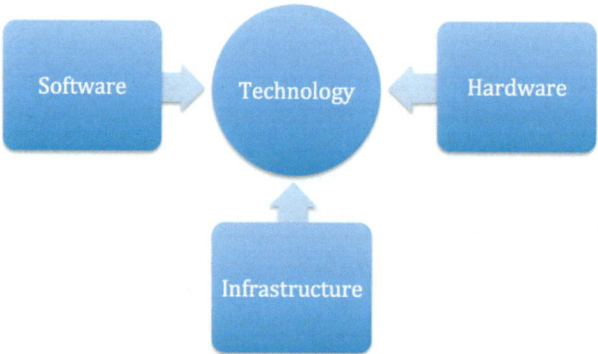

Figure 4: The key aspects of technology

The infrastructure, choice of software, and hardware can determine if the initial steps of ICT integration will enable teachers to develop their TPCK knowledge.

Infrastructure
A good understanding of the available physical infrastructure (e.g. buildings, furniture) is important before decisions are made about the type of the computer technology to integrate. One of the biggest challenges in developing countries is the availability of electricity. In Fiji, up to 300 primary schools do not have access to it (International Telecommunication Union, 2004). Understandably, unless this issue is addressed computers cannot work in schools. Solar energy can be an option. In the Indian State of Uttar Pradesh, solar panels have been used to provide power to computers in schools (BBC News, 2004). But setting up solar panels requires specialist knowledge. The electricity output type is also an issue that needs to be considered. In the case of Fiji, this output is 240 volts. Where electricity is available, the load capacities of the circuits need to be understood. Overloaded circuits can break with blown fuses or become fire hazards. The number and locations of electrical power points is an important consideration. Many existing classrooms were not designed to cater for the electrical needs of computers. So running a roomful of computers with only one or two power points can be problematic. The use of power boards and double adapters with extension cables may not be a safe alternative.

Another important factor is the availability of space in existing buildings that can be used to accommodate the computers. Security of these resources also needs to be considered. In many instances, running computers in dusty surroundings can be an issue. For this reason, the quality of the air needs to be considered. The location of buildings can also be a factor especially if ICT acquisition includes the installation of a wireless network. The distance between wireless access points to classrooms can be an issue if trees and other obstructions get in the way.

Furniture is an important aspect of ICT integration. This is an issue which is sometimes overlooked – especially in developing countries. The issue of ergonomics and workplace health and safety should be a priority. The myth that any furniture will do should be quickly dispelled because inappropriate choices can lead to dire consequences in children later in their lives (Gillespie, 2002). Gillespie added:

> "Children using computers and electronic games may adopt the kinds of sustained and awkward postures that are associated with musculoskeletal disorders in working adults. If they do, the physical demands of extensive use could lead to a wide range of adverse effects on developing children, including visual, neurological and physical changes" (p. 249)

The points associated with the infrastructure are an important step to ICT integration. They may vary from school to school but are critical in terms of making decisions such as what type of hardware should be used.

Hardware

A decision has to be made about whether a school will be equipped with desktops or laptops. These could be either new or secondhand – the former would obviously require a greater financial outlay. Desktops have their advantages over laptops. For example – it is generally cheaper when compared with a laptop of similar specification, is easier to upgrade, has bigger monitors, and are less likely to be stolen. However, they tend to generate more heat, are not portable and require a permanent space. The latter is an issue – because converting an existing classroom into a laboratory would reduce the number of classroom space. While building a new laboratory is an option, this is not always feasible – due to financial constraints. Equipping classrooms with a handful of desktop computers (2-3) creates opportunities for certain types of activities (e.g. project-based learning) but their use by a whole class is not practical. Laptops on the other hand can be easily damaged (if dropped by students) are more likely to be stolen and generally have less power. However, they are more portable and can be used more effectively as a class set. They do not need a fixed space. These practicality factors make them more viable than desktop computers. In terms of freight – laptops are lighter and therefore will cost less to have them transported (when shipped by a donor overseas).

No matter what type of computer is chosen for a classroom, its specification is also an important factor. The processor (e.g. Intel, AMD) is the brain of the computer. Dual and multiprocessors increase the efficiency of computers. Therefore, the best needs to be sought for a given budget. The RAM (Random Access Memory) is the working memory. A 2GB is considered to be the minimum "for every day computing tasks, such as web browsing, editing documents, and even HD video" as long as these options are not opened simultaneously (Escallier, 2012, para. 5). The size of the hard disk drive (HDD) is the next important question. For a primary school, a 60 to 80GB is workable provided appropriate strategies are in place when students engage in "space-hungry" activities such as creating movies. A DVD drive is also essential. A built in modem with wireless capability creates hassle-free opportunities for surfing the net (just in case the Internet is available). In summary, for a primary school – a desktop or laptop option can work provided it has a good processor, with at least 2GB of RAM, 60-80GB HDD, a DVD drive along with a built in wireless modem. In addition, external Hard Disk Drives (HDD), digital cameras, a data projector, and modem for the Internet are also essential tools to make the integration of ICT an effective and exciting experience.

Software

The operating system is an important consideration especially if second hand computers are donated with re-formatted hard drives and no operating systems. With PC's and MAC's the installation of Windows and Mac OS's is the obvious choice. Finding the right drivers for PC's for some of the installed devices can be an issue. A third option is the installation of *Ubuntu* Linux operating (http://www.ubuntu.com/ubuntu/why-use-ubuntu). This is an open source, free software. Where financial resources are a major constraint (e.g. schools in developing countries), this is a significant advantage. Its stability, security, and the availability of free software (including open-source anti-virus and firewall software) enhance its usability for the users. For example, either through *Ubuntu*'s software centre or the "apt-get" tool https://help.ubuntu.com/8.04/serverguide/apt-get.html) software can be either installed, updated, or deleted with ease. Thousands of free applications (including education) can be accessed from the *Unbuntu* website (Figure 5). Provided the schools have Internet access (to download the software), such an option can be quite effective and efficient. The no cost factor is important.

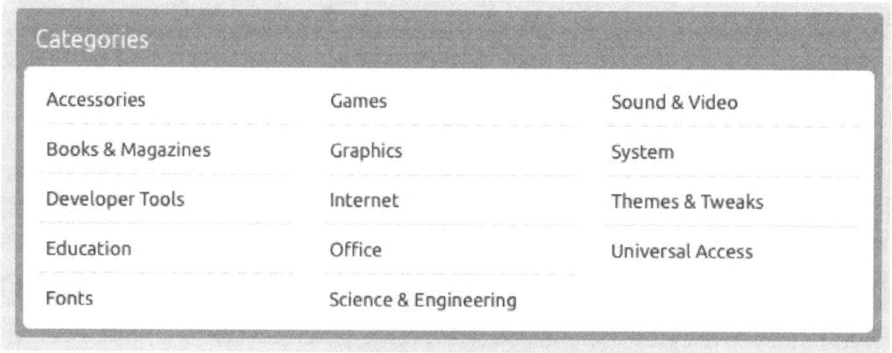

Categories		
Accessories	Games	Sound & Video
Books & Magazines	Graphics	System
Developer Tools	Internet	Themes & Tweaks
Education	Office	Universal Access
Fonts	Science & Engineering	

Figure 5: Software categories in Ubuntu
(Source: http://www.ubuntu.com/ubuntu/features/ubuntu-software-centre)

With PC's and Mac's pre-installed applications such as *Windows Moviemaker, imovie,* and *iphoto* offer a range of options and opportunities. Free downloads such as *Photo Story 3 for Windows* can also be very useful in classrooms. While the acquisition of applications such as Microsoft Office can be costly, a viable alternative would be to use *Libre Office* (http://www.libreoffice.org/) which is an open source software and works across all common operating systems. It is available in more than 30 languages. It has six applications: *Writer, Calc, Impress, Draw, Math* and *Base* which enable the user to engage in activities where they can create documents, spreadsheets, databases, power points and so on. Similarly, the possibilities presented by such software which are free downloads should also be explored to keep the integration initiative low cost.

Once the system has been installed, identifying other appropriate applications for classroom use is important. Three strategies are useful here: (a) free downloads are always the preferred option to keep the costs down; (b) stand-alone programs are more useful in developing countries because they do not need the Internet to run, and (c) where possible, the identified stand-alone applications should enable learners to construct their knowledge in a constructivist-learning environment to facilitate higher order thinking in learners.

Scratch (http://scratch.mit.edu/) is one example of such a program. It enables users to create and share interactive stories, games, music, and art. The value of the opportunities for users and in particular young school children to engage in higher order thinking skills through media-rich tasks using *Scratch* has been explained by a number of researchers (e.g. Maloney, et. al, 2010; Resnick, et. al, 2009). According to Resnick et al: "digital fluency requires not just the ability to chat, browse, and interact but also the ability to design, create, and invent with new media" (p. 62). Designing, creating and inventing are key aspects of higher order thinking skills. The "World Scratch Day" is now run in forty-three countries (including developing countries), which enables participants to not only showcase their problem solving and creativity skills, but also learn from the artifacts created by others. Events such as this can also be organized in countries like Fiji at minimal cost.

Other stand-alone applications such as *SAM* (http://icreatetoeducate.com/) can enable learners to construct and demonstrate their knowledge through stop-motion animations. For example, these animations can be useful for students and teachers to develop their understanding of science concepts (Hoban, 2007). Mind mapping is another useful tool for students to demonstrate their understanding of ideas and concepts. There are a number of programs which can be downloaded. *Freemind* (http://freemind.sourceforge.net/) is an example of a piece of open source software which is relatively easy to use. The value of these tools was highlighted by Cuthell's (2008) investigation of the MirandaNet Fellowship Projects. The results in the 18-month study by Cuthell showed that the use of such tools had "significant impact on the learning environment, on pupil perceptions of learning, and on attainment" (p. 1). More importantly it had enhanced teachers own professional knowledge. But Cuthell pointed out that these results were dependent upon the "pedagogical context in which their possibilities are introduced and modeled" (p. 9). *Google Sketchup* is another useful piece of software, which is a free download from *Google*. It enables students to express their ideas through two and three-dimensional modeling and used is extensively in disciplines other than education. In an investigation of how *Google Sketchup* impacts on upper primary and lower secondary students (n=82) in Turkey, researchers, Toptas, Celik and Karaca (2012) found that the application impacted positively on the treatment group (n=42). These students demonstrated enhanced abilities in mental rotation and spatial visualization when compared to the control group.

The examples (*LibreOffice, Scratch, SAM, Freemind* and *Google Sketchup*) highlighted here are probably a few of the hundreds that could be downloaded for classroom use. These applications are useful in the context of developing countries because they are free downloads and stand-alone programs (no Internet access required). In addition, they enable students to construct and demonstrate their knowledge. There is also some research evidence to suggest how it has impacted on users in other learning environments.

Marrying Technology with Content and Pedagogy

No matter, how simple or complicated the technology, one of the challenges is marrying it with content and pedagogy. According to Mishra and Koehler (2006), there is a need for "a nuanced understanding of the complex relationships" (p. 1029) and is contrary to the views held by some that it is "relatively trivial to acquire and implement" (p. 1025). Several research investigations have highlighted this challenge. For example, some schools are embracing interactive whiteboards as part of their ICT strategy. In South Africa a pilot roll out of this technology was undertaken in one of the nine provinces. An investigation in three of the pilot schools by Slay, Sieborger and Hodgkinson-Williams (2008) showed that teachers and students were enthusiastic about this new technology. However, in view of the cost associated with acquiring the technology, teachers and students lack of ICT literacy in fully utilizing this digital tool was a major concern. Based on their observations, Slay et al. (2008) proposed that teachers' needed to develop appropriate pedagogies before this technology could be effectively used in classrooms. This concurs with Mishra and Koehler's (2009) suggestion about complex relationships that existed between the content, technology and pedagogy.

Understanding the content associated with the school curricula is an essential perquisite to linking it with appropriate pedagogy(ies) and technology(ies). The curricula used in Fijian schools have well defined outcomes and benchmarks across all subjects. The subjects taught are English, mathematics, science, social science, health science, art and craft, music, physical education, and languages (iTaukei, Hindi, Urdu, Rotuman). Every student has a learning record for year level. This provides important details such as the achievement indicators, assessment methods (summative or formative), learning outcomes and achievement methods. The themes in each subject for each school term (there are three school terms per year) are explicit and divided into units. For example, in Year 5, science students focus on "Life Science" "Physical Science" and "Earth Science". The school curricula provide many opportunities for ICT integration. Examples of how this could be done in Year 5 science (using the applications identified in this chapter) are shown in Table 1.

Table 1. Examples of ICT based activities in a Year 5 science class

Theme/ Unit	Achievement indicator (Content)	Technology	Pedagogy
Life Science / Plants	Classify leaves using any criteria.	Hardware: Laptop or desktop Software: Freemind. Product: Students create mind maps	Teacher outlines the task. Students collect some leaves from around the school. Teacher suggests at least one way in which the leaves could be classified. Students propose other classification strategies using mind maps.
Life Science/ Animals	State the advantages of keeping cats.	Hardware: Laptop or desktop Software: LibreOffice Draw Product: Students create a poster	Teacher outlines the task. Working individually, students create a poster-using Draw which outlines why cats should be kept as pets.

Table 1 shows some options of how ICT can be integrated in a Year 5 class. The achievement indicators can be delivered with software that is available at no cost to the schools. Hardware configuration (e.g. Number of RAM, Size of HDD) also does not require any high level of sophistication. Another integration strategy would be through Rich Tasks. Such a task is defined as follows (Education Queensland, 2010):

> "A Rich Task is a culminating performance or demonstration or product that is purposeful and models a life role. It presents substantive, real problems to solve and engages learners in forms of pragmatic social action that have real value in the world. The problems require identification, analysis and resolution, and require students to analyse, theorise and engage intellectually with the world. In this way, tasks connect to the world outside the classroom." (p. 5)

A Rich Task can be created with ICT by designing activities which addresses a number of achievement indicators as shown in Table 2.

Table 2: An example of an ICT based activity which addresses a number of achievement indicators in Year 5 science

Theme/ Unit	Achievement indicator (Content)	Technology	Pedagogy
Earth Science/ Weather	1) Identify basic cloud types. 2) Describe the different cloud types. 3) Observe different cloud types and predict the weather. 4) Identify and describe rain as heavy/light showers and continuous rain. 5) Use rain gauge to measure different rainfall. 6) Display information about rainfall collected from the weather chart in a graph.	Hardware: Laptop or desktop Software: *LibreOffice Calc* Products: Students create graphs and data tables	Teacher outlines the task. Working in groups, students record cloud types and rainfall data in a table in *Calc* over a fortnight. Rainfall data is graphed. Students explain the graph and relate it to cloud types. From this knowledge, students make predictions about rainfall.

Table 2 shows how rainfall data is gathered and graphed using *LibreOffice Calc*. In this activity, at least six achievement indicators in science can be addressed. The richness of the task lies in the fact that it enabled students to draw links between cloud types and make predictions about rainfall. This example also shows how authentic learning can occur in such a technology rich learning environment (Mishra & Koehler, 2006).

Fusing the curricula (Hudson & Chandra, 2010) would be another option where the creation of a product using ICT is dependent upon the seamless merger of a number of achievement indicators across a number of subjects (Table 3). This too leads to the creation of a product which is aligned with the principles of developing a rich task (Education Queensland, 2010).

Table 3: An example of an ICT based activity where the achievement indicators are fused in English and Health Science

Subject/ Theme/ Unit	Achievement indicator (Content)	Technology	Pedagogy
Health Science/ Nutrition/ Basic food groups	1) Classify food into the three basic food groups 2) Explain main sources and their value to the body 3) Explain quantity and quality of consumption	Hardware: Laptop or desktop, digital video camera

Software: *Windows Moviemaker* or *imovie*

Product: Students produce a documentary | Teacher outlines the task. Students work in groups and research on information about food and obesity. They create a storyboard on how they intend to tell their story. Afterwards they assume special roles e.g. interviewer, cameraman, and nutritionist to create their scripts and play their roles in filming the documentary. The final videos (edited using *Windows Moviemaker* or *imovie*) can be showcased e.g. to the parents and students in other classes. |
Health Science/ Nutrition/ Over eating	4) Explain the effects of obesity and malnutrition, and show good eating habit		
English/ Oral communication/ Dialogue	5) Participate in a dialogue 6) Expand ideas 7) Use grammatically correct sentences 8) Compare facts		
English/ Oral communication/ Stories	9) Expand ideas 10) Compare facts 11) Use grammatically correct sentences		

Fusing the curricula presents teachers with opportunities to develop activities that facilitate more efficient use of time and resources in classroom (Hudson & Chandra, 2010). As the example above shows, two significant aspects of English and Health Science can be delivered through a video documentary on food and obesity. This is also a rich design-based activity where students learn by doing and as a consequence are creating an artifact which is closely related to a context and a big idea (Mishra & Koehler, 2006).

The three options presented in Tables 1, 2 and 3 are workable in Fiji provided teachers are given opportunities by their school principals and the Ministry of Education to engage suitably designed professional development workshops. The ICT products, which can be created through these activities are relatively easy to develop and therefore highly likely to succeed in classrooms. Teachers' success with ICT based activities is important because this is more likely to keep them engaged. A complicated challenge can have negative impact on teachers' confidence. As a consequence they are less likely to design and develop technology-rich activities. Challenges and tasks suited to teachers' abilities builds success and confidence.

Layer Three – Sustainability

One of the ways in which ICT integration in countries like Fiji can occur is through donations from organizations and individuals in more affluent countries. This donation strategy should not only include the technology but also incorporate provisions for professional learning. Of equal importance are issues of computers maintenance, replacement, and disposal. However, schools and communities in Fiji should not become dependent on donated digital products. A cycle of dependence for such support is counterproductive. For example, more than US$1 trillion of assistance has been provided to African countries over several decades. This support has made them "worse off" (Moyo, 2009). One of the points made by Moyo is that external assistance should come with explicitly defined expectations. If computers or laptops are given to schools, then the demonstrable outcomes should be clearly outlined.

Instead of creating a cycle of dependence for donated hardware and software, schools should develop their own strategies for self-reliance over time. Relying too much on donated resources can cause far too much disruption to the learning process. For example, if a school is setup with technology resources, over time these will need to be replaced. Relying on a donor can be risky. The donor may choose not to continue with the support. Another donor may be hard to come by and as a consequence the technology driven activities will come to a halt. Or a new donor may choose to provide computers with different operating systems and software packages. As a consequence, schools, which are equipped with such resources, should look to the future and focus their energies on how the digital resources can be replaced once they reach their use-by dates.

A feasible option would be the inclusion of a small levy for computer use for all students. In the Fijian context, such a levy may be acceptable provided: (a) good relations are setup with the community and teachers when a program starts; (b) the program is clearly explained to all stakeholders; (c) teachers are supported with their professional learning; (d) effective learning activities are designed, implemented and showcased with the donated resources, and (e) demonstrable outcomes are made explicit. An investigation undertaken across a number of secondary school sites in South Africa and Zimbabwe by Cawthera (2002) showed that factors such as: (i) the type and quality of technology; (ii) level of teacher professional development; (iii) level of usage, and (iv) infrastructure overheads determined the cost per user. Cawthera (2002) also pointed out that the training of teachers should be an important priority. He believed that low-cost and user-friendly professional development options could be a part of the solution. Even in schools without electricity or landline connectivity, children can access to computers for under $20, provided there were high levels of usage (Cawthera, 2002).

But this outcome can only be realized if teachers are confident enough to embed these technologies in their classrooms. Sustaining technologies should go hand in hand with teachers' professional learning. This can be achieved through a community of practice. Through this community, committed teachers can share their knowledge and experiences of ICT (Wenger, 2006). Teachers can also get feedback on their pedagogical approaches to teaching a certain concept using ICT. Such a network can be created in a school or between schools. Knowledge sharing in this way can over time diminish the need to have external professional learning support. It also can be cost effective. In a study conducted in Costa Rica, Chotto (2010) reported that the professional development of teachers can be effective in distributed communities of practice. Such communities had a positive impact on teachers' knowledge and understanding of educational issues. As a consequence it had an influence on their values, beliefs, and practices.

Chapter Summary

ICT is here to stay. Therefore, it is logical for citizens of developed countries to support their fellow humans in developing countries to develop their knowledge and skills. It is only through such initiatives that the issue of digital divide can be addressed. Consequently more citizens of the world will be able to harness the power of digital technologies and benefit from them.

One of the ways in which knowledge and use of ICT can progress is through the education of children and most importantly those in primary schools. Such an initiative will make a positive contribution towards two of the eight Millennium Development Goals of the United Nations (UNDP, 2012). But for such initiatives to succeed, understanding a country is very important. Developing an understanding of its economy, and education priorities are some of the important considerations. Of critical importance is developing knowledge about its schooling system including students, teachers, and parents and the community.

The issue of content, pedagogy and technology is a complex one. Within the technology domain – the infrastructure, hardware and software issues need to be considered as well. Understanding the school's curriculum and teachers' attitude and knowledge about ICT are important pre-requisites. It is through this understanding that appropriate professional learning activities can be designed. While ICT cannot be embedded in all activities, well thought out rich tasks can create authentic learning opportunities (Education Queensland, 2010; Mishra & Koehler, 2006).

The issue of sustainability should not be overlooked. ICT support to schools in developing countries should also have a sustainability plan. Relying exclusively on external help creates a cycle of dependence. For schools such dependence can be counter- productive.

This chapter has focused on how ICT implementation can occur in primary schools in Fiji. While this chapter does not address the interplay of all the issues and factors associated with ICT integration, the keys ideas presented here can be extrapolated and modified to suit such an initiative in other countries as well.

References

Anderson, J. (2010). ICT transforming education: A regional guide. Bangkok, Thailand: UNESCO.

Arias, S., & Clark, K. A. (2004). Instructional technologies in developing countries: A contextual analysis approach. TechTrends, 48(4), 52-55,70.

BBC News (2004). Solar plan for Indian computers. http://news.bbc.co.uk/2/hi/technology/3623864.stm [viewed 15 Jun 2012]

Bruce, B. C., & Hogan, M. C. (1998). The disappearance of technology: Toward an ecological model of literacy. In D. Reinking, M. McKenna, L. Labbo, & R. Kieffer (Eds.), Handbook of literacy and technology: Transformations in a post-typographic world (pp. 269–281). Hillsdale, NJ: Erlbaum.

Cavas, B., Cavas, P., Karaoglan, B., & Kisla, T. (2009). A study on science teachers' attitudes toward information and communication technologies in education. The Turkish Online Journal of Educational Technology, 8(2), 20-32

Cawthera, A. (2002). Computers in secondary schools in developing countries: costs and some other issues.

http/www.worldbank.org/worldlinks [viewed 10 Jun 2012]

Chitiyo, R., & Harmon, S.W. (2009). An analysis of the integration of instructional technology in pre-service teacher education in Zimbabwe. Educational Technology Research and Development. (57), (6), 807-830

Cristia, J.P., Ibarrarán, P., Cueto, S., Santiago, A., & Severín, E. (2012). Technology and Child Development: Evidence from the One Laptop per Child Program.

http://idbdocs.iadb.org/wsdocs/getdocument.aspx?docnum=36706954 [viewed 10 Jun 2012]

Chotto, M.C. (2010). Designing for change in University Teaching Practices (Unpublished doctoral dissertation). Aalborg University, Alborg, Denmark.

Cuthell, J. P., & Preston, C. (2008). Multimodal Concept Mapping in teaching and learning: a MirandaNet Fellowship project. http://virtuallearning.org.uk/wp-content/uploads/2010/10/MN-Concept-Mapping.pdf [viewed 10 Jun 2012]

Education Queensland (2010). New Basics – The Why , What , How and When of Rich Tasks. http://education.qld.gov.au/corporate/newbasics/pdfs/richtasksbklet.pdf [viewed 1 Jul 2012]

Escallier, P. (2012). The Memory Buyer's Guide: What's the Best RAM for My System? http://www.maximumpc.com/article/features/memory_buyers_guide_whats_best_ram_my_system [viewed 27 Apr 2012]

Fullan, M. (1991) The New Meaning of Educational Change. London: Cassell.

Gillespie, R.M. (2002). The physical impact of computers and electronic game use on children and adolescents – a review of current literature. Work, 18(3), 249 - 259

Government of the Republic of Fiji (2011). https://www.egov.gov.fj/_layouts/images/egovFiji/eGOVdocs/Draft%20National%20Broadband%20Policy.pdf [viewed 18 Jun 2012]

Hepp, P., Hinostroza, J., Laval, E., & Rebein, L., (2004). Technology in schools: Education, ICT, and the knowledge society. Washington, DC: World Bank.

Hietanen, O. (2006). The digital balance between industrialised and developing countries: Futures studies for development. E-Learning (3), 3, 373-380

Hoban, G. F. (2007). Using slowmation to engage preservice elementary teachers in understanding science content knowledge. http://www.citejournal.org/vol7/iss2/general/article2.cfm [viewed 19 Jun 2012]

Human Development Report (2011). http://hdr.undp.org/en/media/HDR_2011_EN_Tables.pdf [viewed 10 Jun 2012]

Hudson, H. (2001). The Potential of ICTs for Development: Opportunities and Obstacles. International Labor Organization, Geneva, Switzerland.

Hudson, P.B. & Chandra, V. (2010) Fusing curricula : science, technology and ICT. In: Sixth International Conference on Science, Mathematics, and Technology Education, 19-22 January 2010, Hualien, Taiwan.

Ifeoma, O.E. (2010). Roles and Actions of School Principals in Managing Curricular Reforms in Nigeria. International Journal of Educational Research and Technology, (1), 1, 85-90

International Telecommunication Union (2004). Bula Internet: Fiji ICT Case Study. http://www.itu.int/ITU-D/ict/cs/fiji/material/CS_FJI.pdf [viewed 11 Jun 2012]

Jamaica Observer (2012). Peru's aggressive laptop plan misses mark. http://www.jamaicaobserver.com/business/Peru-s-agressive-laptop-plan-misses-mark_11880341#ixzz20XvhkCET [viewed 22 Jun 2012]

Kiander, J. (2004), The evolution of the Finnish model in the 1990s: from depression to high-tech boom, VATT discussion paper No. 344.

Kim, H. K., & Rissel, D. (2008). Instructors' Integration of Computer Technology: Examining the Role of Interaction. Foreign Language Annals, 41(1), 61-81.

LeBaron, J., & McDonough, E. (2009). Research report for GeSCI meta-review of ICT in education phase two. http://www.gesci.org/assets/files/Research/meta-research-phase2.pdf [viewed 22 Jun 2012]

Maloney, J., Resnick, M., Rusk, N., Silverman, B., & Eastmond, E. (2010). The scratch programming language and environment. ACM Trans. Comput. Educ. 10 (4), 1-15

Mishra, P., & Koehler, M. (2006). Technological pedagogical content knowledge: a framework for teacher knowledge. Teachers College Records, 108(6), 1017-1054.

Mitchell, C., & Sackney, L. (2000). Profound improvement: Building capacity for a learning community. Lisse, NL: Swets & Zeitlinger

Mitra, S. (2005). Self organising systems for mass computer literacy: Findings from the 'hole in the wall' experiments. International Journal of Development Issues 4(1), 71-81

Mutonyi, H., & Norton, B. (2007). ICT on the margins: Lessons for Ugandan education. Language and Education 21 (3): 264–270.

Moyo, D. (2009). Dead Aid. London: Penguin Books

Nyika A., et al. (2010). Engaging diverse communities participating in clinical trials: case examples from across Africa. http://www.malariajournal.com/content/pdf/1475-2875-9-86.pdf [viewed 16 Jun 2012]

OECD (n.d.). ICT in Innovative Schools: Case Studies of Change and Impacts. http://www.oecd.org/dataoecd/11/11/41187025.pdf [viewed 27 Apr 2012]

Rahiman, M.H., & Naz, R. (2006). Digital Divide within Society: an account of poverty, community and e-governance in Fiji. E-learning,(3), 3, 325-343

Resnick, M., et. al (2009). Scratch: Programming for all. Comm. ACM 52(11), 60–67.

Rogers, E. M. (1995). Diffusion of Innovations (4th ed.). NY: Free Press. 47.

Shulman, L. S. (1987). Knowledge and teaching: Foundations of the new reform. Harvard Educational Review, 57(1), 1–22.

Slay, H., Sieborger, I., & Hodgkinson-Williams, C. (2008). Interactive whiteboards: Real beauty or just "lipstick"?" Computers and Education , 51 (3), p. 1321-1341.

Tessmer, M., & Richey. R.C. (1997). The role of context in learning and instructional design. Educational Technology Research and Development 45 (2), p. 85-115

Toptas,V., Celik, S., & Karaca, E.T. (2012) Improving 8th grades spatial thinking abilities through a 3D modelling program. The Turkish Online Journal of Educational Technology (11), 2, 128 -134

Toluyemi, S.T., & Mejabi, O.V. (2011). Can information and communications technology application contribute to poverty reduction? Lessons from Nigeria. Educational Research and Reviews, (6), 1051 – 1057

UNDP (2012). Millennium development goals. http://www.undp.org/content/undp/en/home/mdgoverview.html [viewed 27 May 2012]

Wenger, E. (2006). Communities of practice a brief introduction. http://www.ewenger.com/theory/communities_of_practice_intro.htm [viewed 14 Jun 2004]

Williams, D., Coles, L., Wilson, K., Richardson, A., & Tuson, J. (2000). Teachers and ICT: current use and future needs. British Journal of Educational Technology, 31(4), 307-320.

The Unheard Voices at Dhaka University

Marianne Georgsen, VIA University College
mage@viauc.dk

Pär-Ola Zander, Aalborg University
poz@hum.aau.dk

Abstract
There is a limit to how much a university can contribute to development if it is impeded by a malfunctioning administration. The public universities in Bangladesh are still largely paper-based in their administration, and their transition to digital working procedures is a great challenge. This chapter challenges a fundamental assumption, namely that administration workers are not capable of contributing creatively to public development. It is implied in literature that the outline of development is already given by experts or can be imitated by studying role models from abroad. This research adopts an action research approach where workshops with university administration workers are carried out, with the aim of generating new ways of doing computer-based administration. The case is University of Dhaka, a prestigious national top university of Bangladesh. The results of the workshops are interpreted through the use of qualitative methods. They demonstrate that the administration workers are capable of envisioning new ways of working, in particular new methods of reducing the number of steps in the workflows. Finally, we discuss other qualities of the administration workers' visions of future practice, such as workflow literacy, staff training, perceptions of top management - and issues which turned out to be difficult to articulate in a workshop.

Introduction & Theoretical Background
There is a limit to how much a university can contribute to development if it is impeded by a malfunctioning administration. The public universities in Bangladesh are still largely paper-based in their administration, and their transition to digital working methods is a great challenge.

Some literature on Bangladeshi administration (Jamil, 1998; Sohban, 2004) has been published, and plenty on the development of the public sector at the macro level. However, in the tradition in which this research is situated, Scandinavian Participatory Design (Greenbaum & Kyng, 1991; Gregory, 2002; Simonsen & Robertson, 2013), the literature that would be most helpful is qualitative research centered on users'/workers' experience, because of high relevance to design (ibid). This can take the form of e.g. ethnographies or descriptions and design proposals from user-driven development and analysis.

The purpose of this chapter is to provide the administrative workers with a voice in the debate about how the future digital working procedures should be designed. Furthermore, we wish to shed light on "the nature" of their views of the future. This may act as a counterweight to popular stereotypes of the Bangladeshi administration and provide a more nuanced picture than e.g. this one:

> "A dozen babus in dhotis were seated in the middle of this chaos, beneath a battery of fans which throbbed out a veritable sirocco of moist air and sent the papers into a whirl of confusion. While some scrambled to catch documents as if they were chasing butterflies, others jabbed a single finger at antique typewriters, pausing after each letter to verify that they had actually hit the right key. Others were talking on telephones that didn't appear to be connected to any line. Many of them seemed to be engrossed in activities that were not, strictly speaking, professional. Some were reading newspapers or sipping tea. Others were asleep, with their heads propped up on the papers that covered their desks..." (LaPierre, 1986, p. 177)

Such is the description from a Western bestseller, depicting Bengali administration work.

People outside of Bangladesh are largely left with depictions in popular culture, where administration is depicted as an alienating, absurd way of working. In fact, very little research is reported from this domain. Ever since its nascency, participatory design has encountered scepticism regarding the prospects of involving people other than experts in the creation of visions of future ways of working. Jungk & Müllert, who themselves were strong believers in the power of common, even unskilled, people, present the viewpoint like this:

> "'Common people' know too little to be able to express 'adequate' sketches of the future. They are too uneducated, their level of information is insufficient, their view restricted…it would require years of education and - as a necessary prerequisite - ability to think abstract, analytically, and placing things in a larger perspective" (Jungk & Müllert, 1991, p. 16, our translation).

We will return to these objections later in the chapter. The discussion is based on the participatory design (PD) understanding that users are competent practitioners. We investigate this through our research project "ePolicyInPractice", situated at University of Dhaka (locally known as Dhaka University, or DU), where we have run a series of Future Workshops (ibid). Here, our pre-understanding was that the administration workers were undervalued resources in the development of the organisation, as well as in the sketching out of new ICT services within the field of higher education. The initiative for the project was taken by an ardent supporter of digitalization at DU, and we agreed that it was an interesting project context. Our partners at DU had ratherlow expectations for their abilities to formulate suggestions, although they did agree that it was important to understand the expectations, skill levels and experience of the administrative workers in order to digitalize workflows at the university. Thus we decided to carry out workshops with administration workers as participants. We believe that researchers and professionals with limited experience of Bangladeshi administration workers may bring to the table pre-understandings similar to ours. This can also be said for Bangladeshi experts who may hold everyday experience, but have not reflected on their experience in order to produce systematic knowledge about administration workers at Bangladeshi universities.

The chapter is structured as follows: First, we describe the general context and argue how the accounts and ideas of administration workers' remain an unexplored theme in the ICT4D literature. This is followed by a description of the method used and the data created in the fieldwork. The subsequent analysis of data places emphasis on identifying and presenting themes in relation to the further design of ICT support at DU, which the participating administration workers felt were important.

Dhaka University and its Administration Work

Dhaka University is a public university and one of the most prestigious higher education institutions in Bangladesh. It offers study programs in all the academic areas that one would expect from a large university. It is based in Dhaka, but has "constituent" colleges throughout the country, e.g. in medicine, which formally also belong to the organisation. By national standards it is doing well as far as research is concerned. Shifting governments have traditionally prioritized DU in their resource allocation, and DU is thus relatively rich in resources, as regards both staff and buildings. However, DU is struggling to establish itself in the top rankings of international standards.

Since the atrocities carried out during the Independence war, DU has held a unique position in Bangladeshi society. During the war, Pakistani military troops elimininated hundreds of students and teachers at the 1971 massacre at the beginning of the then West Pakistan's (now Pakistan) attempt to counter the rebellion in East Pakistan (now Bangladesh). To this day, this is an important part of the identity of DU, and the university remains an important site for political struggle. The top management is politically appointed, and almost all teachers have party membership in one of the two major political parties. This means that all change processes are intertwined with the party-political game. However, the leading position of DU also means that its changes are often adopted by other universities, so the successful digitalization of DU is likely to have spin-off effects. This is, at least, the self-perception of all stakeholders that we have met in our fieldwork. A further complication (but also a strategic opportunity) is that the current government (in 2011, when this work was carried out, the government was led by the so-called Awami League) is strongly promoting digitalization of many areas in society. Although not explicit in the data, we argue that the institutional, historical and political contexts of DU are important for our understanding of the case. The current political situation at DU, we believe, is helpful in making it possible to address issues and problems.

The Administration Worker

As mentioned before, the structural conditions of administrative work in Bangladesh have been extensively described, and to some extent also its culture. However, the practice and wishes of administration workers are hardly at all dealt with in the academic body of knowledge. The needs of the workers seem to have been neglected, as the existing research has not aimed to be design-oriented. Below, we will give a short description of what we understand by "administrative work". The base of administration workers at Dhaka University is more heterogeneous than first anticipated by us when launching our investigation. Our initial contact persons (all university faculty and/or managers) spoke of the administration workers as a homogeneous mass, and this influenced our pre-understandings.

The tasks of the administrative workers include filing and processing applications; keeping financial records; recording, processing and presenting administrative data; helping students, faculty, and managers fill in applications; assisting when questions are asked about a specific case; learning and applying new regulations; and sometimes handling special cases where it is not clear if and how existing rules apply. A few areas have undergone computerization; however, in the vast majority of cases, coordination between the involved parties is mediated by printed paper. To add to the toil of the paper handling, very often papers need a seal of approval or authentication, which involves a senior office manager, a director or a dean.

Senior workers refer to themselves as officers (in English), typically dealing not only with processing but also part-time with some analytical tasks or other managerial duties. Some of the senior staff (not only key advisors of the top management, or the managers themselves) are highly educated, some even graduates from Dhaka University. The upper middle management within the administration is generally referred to as deans (these are elected by faculty) and directors (these are appointed). Although administration workers are clearly also part of the administration workforce, the discourse around these does not include deans and directors.

The lower level positions may be referred to as "administrative support staff". This group takes orders from 'officers', and they often have assistants below them as well. Finally, there are the so-called "class 4" workers (sometimes derogatorily called "peons"), who carry out practical tasks such as paper delivery and tea making, and run other errands for senior staff and faculty such as buying cigarettes or delivering messages. Yet the concept is complex for someone who is non-Bangladeshi - as an example, policemen are also "class 4" workers, so this is not a uniform group of people in the society of Bangladesh. The reference to policemen as class 4 workers testify to the fact that it is impossible to think of the totality of this group of people as completely powerless or uneducated. For instance, one of our class 4 workers also has children who successfully applied to DU, so this is also not a group of people whose families are always uneducated and non-analytic, as they are often described. On the other hand, many "class 4 workers" speak little English and may be functionally illiterate (and ICT illiterate too).

The Role of Universities in Development

The role universities play in societal development is a complex and well-researched one, and a description of this could easily expand into an entire book.

The role of the administration is generally overlooked, however. This is unfortunate, because in most teaching innovations and most student activity the administrative workforce represent one of the stakeholders. Furthermore, a flexible administration is a necessary precondition if the relation between the university and the surrounding society is to be altered.

Therefore, this study is relevant for at least one part of the ICT4D community, namely those who deal with higher education and ICT. However, for the purpose of this discussion, in the case of DU, it will suffice to introduce this simple explanation of development:

Efficient administration leads to universities that accomplish their functions. One of the purposes a university can accomplish is that of contributing to sustainable development (Stephens et al., 2008). Exactly how that function works can be debated (Fincham, Georg, and Holm Nielsen, 2005), but this is not something we aim to solve here. In any case, our stance is that efficient administration contributes as a catalyst to sustainable development.

The catalyst model can be criticized, e.g. from the point of view of the Triple-Helix approach (Etzkowitz & Leydesdorff, 1997; Saad & Zawdie, 2011; see also Sanchez in this book). Based on this literature, one could argue that the ideal administration should be designed to support collaboration across organizational borders. This will question the simple explanation given above, as it is not possible to say anything about development before taking a stance as to which functions a university should support. As an example, within the triple-helix paradigm, a university administration needs to be fast and flexible in case of a business opportunity with only a small window of opportunity (Wallin, Lavagno, and Zander, 2004). In line with this thinking, it would be tempting to launch a project that creates truly radical change and takes DU to the forefront of administration worldwide. Triple Helix notwithstanding, we believe radical change of this kind to be risky, especially when there is no strong perceived need for it among the actors, and it would most likely also be in opposition to the participatory design-approach inherent in our methodological approach. Rather than imposing research goals on the activity of the administration workers, the research project is formed by their needs: from within. We have not come across any students or teachers who ask for radical changes or even see this as a possible far future - what they want are reasonably fast responses as well as transparency in case processing. Flexible ICT systems and open boundaries come across as severe challenges even for advanced administrations that have pursued this for several years, and we take the approach (supported by all stakeholders) that the time for such change has not yet come for DU.

This discussion can be summarized to conclude that universities have a role within development, and the administration is important in this role. It should not, however, be understood as a requirement that DU's administrative change projects must aim for compliance with the most appraised organizational models of universities.

Method

The research reported here is part of an large action research project called ePolicyInPractice (Zander, Georgsen, & Murshed, 2011). On a theoretical level, the purpose is explorative: to understand some of the effects of digitalization in higher education on the institutional level. On the practical level, the overall goal is to improve the digitalization of Dhaka University, in a "reformist Participatory Design" way (Bødker & Zander, 2012; Shapiro, 2005) where both management and worker stakeholders gain from the project. In concrete terms this means that we are aiming for an improvement of the users' technological working conditions in a way that takes their needs and visions into account.

We have involved administration workers actively in the process through methods that let them enact their experience and tacit knowledge, and the aim is also that they develop realistic expectations for technology. As mentioned in the introduction, this is a project in the spirit of participatory design. This research approach emerged in the 1970s in Scandinavia, and became widespread in the West in the 1990s. Recently, an increased interest has emerged as to what the approach can accomplish in developing countries as well (Zander, 2011) with the forthcoming PDC 2014, the world conference of the PD community, symbolically placed in Namibia. This research approach is a kind of interventionist research, and has the following significant features:

- A focus on concrete mock-ups (see example below), which makes discussions tangible, and enables a discussion about specific, personal experiences (Kyng & Ehn, 1991). An example of a concrete mock-up is when participants discuss the use of mobile phones for scanning, and a scenario is enacted where old mobile phones are used, and scanning labels are provisionally constructed. Another example is when an envisioned web site interface is represented in a workshop by an ad-hoc drawing in order to explore what-if situations in people's everyday lives. The key methodological underpinning is "an insistence on concrete experiences as the basis for theoretical work" (Kyng, 1996, p. 32).
- Related to being concrete, PD also advocates the importance of local action, possibly paired with action on a central level. Change should not be imposed from above, but be anchored in local motivation, e.g. felt needs that are not being satisfied (Kanstrup, 2005).
- An emphasis on engaged scholarship. The researchers are involved in and take a stance in the real-political situations which relate to the research project. A stance can be to take the workers' perspective (Ehn, 1988), or in some cases trying to find a win-win situation in a complex stakeholder situation (Bødker & Zander, in review). But a top-down manager perspective is never taken, nor a detached, descriptive approach. Some ambition of change is always involved.
- Building realistic expectations as to what can be achieved. ICT (information communication technologies) can accomplish many things, and many organizations where change seemed impossible have in fact changed. However, for a sustainable effort for change to take place, realistic expectations are necessary (Bødker, Kensing & Simonsen, 2004).

- Contradictions as a fundamental condition for social reality, and also a resource and catalyst for future action (Gregory, 2002). Contradictions can be productively used for framing discussions. They can also be seen as the catalysts of motivation for change. If a social system contains irreconcilable forces, individuals will be placed in double-bind situations (Engeström, 1987) where they will not feel comfortable. When having to cope with these situations, they may invent new modes of work, and it may be fruitful to analyze these modes of work in the design process.

The primary method employed was workshops. Subsequently we have conducted interviews, which can be used to contrast and substantiate the interpretations of what took place in the workshops. We were two facilitators (the authors), one local organizer and two translators. The latter were carefully instructed in the project goals, and encouraged to intervene if they assessed that the process went astray. The working language was Bengali when facilitators were not around. Facilitators and participants discussed in English or in some cases through simultaneous translation.

The workshops with the administrative staff went on for two consecutive days, since we were informed that the participants could not be away from their offices for a full day. Instead, we worked with them for two half days. The intention of the workshop was to go through two phases of the future workshop (critique of existing practice; and ideas about the future) (Jungk & Müllert, 1991). The third phase, the so called realization phase, was left out, as the main purpose was to try out the scope for user involvement in the process of pinpointing shortcomings in the current work practice, as well as in the creation of new ideas. The idea was to let the critique phase determine the focus of the remaining part of the future workshop, e.g. to find out what workflows to rethink and redesign. The intention was also to document a number of ideas or visions which were also detailed in their level of description. Furthermore, we were aiming for the outcome of this workshop to be used as a basis for further field observations.

To start out the fantasy phase, participants were asked to engage in a group-based game, using Lego bricks as a tool for design, in this case to illustrate something which each person liked about his/her work (LEGO, 2012). One person would build something, the others in the group were to guess what it was, and this was followed by a short discussion before the next person was asked to build something. By doing this, we achieved the simple purpose of letting the participants do something fun and serious at the same time. Most participants were amused by the playful exercise, although some senior participants were a bit hesitant. For them it was an unusual social situation; but their later participation did not indicate that it was detriment to their engagement. It should be noted that the Lego exercise was not intended for generating data for design proposals, but their output is still helpful to get an idea how the administration workers are capable of creativity, quick sketching and informal representation.

The warm up-activity was followed by a collective brainstorm where participants described organizational routines that they found to be unproductive or bad in other ways. These procedures were described in a short form, and the majority of time and effort went into trying to come up with ways of improving these procedures. On the second day of the workshop, the groups would repeat the warm-up exercise, this time they were asked to collectively illustrate the office of their dreams, using Lego and pen and paper. Following this, the participants worked in groups with developing ideas of how to improve some of the problematic procedures identified the previous day (see Picture 1 for examples). Participants were then asked to produce storyboards (Gruen, 2000) to illustrate the new improved workflows and practices. Storyboards were chosen because they are easy to exemplify (given most of these techniques would be novel to the participants, we were concerned with ways of giving good instructions); a story board does not focus narrowly on the form, it is fast to produce, and it allows almost full user control in terms of style and level of detail.

Picture 1. Example of illustrations of future offices from the admin workshop

The administration workers came from various departments, and the advantage of this was that they could verify whether an issue raised was indeed a common problem in the organisation, or whether it was a local-department problem.

Much of the data makes little sense in itself (more information is needed to understand what 'the registrar building' actually is?) and it would also be difficult to participate in discussions without any background knowledge. Therefore we also conducted some interviews and observations in order to contextualize the workshop data. An overview of the data can be found below.

Overview of Data

From the 2-day workshops with administration workers:

- Pictures of admin workshop
- Workshop notes
- Audio recordings of presentations of group work, day 1, and presentations of group work, day 2
- Posters prepared by the groups presenting their work
- A small paper prototype
- Condensations of the critique phase
- Reflections from the workshops from all involved

Follow-up data (interviews and observations):
- Interview with an administration worker/a flowchart of a particular workflow
- Two interviews with class 4 workers
- One day of parallel observations of seven administration workers in various parts of DU

Analysis of Data

The workshop data were subsequently transcribed and interpreted. Whereas most of the interpretation work was qualitative research common to the field, we would like to specify how we dealt with silences, i.e. issues which were not touched upon in the workshop discussions. Often it is as interesting to note what is not said as what is actually said. This may point to issues that are very design-relevant but difficult to probe into via workshops in this domain. The design-relevant silences can be of several types:

1. Something may "fail" to be discussed because the topic or information is deemed irrelevant or lacks salience for the participants. To some degree, this is mitigated by a good workshop introduction and contingent facilitation. Furthermore, the critique phase of the future workshop may increase the understanding of the problem amongst both participants and facilitator. Conversely, obvious topics also make for silence. (Poland & Pederson, 1998, p. 306). Methodologically, this means that transcript passages with "little content" are markers of this. (the concept of 'load shedding' is one such issue in parts of these discussions). It may, however, be design-relevant for technical reasons, and what is obvious for the participants may be overlooked by designers at a later stage in the process.
2. A person may lack the specific vocabulary to articulate something that he or she has experienced. We tried explicitly to counter this with the introduction of concepts into the future workshop.
3. Categorical silence - when there is no understanding (maybe no vocabulary either). We also alleviated this by the concept introduction.

However, before discussing our findings, some things should be considered as rival explanations. Poland & Pederson (1998) discuss some alternatives:
1. Due to cultural insensitivity. Participants withhold their speech because of thoughts such as "I do not talk to you about this because you seem to talk about it in an inappropriate way or time" or similar considerations.

2. To this we would like to add the risk that the facilitators are perceived as the "long arm of management" and it would be bad tactics to describe some aspects.

Due to space restrictions, it is not possible to present the evaluations of the rival explanations here, but they have been taken into consideration in the analysis. It was important for us to reflect on the possibility offered to enact and discuss all issues; but for this to happen, our cultural capital was insufficient.

What the Workers Envisioned, and How

Descriptions of Future Use

The administrative workers were able to identify a number of potential areas for digitalization:

Table 1. Potential areas for digitalization

4.	Hall admission
5.	Student information (schedules, exams results, etc)
6.	Administrative "one-stop service" process for teachers and students for applying for and obtaining admission for studying PhD or MPhil degrees.
7.	Allocating residential facilities to staff

From the outsider perspective of the authors, all these areas seem to be reasonable organizational development projects with IT support. Consider the following example, given by some of the participants as a short presentation to the entire group in the workshop:

"These are our thoughts on "student information service". First, we want to make a database. The student applies online for his admission test. Then, the database system retrieves information from various sources. For the [admission] exam, he will contact the dean's office. The dean's office will check his merits and the exam room and the dean's office will send the information to the student, and send the student to the department. The chairperson will decide class size and routine. The department also sends the information to the database. Then the student can finally go to the hall office. The hall office will check all his documents. They will scan through the application. If all his documents are correct, they will send a message to the central database, and the student will receive an email. All his information will be in it, and the application procedure will be completed. The database will send a claims processing number, a password, and the student will sit at a computer, anywhere on the planet, and access the system. He will provide password and name. Passwords may change. After logging in, he will see his name and hall number. What kind of information does he need? Several boxes are here..."

Picture 2. Sketch illustrating a "student information service procedure"

There may be obstacles to this vision, such as legal requirements, and there is no analysis as to how this benefits the organization as a whole. Nevertheless, such proposals can serve as excellent ideas to elaborate upon. We find that criticizing the worker for having restricted viewpoints (as mentioned in the introduction) is not fair, since this was not the task they set out to solve in the future workshop.

An interesting objection is whether "management" was already thinking in ways similar to what was proposed by the workers. Our research was framed also by meetings with top management, and we held additional workshops with them (still to be reported in an academic format). However, the top management seems to be aware of the great scope for improvement through ICT, but (for natural reasons) they lack the detailed knowledge necessary to formulate such a proposal. The middle management (e.g. directors) often have detailed knowledge, it may be argued. But in none of the areas listed have we seen any initiatives towards digitalization from middle management. An area in which the situation differs is in accounting, where an ambitious IT project has been launched.

The type of IT-based work environment the workshop participants are dreaming of looks like this:

- Training is provided for those who need it in the form of courses.
- Top managers and the heads of department have understood at a strategic

level what IT can do, and are also using the systems themselves.
- IT has provided an efficient bureaucracy (in the positive sense of the word) with clearly defined roles, and with information flowing in well-defined workflows.
- Above all, it is faster than the present way of handling the cases.
- Email, web and text messaging are the main media used for case processing, and face-to-face interactions also take place.
- There is no corruption. The primary users of the system (students and teachers) know the status of their cases.

The remaining part of this analysis section is ordered in themes emergent (not theory-driven) from the analysis of our data.

The Foregrounding of Training

Administration workers are seen as lowly educated people at DU, and this prejudice may imply that they are uninterested in learning new things. The workshop clearly showed that the supposedly uneducated people were quite willing to receive training. The participants were generally quite interested in learning more about ICT and the ways in which it can be integrated into administrative work. Contrary to prejudice, they were active when concepts were explained to them, even if it had no clear future impact on their particular jobs. In short, they were engaged learners.

In the minds of the administration workers, ICT is above all a question of possessing the right skills, although participants did not elaborate on exactly what kinds of skills they meant (is it how to use an operating system, general office skills, or communication conduct in emails?). The administration workers anticipate that competence development is necessary, and they link this to training.

When the workshop was organized, considerable resources were spent on the possibility of issuing certificates to acknowledge participation. This was not promised to the partcipants beforehand, so we find it safe to assume that the participants did not participate solely in order to acquire a certificate. It is clear, however, that certificates in general are an important part of the culture in Bangladesh, and this tendency is even stronger at a university. So clearly this is (correctly used) something that can be used as a motivator. On the other hand, it is also a sign that self-paced competence development, based on the initiative of the individual, is not what the administrative workers envision. Little allegiance was paid to the viewpoint that learning is something that takes place as part of everyday work.

Concerns about the Role of Top Management

When we asked the participants what were the key obstacles to digitalizing administration, the support of top management for ICT projects scored as number two on a prioritized list of "dead-ends of digitalization". This issue was the top concern in one of the groups, and was broadly agreed upon among the 15 caseworkers in the workshop. This perception may carry some extra weight, due to the fact that many of the participants worked in locations they shared with people from the upper levels of management. The issue was fleshed out in some detail in the discussions. The workers believed that digitalization needs to be promoted by the top-level management. Many administration workers will resist new IT systems if these are not promoted by upper management. A deeper understanding of the factors behind this mechanism is interesting in itself but it falls outside the topic of this study. It is of interest to note, however, that the pessimistic scenario is that the key managers do not understand the technology, and hence they will not be truly motivated to support the digitalization process. And even if they were motivated, they would not come across in a convincing manner if they displayed an apparent lack in computer skills. One of the authors of this chapter has visited several offices of the upper management, and often they were without computers. It is quite likely that the administration workers have made the same observation, and draw their conclusions from this experience. As one participant phrased the condition for resistance: "...if everybody starts using the system but it becomes apparent that the top managers are not dealing with [i.e. using] computers...".

Besides the questions of leadership, the non-involvement of managers is also important when imagining future modes of working. Dhaka University is a hierarchic organization (especially compared to Western universities), and the case workers do not envision an organisation using ICT which will result in shorter lines of command. Many workflows have the vice chancellor or the treasurer as one of the nodes, even if this is only for the purpose of approval or disapproval. The main thrust of digitalization at DU is to achieve faster case processing (see also discussion above in this section). A workflow that has been partly digitalized but where managers live in "paper-based pockets" inside it may miss this point.

Based on these examples, we find that the administration workers' concern about involvement of the top management is in many ways central for their imagination. A future way of working must also include the ways in which the top management is involved.

Workflow Literacy

Early in this chapter we mentioned that input from the bottom-level of the workforce is often omitted because the latter is perceived as lacking abstract and analytical skills. Perhaps the concept of workflow is the most archetypical concept of abstraction of everyday work that exists. In the richness of particular actions, exceptions, iterations, emotions and human relations that we call work, some boxes and arrows are taken to represent this, and as a result, all personal idiosyncrasies are hidden.

For the administration workers, the default way of collaborating was, nonetheless, the workflow. This was a tool they were familiar with and which they resorted to in their discussions and when they assumed that they were to deliver their output to the rest of the group and to us. The workers are able to identify a wealth of concrete suggestions of how workflows could be significantly shortened. Most clearly we see that they become frustrated with the many steps in the procedures, which serves as a motivator for them in producing ideas and solutions.

All in all, the conception of the administration worker as universally unable to think analytically and abstractly is incorrect. The point we would like to make is, however, that we did not find that the workers have universal abstraction abilities. The workshop had a narrow focus, and it may be that the workers would have had problems in applying other abstract concepts. However if they can use the workflow concept aptly, it seems reasonable to expect that they can probably appropriate many other concepts as well.

Notable Absences

In the research perspective we are aware that we may be theoretically sensitized to the field of digitalization of administration. From this perspective, it was interesting to note a number of "absences". We found that the administration workers were silent on the following issues:

1) Direct organizational and economic consequences. The most obvious consequence is workforce reduction or the change of roles. However, generally staff reduction is not perceived as a big threat at Dhaka University. Many workers have seen public sector employers that keep their staff despite the fact that dismissal would be possible from an efficiency point of view.

2) Motivational issues were almost non-present. Members of the organisation have later suggested that this is because the norm in this sector is that the worker does what he or she is ordered to do. A large share of the Bangladeshi work force is simply motivated by the payroll and the threat of absolute poverty. However, one of the recurring topics was the fast processing of cases. You do not have to be trained in work psychology to be aware that you work harder when work is perceived as fun or meaningful. As the administration workers were very concerned with the speed of case processing, it is remarkable that the issue was never discussed. As an ice-breaking and creativity-unleashing exercise at the beginning of the second workshop we asked the participants to build their "favorite future office". These offices contained things that were pleasant and important for their wellbeing at work, but not core to the work tasks, such as fans and sofas.

3) Visual design of the systems. Maybe this is perceived by participants to be an irrelevant detail. It may also be noted that most administrative work spaces at DU are relatively sparsely decorated and impersonal (or free from non-professional self-expression). The exception to this are a few simple Islamic decorations and photos of Sheikh Mujibur Rahman, the founding father of the nation (and belonging to the current ruling party).

4) Advantages to be expected from an increased overview. For instance, no one mentions ease of prioritization and more efficient allocation when all cases are visible and possible to order quickly in the system. No one mentions possibilities of benchmarking between departments. Although such technologies can be used by management to enforce taylorism at the expense of the ordinary worker, a lack of awareness about this possibility and the "win-win" benefits it can yield seems to prevail. Better prioritization can also lead to reduced stress and an administration that is held in higher regard. One project at DU is work-

ing with digitalization of accounts across departments, which will provide a better financial overview for the top management. Some participants worked in accounting and must have known about this project. As they did not mention it, it seems likely that this benefit has not been realized (or embraced) by any of the people in the workshop.

5) The feelings and experience evoked by interaction with the system. This was explicitly encouraged at the workshop, but was little touched upon. We speculate that this is due to the fact that it is so unusual to discuss these issues, and more structured techniques must be used if a workshop is to provide any interesting data or ideas relating to emotion.

6) Almost no discussions of winners and losers of the technologies took place, nor did other terms similar to Grudin's first principles (Grudin, 1994) emerge. This is interesting since the silence occurred despite the fact that we prompted for "win-lose" situations. We held a similar workshop with teachers at DU, and they readily discussed these issues. The workshops were confined to four hours (against the original suggestions from Jungk & Müllert (1991)). With more time, it would have been possible to discuss the proposed solutions in more depth. This could involve a stakeholder aspect in which the consequences for all stakeholders could be perused.

7) Strikingly few suggestions of good training were proffered; it is clear that awareness of the need for training is widespread, but the solutions remain unknown. This is not a particularly sensitive topic. The most plausible mechanism seems to be that the workers have simply not seen a large variety of training approaches (different ways to conduct a course, organizing helpdesks, super users, etc.) - or at least, these concepts are not ready-at-hand.

Finally, it cannot be ruled out that the silences were due to what can be seen as culturally insensitive handling. Probing may have been too direct, or insufficiently insisting. Asking for elaboration on a participant's opinion can be interpreted as rude questioning of his or her authority and cause resentment, and so on. Facilitators and organizer (professor at DU) knew each other well, and the organizer did not report on any blatant mistakes. But even if we might have hampered the view sharing of participants, the "notable absences" are still relevant to report. The notion that visual design and motivation get suppressed in these workshops is so important that it requires specific attention. If we ('we' as in a combination of Bangladeshi and Scandinavian facilitators) were culturally insensitive, it is likely that others will make the same error. An obvious situation is future cross-cultural designer teams operating in a similar context.

Discussion and Conclusion

This chapter began by examining how administration workers act when engaged in developing future modes of work at their university. The analysis above shows that they are able to think in a way that is both abstract and analytical (in terms of workflow design), and seen as a group, it contains individuals that are highly educated or come from educated homes. From a participatory design perspective, it is important that competent co-designers can be added, not that they are statistically representative (Bødker & Grønbæk, 1992;

Von Hippel, 1986). They can articulate sketches of future ways of working that are worth taking seriously.

The administration workers are admittedly restricted in what they highlight as important in their future visions. However, their ideas from the workshops do not demonstrate a mere incapability of seeing the points of view of others, nor do they indicate a narrow self-interest. To a large extent, what the administration workers leave out are aspects of their own experience and practice, such as e.g. emotional characteristics or specific antagonisms at the workplace. When participants are stereotypically accused of having a restricted view (Jungk & Müllert, 1991), this is a relative statement. It is common in information systems development to rely more on accounts of work supplied by middle managers and experts. But the overview of e.g. middle managers is really just another perspective, which becomes clear when these managers are unable to give valid feedback on hands-on evaluation of prototypes in daily work situations (von Hippel, 1986). Furthermore the generally hierarchical nature of DU and the public sector in Bangladesh renders it inconceivable that this perspective will not have an influence on every system development project anyway. In any case, it cannot be ruled out that other design techniques and methods would generate the articulation of administration workers' knowledge and interests beyond those stated here.

Finally, it is interesting to notice that the administration workers' sketches of the future and their discussions are often centred upon efficiency and transparency. Some design literature has warned against this as it leaves the work easier to refactor (e.g. Suchman (1995). With well-defined work flows, roles are thoroughly specified and it is easy to train new candidates to comply with their roles, and many types of taylorist measures can be taken. But instead of patronizing workers, it is instructive to look more deeply into the reasons why transparency is desirable. One assumption is that in a working climate that is so politicized, there may be a longing for a way to demonstrate work skills. Making work visible and competitive can of course deteriorate into sometimes absurd work life conditions as in some call centers (Cederström, 2009), but this is worth pursuing in future research.

References

A2I programme. (2010). Strategic priorities of Digital Bangladesh. Retrieved from www.basis.org.bd/resource/Digital-BD-STRATEGY.pdf

Azizuddin, M. (2008). Public administration reform in Bangladesh - Challenges and prospects. Dhaka: Chowkash Printers.

Bødker, K., Kensing, F., & Simonsen, J. (2004). Participatory IT design: Designing for business and workplace realities. Cambridge Mass.: MIT Press.

Bødker, S., & Grønbæk, K. (1992). Design in action: From prototyping by demonstration to cooperative prototyping. In Design at Work: Cooperative Design of Computer Systems (pp. 197 – 218). Mahwah: Lawrence Erlbaum Associates.

Bødker, S., & Zander, P.-O. (in press). (When) Scandinavian Democracy Meets Web 2.0. Scandinavian Journal of Information Systems.

Cederström, C. (2009). The other side of technology: Lacan and the desire for the purity of non-being. (PhD thesis, Lund University). Lund: Lund Business Press.

Ehn, P. (1988). Work-oriented design of computer artifacts (PhD Thesis, Umeå University). Gummesons: Falköping.

Engeström, Y. (1987). Learning by expanding: An activity-theoretical approach to developmental research. Helsinki: Orienta-Konsultit Oy.

Etzkowitz, H., & Leydesdorff, L. A. (1997). Universities and the global knowledge economy: A triple helix of university-industry-government relations. London: Pinter.

Fincham, R., Georg, S., & Holm Nielsen, E. (2005). Sustainable development and the university: New strategies for research and practice. Howick: Brevitas.

Greenbaum, J., & Kyng, M. (1991). Design at work: Cooperative design of computer systems. Hillsdale: Lawrence Erlbaum.

Gregory, J. (2002). Scandinavian approaches to Participatory Design. International journal of engaging Education, 19(1), 62–74.

Grudin, J. (1994). Groupware and social dynamics: Eight challenges for developers. Communications of the ACM, 34, 93–105.

Gruen, D. (2000). Storyboarding for Design: An overview of the process (Technical report). IBM Watson Research Center. Retrieved from http://domino.watson.ibm.com/cambridge/research.nsf/0/ebcd159a81a43e36852569200067d59e/$FILE/Techreport%202000.03.PDF

Jamil, I. (1998). Administrative Culture in Public Administration: Five Essays on Bangladesh. ☺Report 9801. LOS-center report.☺

Jungk, R., & Müllert, N. (1991). Håndbog i fremtidsværksteder (2. udg.) [Future Workshops]. Copenhagen: Politisk revy.

Kanstrup, A.-M. (2005). Local design - an inquiry into work practices of local IT supporters (PhD Thesis, Aalborg University).

Karim, H. N., Mina, Q., & Samdani, G. (2011). Going digital: Realizing the dreams of a digital Bangladesh for all. Dhaka: University Press.

Kyng, M. (1996). Users and computers: A contextual approach to design of computer artefacts. DAIMI publication series.

Kyng, M., & Ehn, P. (1991). Cardboard computers - Mocking-it-up or hands-on the future. In Greenbaum & Kyng (Eds.), Design@work (pp. 169–195). Hillsdale: Lawrence Erlbaum.

Lapierre, D. (1986). The city of joy. London: Arrow Books.

LEGO (2012). LEGO serious play. LEGO. Retrieved from http://www.seriousplay.com

Poland, B., & Pederson, A. (1998). Reading Between the Lines: Interpreting Silences in Qualitative Research. Qualitative Inquiry, 4(2), 293–312.

Saad, M., & Zawdie, G. (2011). Theory and practice of the triple helix system in developing countries: Issues and challenges. New York: Routledge.

Shapiro, D. (2005). Participatory design: The will to succeed. In Critical Computing proceedings (pp. 29–38).

Simonsen, J., & Robertson, T. (2013). Routledge international handbook of participatory design. New York: Routledge.

Sohban, R. (2004). Structural dimensions of malgovernance in Bangladesh. Political and economic weekly, 39, 4–10.

Stephens, J. C., Hernandez, M. E., Román, M., Graham, A. C., & Scholz, R. W. (2008). Higher education as a change agent for sustainability in different cultures and contexts. International Journal of Sustainability in Higher Education, 9(3), 317–338.

Suchman, L. A. (1995). Making work visible. Communications of the ACM, 98, 56–64.

von Hippel, E. (1986). Lead users: a source of novel product concepts. Management Science (32:7), 791–805.

Wallin, E., Lavagno, E., & Zander, P.-O. (2004). Lessons for learning regions. Lund: Office for Continuing and Distance Education.

Zander, P.-O., Georgsen, M., & Nyvang, T. (2011). Scandinavian Participatory Design - Beyond Design, Beyond Scandinavia. Presented at the The Joint Nordic conference for the Nordic Development Research Associations, Copenhagen. Retrieved from http://www.fau.dk/NC/Abstracts_and_papers/Papers/W9_paper_Zander_Georgsen_Nyvang.pdf

Zander, P.-O., Georgsen, M., & Murshed, S. M. (2011). ePolicyInPractice report I - Inaugeration and future workshops (eLearning Lab Publication Series No. 28). Aalborg: Department of Communication and Psychology. Retrieved from http://www.ell.aau.dk/2011/12/08/no-28-epolicyinpractice-report-i/ell-28-epip-i/

Part III

Learning with ICT

Learning as Negotiating Identities. Applying Wenger's Identity Theory to Inform Designs for Learning to Use ICT in a Developing Country Context

Aparna Purushothaman, E-learning Lab, Aalborg University
Email: aparna@hum.aau.dk

Abstract

This chapter discusses how Communities of Practice (CoP) can contribute to the field of ICT4D. The chapter will explore only the identity aspect of CoP and not the concept as a whole. The perception of learning as becoming can to a high extent contribute to learning for students who are novice users to use the Internet in an ICT4D scenario. How this approach to learning can contribute to ICT4D, is explained based on an empirical study done at a university in Southern India with a group of master's students. Learning as experiencing the Internet and constructing identity of what it means to be an Internet user can bring more effective results. The use of Wenger's theory of social learning is barely explored in the field of ICT4D. The chapter hopes to fill this gap by throwing light on how the concept of constructing identity through informal learning can contribute to the field of ICT4D on a micro level through an intervention-oriented research approach.

The Internet – the Inevitable ICT Tool

Of all technologies, the Internet is the ICT tool which has penetrated diverse fields such as education, healthcare, insurance, hospitality industry, job markets etc. Few technologies have had such a global impact cutting across a wide range of sectors and within diverse socio-economic groups like the internet-based technologies and the World Wide Web, which are expanding at an exponential rate (Hill et al., 2004). The Internet can be defined as an "unsurpassed repository of information of all kinds – from specific to general, from minutiae to trivia to depth of detail, to historic and up-to-the minute" (Nwagwu et al., 2009). The Internet provides ways to complete the daily tasks, to gather information and is also a source of entertainment and it touches upon every aspect of our lives (Amichai-Hamburger, 2002). The Internet is viewed as a "virtual laboratory" with its ability to bring people together in a virtual space, its usage as a communication medium and its capacity to collect enormous amounts of data (Sklar & Pollack, 2000). In the twenty first century, the educational and economic development of a society depends on citizens' attitudes towards using and learning to use the Internet (Tsai et al., 2001). The global economy is transforming into an Internet economy (Ramayah et al., 2003). Because of the significance of the Internet in developing countries across the globe, the Internet has generated an upsurge of interest in ICTs among development scholars in researching how ICTs might be applied in developing countries regarding development efforts (Heeks, 2009).

With the emergence of Internet technologies, knowing how to use Internet has become a pre-requisite for students of this generation. As Owston (1997) has stated: "Nothing before has captured the imagination and interest of educators simultaneously around the globe more than the World Wide Web". The Internet can exponentially increase the knowledge base of teachers and students by connecting them to information resources which are far beyond the physical confines of the classroom (Kumari, 1998). Educational institutions around the world are investing in Internet infrastructure and technologies and encouraging the use of both computers and the Internet for supporting courses, research, and distance education, making computers and Internet access and skills critical for students (Nwagwu et al., 2009; Schumacher & Morahan-Martin, 2001). Researchers around the world use the Internet on a daily basis in search of work by other researchers as well as making their own research work available to the research community across the globe (Edwards & Bruce, 2002). "Technology is challenging the boundaries of the educational structures that have traditionally facilitated learning" (Sam, et al., 2005, p. 205). The value of the Internet as an ICT tool to support teaching and learning has gained prominence in recent years (Hill et al., 2004)

Internet skills and literacy are becoming increasingly important in the new information age and those who do not have these skills are economically and educationally disadvantaged (Edwards & Bruce, 2002; Schumacher & Morahan-Martin, 2001; Tsai et al., 2001). One of the main challenges which developing countries face is to get access to the Internet and other ICT technologies. The lack of access to technology for citizens in the developing countries reduces their chances of effectively participating in the new information age and of reaping the benefits of the Internet and other ICTs.

Digital Divide – the Real Hitch for Internet Use?

Though the information and communications technologies are driving globalization, they are also separating the world into the connected and the isolated (UNDP, 1999); a fact that was identified thirteen years ago by UNDP still holds relevance today. Even though the growth of ICT has been exponential, it has not been evenly distributed within countries or around the world, which makes people from these countries unable to take advantage of ICT as they do not have access to it (Kozma, 2011). In this chapter, the usage of ICT/computers/technology also include Internet access, since the Internet is primarily computer-based and experience, skills and attitudes towards computers logically should affect experience, skills and attitudes towards the Internet (Schumacher & Morahan-Martin, 2001). Internet use can be argued to be a natural extension of computer use since access and use certainly involves using a machine or technology (Durndell & Haag, 2002).

Digital divide is a gap or difference in usage of ICTs, computers and the Internet by people (James, 2004; Mehra et al., 2004). Digital divide signifies the gap or separation between "the haves" who have access to digital and communication technologies and "the have nots" who do not have access to digital and communication technologies (Dewan & Riggins, 2005; Edwards & Bruce, 2002; Hargittai, 2004).

The literature on digital divide indicates that there are two types of digital divide. First order digital divide places emphasis on the access statistics that show disparities in usage (Dewan & Riggins, 2005; Hargittai, 2002; Warschauer, 2002). Second order digital divide is characterized by "inequality in the ability to use ICT among those who already have access" (Dewan & Riggins, 2005, p. 300). Scholars came out with the second dimension because they found that the problem of digital divide is not only about the physical access and connectivity, but it also includes a complex array of factors such as education, content, language, skills to use the available technology and socio-cultural factors which influence their usage. (Dewan & Riggins, 2005; Dimaggio, Hargittai, Celeste, & Shafer, 2004; Hargittai, 2002; Warschauer, 2002)

The second order digital divide can bring about more challenges for students of this generation because of lack of skills and knowledge. Second level digital divide can be abridged by developing students' networked competence where students develop the skills to identify, retrieve and use information from the Internet efficiently. Information navigation skills and ability to filter and determine which is the needed information is a prerequisite for individuals of the networked age (McClure, 1994). However, learning how to use the Internet is not an easy task because of the diverse paths of navigation and usage options (Iske et al., 2008). Learning to use the Internet can be difficult for novice users as an Internet search can give inconceivable volumes of information which are unstructured making it look chaotic (Edwards & Bruce, 2002; Lazonder, 2000). What makes it more challenging for novice users is that the problems that are applicable to an information system, like disorientation, navigation, inefficiency and cognitive overload are multiplied on the Internet (Uden et al., 2001). Thus, searching the Internet and getting adequate and relevant information is a complex process which requires great amounts of specialized searching skills. Surfing from one hyperlink to another will not bring optimal results and require specific navigation and browsing skills in order to find the most relevant information (Savolainen, 2002).

As learning and using the Internet is influenced by the socio-cultural factors in developing countries, learning needs and theories that describe learning principles and processes should be reflective of underlying social environments (Siemens, 2004). This chapter discusses how a learning approach based on the identity concept of CoP can contribute to understanding the learning process of how to use the Internet for students in an ICT4D scenario in order to address the issues of second order digital divide.

How can CoP Contribute to Learning ICT in a Development Context?

This chapter takes the position that viewing ICT4D projects through the lens of the theoretical construct of identity can contribute significantly to development efforts of interventions. CoP's concept of learning as negotiating identities can provide the practitioners the means to understand how informal learning happens within projects. If informal learning is the primary focus of intervention, it can potentially provide more appropriate ways to understand empowerment, social change and participatory production within ICT4D (Foster, 2011).

In CoP, learning is a way of negotiating identities and this concept of identity is neither individualistic nor abstractly institutional or societal. Rather CoP focuses on the lived experience of identity that has a social characteristic – it is the social, the cultural, the historical with a human face (Wenger, 1998). Wenger's concept of identity, through linking learning and identity formation, addresses learning mainly as a process of shifting participation in cultural practices (Nasir & Cooks, 2009). This can be very much significant in ICT4D learning scenarios as there are scholars of the opinion that there is lack of attention on cultural beliefs and their impact on ICT adoption in developing countries (Albirini, 2006; Loch et al., 2003). Studies show that cultural perceptions toward technology influence the acceptance and future usage behavior of the users (Chen et al., 1999; Leidner & Kayworth, 2006; Loch et al., 2003; Straub et al., 2001). Also, in the context of developing counties there is lack of in-depth understanding of people's ideas, beliefs and values about technology, which brings challenges for the designers for successful acceptance of technologies (Straub et al., 2001). In CoP, negotiating new identities through learning is viewed as changing our ability to participate, belong and negotiate meaning that are embedded in the context, culture and history and can help the practitioners to have a better understanding of how people can be made to use ICT effectively. When it comes to using the Internet, the specific ICT tool that this chapter focuses on, the answer to why people are not using the Internet can be attributed mainly to two reasons; that they do not have access or that they do not use the available Internet access facilities. Concerning second order divide in Internet usage, it is the lack of ability to use and extract information from material available on the Internet (Hargittai, 2002). The issue of second order divide can be addressed by adding the social dimension to describe the digital divide where the concept of a 'digital divide' is looked at from a different angle and where technology access is seen in terms of social inclusion to encompass the wide range of factors such as the physical, digital, human, social resources and relationships (Warschauer, 2002). Any kind of learning which involves the use of the Internet in a development context should thus address the social and cultural dimension of learning, and this is where CoP comes into the picture as constructing identity through learning is concerned with the social and the cultural formation of the person and addresses issues of gender, class, ethnicity, age and other forms of categorization (Wenger, 1998, p. 13). This approach to learning can particularly benefit learning Internet usage in an ICT4D scenario projects as each ICT4D project is unique with its own composition of features that are embedded in the socio-cultural setting, and so perceptions and attitude towards learning to use the Internet will be distinct for the participants in different projects. The theory of identity in CoP can bring new insights on how people learn to use the Internet, as identity is a way of how participants negotiate meaning with respect to Internet use; this negotiation of meaning occurs in how they interpret the experiences of Internet usage and how they understand and see themselves as Internet users in their social context.

Certain scholars argue that some people have a tendency to stay away from technology because of fear, anxiety about the current use or anticipation of the intended use, negative attitudes or particular negative cognitions and self-efficacy beliefs (Rosen & Maguire, 1990; Sam et al., 2005; Tekinarslan, 2008). Other scholars have found that higher anxiety levels when using a computer negatively affects computer learning skills (Harrington et al., 1990; Torkzadeh & Koufteros, 1994). Internet anxiety is closely related to computer anxiety (Joiner et al., 2005). Individuals with lower computer anxiety tend to show a more positive attitude towards the Internet (Sam et al., 2005). When individuals have more positive attitudes toward computers they tend to have more positive attitudes toward web environments (Liaw, 2002). Studies also show that students' Internet attitudes will influence their choice of Internet-related careers or activities (Tsai et al., 2001). Internet self-efficacy is a very crucial factor to close the digital divide that separates experienced Internet users from novices (Eastin & LaRose, 2000; Savolainen, 2002).

When students do not use the Internet because of negative attitudes, fear and anxiety, teaching them how to use the Internet can be quite challenging. In such learning scenarios, formation of identity through learning to use the Internet can bring more effective results. Thus, the students can develop a sense of belonging in being a user of the Internet rather than merely having the ability to use the Internet in abstract, which in turn can make them realize that it is the difference in being an Internet user that can bring change to their lives. This approach to developing a sense of who they are as internet users is very useful when learning to use the Internet, because the focus on the process and experiencing Internet usage can bring more favorable attitudes for the students compared to a skills-based approach to teaching and learning about the Internet, which lacks power because of the changing nature of both the technology and Internet content (Edwards & Bruce, 2002).

Wenger states that learning is an integral part of living and being in the world, and the problem is not that we do not know this, but rather that we do not have systematic ways of talking about this familiar experience (Wenger, 1998). An adequate vocabulary is important because the concepts we use to make sense of the world direct both our perception and our actions. Even though informal learning is a crucial component for the success of ICT4D based projects, it is rarely acknowledged in literature (Foster, 2011). Foster argues that most of the practitioners in ICT4D view their work through analysis of products, while the process and informal learning concepts are only addressed peripherally and are not emphasized sufficiently. The theory of CoP can help development scholars and project managers to gain the necessary vocabulary to address the process and learning issues in informal learning environments and thus opening up new ways for understanding how to use ICT based tools in a development context.

Learning as Negotiating Identities

Wenger's concept of CoP is based on the concept of social learning. CoP emerges from situated learning theory, which is an answer to an alternative approach to the dominant cognitive perspectives on learning. Situated learning theory considers learning, not as a process of socially shared cognition that results in the internalization of knowledge by individuals in the end, but as a process of becoming a member of a sustained community of practice (Lave, 1991). The theory of situated learning claims that knowledge is neither a thing, a set of descriptions nor a collection of facts and rules, but rather describes knowledge as dynamically constructed as we conceive of what is happening to us (Clancey, 1995).

In CoP, learning is seen as a form of social participation, which is not confined to just local events of engagement in certain activities with certain people but also encompasses the process of being active participants in the practices of social communities as well as the construction of identities (Wenger, 1998). Wenger describes that this social participation determines what we do, what we are and how we interpret what we do.

Wenger's social theory of learning has four main components (Wenger, 1998):
- Meaning: a way of talking about our (changing) ability – individually and collectively – to experience our life and the world as meaningful.
- Practice: a way of talking about the shared historical and social resources, frameworks, and perspectives that can sustain mutual engagement in action.
- Community: A way of talking about the social configurations in which our enterprises are defined as worth pursuing and our participation is recognizable as competence.
- Identity: A way of talking about how learning changes who we are and creates personal histories of becoming in the context of our communities.

This chapter focuses on the identity element of the CoP, where learning is viewed as negotiating new identities that are both situated and dynamic. According to Wenger, the basic principle of learning is not only about accumulating knowledge and acquiring skills and competencies, but it is also about identity formation and modes of belonging. Wenger describes that identity includes one's ability and inability to give meanings, which describe the communities, and one's form of belonging. Learning is ultimately about the kind of person we become. Wenger argues that since learning transforms who we are and what we can do, it is an experience of identity. Through this formation of identity, learning can become a source of meaningfulness and of personal and social energy. Thus, any form of learning involves a change of identity for the members of the community.

Research Context

The learning framework proposed throughout the chapter is based on data drawn from an ethnographic action research study done at a university in

Southern India at their Department of Women's Studies with thirteen female master's students. The students in the research context were mostly novice users as the process of learning to use the Internet was new to many. The department followed a traditional classroom teaching methodology. The department had only one PC with Internet connection but the curriculum did not have any learning activities that demanded students' engagement with ICT. Therefore, the students did not use the Internet for any of their academic endeavours. Students were given Internet training and each training session was followed by an action research workshop. The Internet training was designed based on Blooms digital taxonomy of learning domains (Churches, 2007, 2008). It was not about making them experts in searching and retrieving information, but about making them understand the process involved in getting accurate information and developing the lifelong skill of reflective and critical thinking ability in using the Internet.

Figure 1 below shows how the Internet training and action research workshops were designed for the research study.

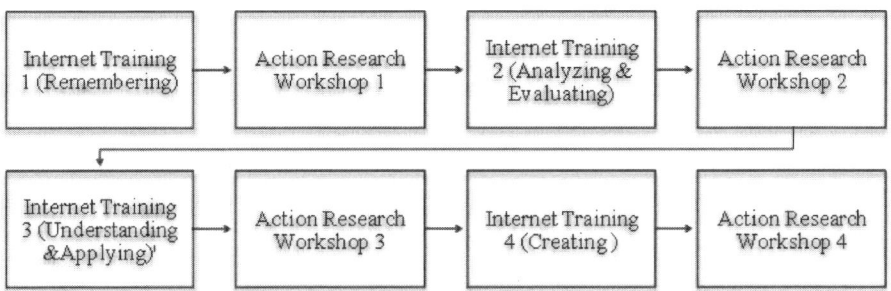

Figure 1. Design of Internet training and action research workshops

In the research context, the students who were grouped to learn about the Internet is identified as a CoP as it fits the definition of CoP stated by Wenger, "Communities of practice are formed by people who engage in a process of collective learning in a shared domain of human endeavor" (Wenger, 2006). The essence of a community of practice for Wenger is that, through joint engagement in some activity, an identified group of people comes to develop and share a practice. Even though the group was not a planned or cultivated CoP, the students practiced joint problem solving, requested information collectively and sought shared experience. These activities match some of the examples of activities within a group which are identifiable with a CoP (Wenger, 2006).

Moreover, I recognized the virtuous circle that is particular to a CoP (Thompson, 2005), as I observed that the more the students participated in online activities, the more they learned and the more they could identify with the Web World and subsequently became more motivated to use the Internet . So, the group of students in the research study was in a way an indirectly seeded CoP (Thompson, 2005).

The research study does not focus on exploring the internal dynamics within the CoP but on how learning occurs through negotiating identities within the group, that is through engagement and shared learning. Students were divided into small groups and were given Internet training five days in a week during a three-and-half-month period. Apart from this, students were encouraged to use the Internet in pairs or groups and learn from each other. Each training session was followed by an action research workshop where students through mutual discussions shared their experiences and reflected on the process of how they obtained information from the Internet, on problems faced in getting the correct information, what searching strategies they used and how they could improve the searching process in order to get better Internet search results. In the end of the research study, the students reflected on which changes the training and action research workshops brought for them as Internet users. Even though the students were brought together for the purposes of learning to use the Internet for a three-and-half-month period, there was sufficient mutual engagement between the students and informal shared learning occurring in the group. Wenger states that it is not the duration which matters, as short-lived communities may exist, but the occurrence of sufficient mutual engagement in pursuing an enterprise to share some significant learning (Wenger, 1998, p. 86).

Identity change for the students in the research context was viewed in the same manner as how Wenger describes identity as a "way of talking about how learning changed who we are" (Wenger, 1998, p. 5). The study researched how students through mutual engagement identify being an Internet user in relation the wider CoP that they belong to, which is the World Wide Web or the Internet. This is important considering the fact that they were actually learning is a lifelong skill that has wider implications for their life, and which was not just confined to the immediate group that they belonged to at the time.

The data discussed in this chapter was mainly collected through students' responses in group and informal interviews and observation. The questions asked did not have any direct relation to CoP. Data analysis found that the statements made by the students reflected Wenger's view of identity through learning. So, a second analysis was done with a focus on the theoretical lens of identity from Wenger's CoP theory in the analysis of the students' statements, particularly on how they perceived a change or transition through learning to use Internet. The analytical components of identity described by Wenger will be discussed in connection with the data from some of the students' reflections and observation from the empirical studies. Thus, I will discuss how students see who they are and what they can do by learning to use the Internet and thereby identifying themselves with the wider CoP of the Internet world based on the analytical components of identity.

Negotiated Experience

For Wenger, identity emerges by negotiating the self. Identity is a "layering of events of participation and reification by which our experience and its social interpretation inform each other" (Wenger, 1998, p. 151).

In the group interviews Tahira expressed her transition in the form of gaining the courage to go alone to an Internet café:

"I have never gone alone to a public center [café]. I have not used the

Internet alone... was doubtful if I could. I had only little knowledge about the Internet, but still had a fear of using it and was confused about some things. Now that has changed. I have that confidence and my fear has reduced".

For Tahira the experience of identity was not an object in and of itself, but a constant work of negotiating the self. For Mubeena the identity change that she experienced concerned knowing more than her friends and thus changing her self-perception of being inferior to her friends:

"There are two other friends of mine. The three of us went to the computer course together before. One is studying law and the other one is married. Now I know more than they do. When I go home on weekends, I check if these two friends are at home, and if they are available, I visit their homes first. I discuss the Internet training and workshops with them...We shared the Google docs, right? I told them about it and they were like...ohh you have learned everything".

This event jolted her experience of participation and brought into focus a negotiation of identity which is reflected in her final comment "The biggest happiness is that I could feel superior in front of them."

Community Membership

Wenger states that membership in a community "constitutes our identity, not just through reified markers of membership but more fundamentally through the forms of competence that it entails" (Wenger, 1998, p. 152). When members in a community know that they are in a familiar territory, it gives them the feeling that they can handle themselves completely. For Deepa and Saritha it was about an experience and a display of competence:

Deepa: "I have never thought of creating my own blog and sharing my opinions and viewpoints online. Now I add to my blogs when I go home. I have a great love of art...so I search for images... then for listening to songs... and for browsing UN [United Nations] sites...now my urge to do it has increased."

Saritha: "I have created an email account. I have added all seminar topics to the email account.... It's a great thing. I can access information whenever I want as it is saved there"

For some students, identity was also manifested through confronting the unfamiliar. What they learned was foreign or opaque to them, as Wenger terms the experience. Wenger states that membership in a community of practice translates into an identity as a form of competence, through the familiar as well as the unfamiliar (Wenger, 1998).

Anuradha reflected that: "In the beginning I didn't know anything. I hadn't even heard of Google Scholar or Google Books. I had heard of Google Maps and Calendar but did not know how to use it. Had not seen or used it. I had difficulties with handling the mouse properly. I am telling you this openly. Now I can handle it properly and it's better….and coming to typing speed. I had lot of difficulties."

How identities are shaped by realizing the unfamiliar was also stated by Deepa, who was quite acquainted with using the Internet prior to the training and workshops:

"Before there were lots of tools I had just explored and clicked on out of curiosity…there were times when it was useful …but sometimes I leave it like that… See this Delicious [an online social bookmarking service], I have never heard of it before. I came to know that it's so useful. Then Google Forms, Google Docs, even though I have heard of them … I did not know this much. Then sharing, I did not know that we have to type the email id to get it shared. I have done Boolean search two or three times before, but did not know the exact tricks of searching. Then Mindmeister, I did not even know that there is an application like that".

Here she is reflecting on what she could not do or perform on the Internet, which is what Wenger describes in arguing that our identities are constituted through learning not only by what we are but also by what we are not (Wenger, 1998, p. 164).

Learning Trajectories

Wenger states that there should be inventive ways of engaging students in meaningful practices by providing access to resources that can enhance their participation and opening horizons, so that they can put themselves on learning trajectories they can identify with (Wenger, 1998, p. 10). Wenger identifies five types of trajectories:

1. Peripheral trajectories, where members cannot participate fully, but their type of access to the community of practice contributes significantly to their identity.
2. Inbound trajectories, when newcomers join with the expectation of becoming full members even though their present participation may be peripheral.
3. Insider trajectories, when full members renegotiate their identities calling for new demands, inventions and events for the purposes of adding to the existing practices.
4. In boundary trajectories, members link different communities of practice.
5. Outbound trajectories involve members planning to move out of a community of practice, developing new relationships and finding a new position with respect to the community.

The learning trajectories of the students in the group were mainly reflected as inbound and insider trajectories. Jasna and Bindu were two students who explicitly identified themselves with inbound trajectories.

Jasna: "Compared to before I can say there has been lot of improvement.

> Earlier it was difficult typing my name even. I can type my Gmail id. I did not even have a Gmail id before. Likewise a lot of improvement, but I am really interested to use it since I know now".

> Bindu: "I did not even know how to search. Now I know how to search. If I get a seminar topic, I know how to go and search information. I don't have enough speed to do an Internet search. I have tremendous fear and I still get confused about what to take from the Internet. But I really have the desire to learn more now and use it later in the future."

Jasna and Bindu's identities are invested in future participation. Even though their present participation may be peripheral, which means that they do not participate fully, their access to practice becomes significant enough to contribute to their identity. Even though their Internet skills are still limited, they are motivated to participate fully in online environments in the future. This is what Wenger argues in saying that sometimes "[e]ven a very peripheral participation may turn out to be central to one's identity, because it leads to something significant" (Wenger, 1998, p. 155).

Some students identified themselves as being in the insider trajectory because even though they are close to the center of participation, they renegotiate their identities with new demands, events and inventions. This can be seen in the statements by Soumya and Mubeena who were quite familiar with using the Internet prior to the course:

> Soumya: "I know the format and all ... like when I have gone to other seminars, I have noticed that I know some tricks. I was trying to make a presentation for the seminar topic. I tried to make a presentation style. Presenting in front of a group... in the next two weeks I need to take a class...I think that it's an opportunity. Got to know many techniques to search and find information fast. Got to know tools... I feel that my speed in using the Internet has improved".

> Mubeena: "First time I am doing a PowerPoint while simultaneously searching information on the Internet. I could do that. Even though I did it wrong today, I know how to do it and feel confident that I can do it better in the future... Next seminar ... I am definitely going to present in PowerPoint."

For Mubeena, doing a PowerPoint presentation while searching for information on the Internet, was a new thing. Even though she had experience with the Internet, she now feels confident to do it more efficiently in future and she was also planning to do a PowerPoint presentation for her next class seminar.

Thus, students' learning trajectories were identities conceptualized in terms of understanding what they knew, where they are and what they could do with learning to use the Internet.

Nexus of Multimembership
Wenger states that identity is an experience of multimembership and is defined

by the way people put their effort in reconciling various forms of membership so as to maintain one's identity across boundaries (Wenger, 1998, p. 158) An analysis of the data revealed that some of the students had a conflict in maintaining the identity as an Internet user, which was a result of the patriarchal gendered roles which was pertinent in the society that they belonged to. This was mainly identified when the students were asked about the future usage of the Internet, they reflected on how their identity being women conflicted with becoming an Internet user. In CoP, learning is viewed as influenced by the structural divisions like class and gender which are reflected in communities which facilitate or restrict access to resources, activites and technology (Contu & Willmott, 2003). In this research context, these structral division of being a women constrained their learning opportunities. Similarly, some of them see going to an Internet café as a barrier.

> Jasna reflected that: "Going to an Internet café and all ... I don't think it will be possible... there will be a limitation."

Anuradha also expressed that going to an Internet café will be difficult for her:

> "I do not have the opportunity to use the Internet at my place. If I want to use the Internet, I need to go to town. It is a little difficult and I will not be allowed to go and do that. I have some issues like this at home."

These conflicts were the result of belonging to multiple communities, and that is very significant in understanding how learning to use the Internet or any ICT tool is influenced by belonging to different communities in a developing country scenario. Maintaining an identity across boundaries requires work and this work is not an independently defined boundary but at the core of what it means to be a person (Wenger, 1998, p. 160). Being women, they also experienced conflicting identities because of the patriarchal gendered roles in the society which was reflected in their responses to questions about the parental influence and what difference it makes if the trainer or facilitator would have been male. This was reflected in the statements by Lakshmi and Hima.

> Lakshmi: "When I told my parents at home that you were going to give some training at an Internet café, first thing which dad asked me was: 'who is going to teach?' ... I told him that it's you [meaning a woman]...and see even my younger brother asked: 'who is taking it for you?'"

> Hima: "If it is a male, they won't allow me at all. In my house they won't allow... I have four brothers!"

The students have to reconcile the different forms of community memberships which they carry, and their participation is influenced by the different communities in which they are involved. Participation and learning to use the Internet will be constrained for the students in this research study due to their gender and thus their belonging to other communities as daughters and sisters.

Local and Global

The practices in a community are not confined to the local but to a broader context (Wenger, 1998, p. 162). Similarly, identity formed in a specific community of practice is not just enclosed to that community. For the students in the research study, what they learned in the training sessions and action research workshops should fit to a broader scheme of things. Thus, identity is always an interplay between the local and the global.

For Saritha applying the skills in a broader context was contacting a foreign author through email, which when communicated to her teacher resulted in a positive response that made her happy:

> "One thing is that when we did that search and got authors' emails... and when I told mam then she said: 'you are getting the effect so fast,' and mam told me: 'you could send the mail again... you could have told about our Department of Women's Studies."

This clearly reflects what Wenger describes through the local-global interplay, that broader categories and institutions attract our attention because they are often more publicly reified than the communities of practice.

Soumya used her new skills to follow her favorite authors on Twitter where she found out how her engagement fits into broader enterprises. She explained:

> "I have studied literature...so I like authors, and people like Paulo Coelho and Alice Walker all are there on Twitter... I can add them now."

This is in line with what Wenger refers as directing the local energy to create global relationships.

In learning to use the Internet, the CoP can thus help the students to construct identities of who they are as users of the Internet and what potential they have as Internet users with respect to the community which encompasses the particular socio-cultural setting that they belong to because learning is socially situated in CoP. From the perspective of an ICT4D learning concept, the notion of learning as a process of becoming can have a great significance in learning to use the Internet as knowledge and competencies gained through learning are not in abstracts but in the service of identity. When students learning to use the Internet develop an identity of who they are as Internet users through experiencing the Internet, then it can bring motivating outcomes to continue using the Internet in the future even after the project is completed, which can bring sustainable results for the project. To understand the process of learning through forming identities, learning environments need to be designed so that students can construct identities through learning to use the Internet.

Designs for Learning to Use the Internet in an ICT4D Context

In ICT4D, the design is very critical for the successful adaption and future usage of ICT by the people to whom it is introduced. Heeks (2002) identifies a design-actuality gap as one of the substantial reasons for the failure of ICT projects in developing countries, where there often is a mismatch between the project design and the local realities. The challenge for designers of technology for developing countries is that the indigenous cultures are deeply rooted and in each country, people's usage of technology will be very diverse reflecting the cultural components that they possess (Avgerou & Walsham, 2000). In CoP, the focus is on the culturally specific forms of participation and reification that exist in a particular community (Jørgensen & Keller, 2007) and can thus contribute significantly in the design for learning to use ICT in a development context.

This chapter contributes with a design for learning to use the Internet based on Wenger's learning framework. Designs for learning to use the Internet should not only focus on providing access to and training for learning how to use the Internet, but it should also facilitate modes of belonging, engagement, imagination and alignment so as to understand the process of learning and its effect on identity formation for students.

In Wenger's view: "learning cannot be designed, it can only be designed for what is facilitated or frustrated" (Wenger, 1998, p. 229). Wenger proposes a learning architecture based on his analysis of learning at the level of practice and identity. Wenger's learning architecture is not prescriptive but rather provides an outline for a community to grow productively (Coto, 2010). When learning is viewed as developing identities through different forms of involvement and modes of engagement characteristic to local contexts of activities (Gherardi et al., 1998), it can provide new learning opportunities and thus allows the students to come up with new ways of approaching the barriers for using the Internet in their local context.

Components of the Learning Framework

Wenger defines three modes of belonging as the main infrastructural components of the learning framework: engagement, imagination and alignment. For Wenger, a design for a learning environment should provide facilities for these modes of belonging that will help to make sense of learning and identity formation. A design for learning to use the Internet should thus enable providing scope for the three modes of belonging so as to facilitate constructing identities for the students as Internet users. The facilities of the modes of belonging for a learning environment where the ICT tool is the Internet in an ICT4D scenario have been developed based on inspiration from the work of Brosnan & Burgess (2003), Coto (2010), Cousin & Deepwell (2005), Jørgensen & Keller (2007) and Wenger (1998).

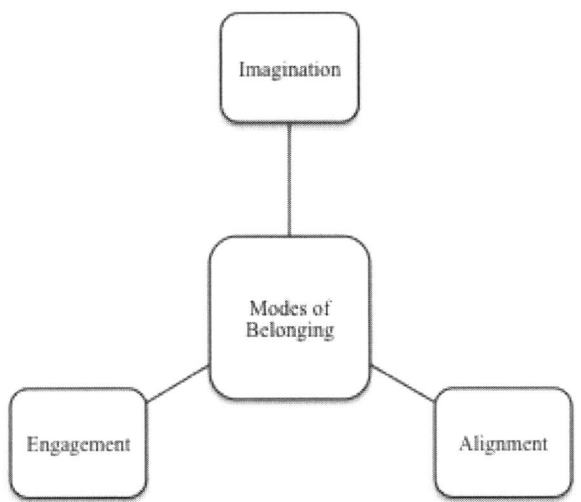

Figure 2 shows the three modes of belonging as proposed by Wenger

Engagement
Engagement from a belonging perspective is considered as the ability to take part in meaningful activities and interactions, in the production of shareable artifacts, in community – building conversations, and in the negotiation of new situations (Wenger, 1998, p. 184). Engagement is vital as it is the starting point of any enterprise (Coto, 2010) and it is different from the other two modes of belonging as it demands direct involvement (Jørgensen & Keller, 2007). For the students learning to use the Internet, their direct experience with the Internet comes through engaging in various Internet activities with various tools and applications that can contribute significantly to shaping their identities. Through engagement, the students come to know who they are in relation to an Internet environment and the digital world through direct involvement. Engagement also involves accumulation of a history of shared experiences as well as making a sense of interacting trajectories that shape identities in relation to each other.

Engagement is a fundamental component in designs for learning as being part of or engaged in a community is what makes a person a member of the community. Wenger describes that "in order to support learning, engagement requires authentic access to participative aspects (access to and interaction with other participants) and reificative aspects of the practice (access to symbols, tools, language, documents etc.) in concert" (Wenger, 1998, p. 184). In terms of use of technology, engagement and participation at the local level is very much needed for its effective use (Nardi & O'Day, 1999).

Facilities of Engagement for Learning to use the Internet in an ICT4D Scenario
Wenger proposes three infrastructures, namely mutuality, competence and continuity, to support the process of engagement in a learning environment. The facilities of engagement that can foster learning to use the Internet aimed

at students who are novice users or with limited knowledge of the Internet in an ICT4D scenario could be as follows:

- The starting point for supporting engagement is what Wenger calls "interactional facilities" which should be offered through proper spaces. In an Internet learning context, providing Internet connection is a core requirement. Interacting in virtual spaces can be encouraged once the students are confident enough to use the Internet.
- A number of informal sessions where students can talk without inhibitions about their perceptions of the Internet. Students should be given opportunities to reflect on how they perceive the Internet. This type of activity can bring diverse ways of understanding how to make the students use the Internet, which is very much situated and context specific.
- For the design element of competence in supporting engagement, opportunities for activities relating to various tools of the Internet must be provided. These activities can provide the scope for applying the Internet skills the students have learned through the intervention of Internet training and workshops.
- Interactive sessions in the form of brainstorming sessions where the students are given opportunities to discuss the difficulties faced in finding information on the Internet. Attention should be given to the process involved in searching, which will help to develop their reflective skills rather than focusing on correct information in abstracts.

Imagination

Imagination in Wenger's words is "creating images of the world and seeing connections through time and space by extrapolating from our own experience" (Wenger, 1998, p. 173). Imagination may be viewed as the process whereby participants integrate past, present and future and see themselves as part of stories which involve other people other than those with whom they engage (Jørgensen & Keller, 2007). Imagination could be an important component of the students' experience of the digital world and how they see themselves in it. When the students are given opportunities to think and reflect on what their Internet usage experience before the project was, how they see themselves now using the Internet and how they imagine they would be using it in future, this process of reflection of the past, present and future can potentially shape their identities and create new learning trajectories.

Imagination affects how we experience our identity and the potential for learning inherent in our activities (Wenger, 1998). Imagination helps us in seeing our own practices as continuing practices that reach far in to the past and can thus help to visualize and explore novice developments, alternatives and future opportunities. When the students start to make connections between current Internet learning and their future opportunities in life, it can bring new learning situations of how to use the Internet for them, which in turn can expand their choices in life. Imagination requires the ability to disengage and move back and look at the engagement from the eyes of an outsider. Wenger says that for imagination to thrive we need to dislocate participation and reification to reinvent ourselves so as explore new relations and to try new identities (Wenger, 1998).

Facilities of Imagination for Learning to Use the Internet in an ICT4D Scenario
According to Wenger, "[i]magination requires some degree of playfulness" (Wenger, 1998, p. 185). From a CoP perspective, imagination should include facilities of orientation, reflection and exploration. Facilities of imagination for learning to use the Internet for students in an ICT4D learning scenario could:

- Encourage thinking in alternative ways for learning to use the Internet. These discussions can bring new insights and is in line with the point Nardi & O'Day (1999, p. 75) has emphasized: "just talk has the power to change things". These discussions can bring diverse sets of perspectives which can inform the design for learning to use the Internet by a different group of students in the same educational context as a university or school.
- Inspire traveling across the borders of how the participants see themselves using the Internet in the future. This can be realized through for example participant-produced drawings, as the cognitive process that participants use when they are asked to draw is different from when they are asked to verbalize or write about their experience (Kearney & Hyle, 2004). This is an apt method for imagination as it includes "fantasies and withdrawal from realities" (Wenger, 1998, p. 177), and drawings enable getting an insight into a respondent's most salient idea or perception without limitation (Nossiter & Biberman, 1990).
- Provide scenarios where the students are encouraged to think of which tasks in everyday life could be done using with the Internet and also making them reflect on how they do those tasks now. These ways of thinking about doing things in the absence of the Internet can make them appreciate the potential value of the Internet in their daily lives.

Alignment

Alignment is about "coordinating our energy and activities in order to fit within broader structures and contribute to broader enterprises" (Wenger, 1998, p. 174). Wenger states that similarly to imagination, alignment is a mode of belonging that is not confined to mutual engagement. Alignment assists to strengthen our power and aids in realizing the possible. Apart from the academic activities, which is their immediate concern, the students who learn to use the Internet should be given opportunities to experience the broader context, which may affect their lives in the future The students should be presented to the ways in which the Internet could fit into other aspects of life in the present and into larger aspects of life awarding more opportunities in future. The work of alignment is to connect the local efforts to broader styles and discourses that allow learners to invest energy in them (Wenger, 1998, p. 186).

Facilities of Alignment for Learning to Use the Internet in an ICT4D Scenario
Since alignment is basically about coordinating perspectives and action so as to achieve a common goal within the community, it requires the ability to com-

municate purpose, needs, methods and criteria. Wenger proposes convergence, co-ordination and jurisdiction as infrastructures of alignment to facilitate learning. Below are some of the facilities of alignment that should be considered from the perspective of learning to use the Internet in an ICT4D:

- Ensure that the students are aware of the role Internet plays in the global context, such as how students across the world use the Internet for academic activities.
- Encourage students to reflect on their experience of how being a member of multiple communities affects their Internet usage. These reflections can help them to think about and coordinate their energies of how obstacles best can be overcome, so that they know what it takes to become an Internet user in the digital world.
- Reinforce the need of the Internet and which advantages it can bring after they leave the university, such as how they could use the Internet in looking for career opportunities or completing online tests for jobs etc.
- Encourage the students to think about the policies and regulations related to using the Internet in a broader scenario. This could for example be to make them aware of Internet etiquette. Preece (2004) states that "[n]orms, including rules of etiquette, are learned through experience in a community".
- Examine opportunities for interacting with other groups who have similar learning experiences in using the Internet. By sharing experiences, the students can benefit from negotiating meanings and identities in different settings (Wenger, 1998).

Thus, a learning framework which facilitates the three modes of belonging, engagement, imagination and alignment, can help the students to negotiate identities as Internet users. Moreover, the design provides the scope to facilitate effective use of the Internet by the students even after the project is completed, as the learning environment provides opportunities for students to develop identities that can motivate them to use the Internet in future even though they may not become experts in using the Internet through the course of the project.

Conclusion

By applying the identity concept of CoP to understanding the process of learning, a language is provided for ICT4D scholars to talk about the informal learning process that occurs in projects and interventions which are aimed at making participants learn to use the Internet. The identity theory of CoP can contribute to learning scenarios in ICT4D contexts, such as learning to use the Internet, where people commonly stay away because of indifferent attitudes and perceptions towards the Internet. In addition, when learning is viewed not just as gaining skills and competence in using the Internet, but more so as an experience of identity, students will view learning to use the Internet as less stressful and complicated. Wenger's social theory of identity not only helps to narrow the focus to the person from a social perspective, it also extends the focus beyond the communities of practice calling attention to a broader process of identification and social structures which can very much contribute to learning to use the Internet in an ICT4D scenario. For the participants of the project, developing a sense of identity and a sense of self, that is what type of Internet users they are with respect to the practices of the wider community which is the web or internet world, was very significant.

Designing learning environments for students which can facilitate creating identities through learning to use the Internet by focusing on the three modes of belonging, engagement, imagination and alignment, as proposed by Wenger can help development scholars in understanding how socio-cultural factors shape learning to use the Internet in specific ICT4D contexts. This kind of understanding of the process and best practices in informal learning is missing in ICT4D literature (Foster, 2011). Thus, understanding the process of informal learning based on the identity concept of CoP can bring better results for the interventions based on using the Internet by novice users in an ICT4D context. Though the context of the research study was a university with master's level students as participants, the design could be adapted to learning contexts of using any other ICT tool, where the participants are first-time users or people with limited knowledge about ICT, taking into consideration the nature of ICT and the cultural beliefs and attitudes towards the ICT tool which is introduced.

If the ICT4D projects face the challenge of limited time and funding, it may not be possible for the development scholars and project managers to give a full-fledged training in using the ICT introduced. In addition, there is a risk that the people do not have the motivation to use the ICT introduced once the project is wound up, thus challenging the sustainability of the developmental interventions. When participants are encouraged to view learning as process of social participation and a form of belonging, participants start to identify themselves as users of ICT in the future, which can result in creating favorable attitudes and positively influence them to use the ICT.

Future research can provide more scope to understanding how a CoP works and to examine the dynamics of the group which is learning to use the Internet in an ICT4D learning context. Moreover the framework developed is based on the data extracted from the field studies and has not been applied to an existing CoP. By applying the Wengers framework on an existing CoP in a developmental country context can throw more light on what context specific factors needs to be considered for applying the framework in a developmental scenario which involved learning to use ICT/Internet.

References

Albirini, A. (2006). Cultural perceptions: The missing element in the implementation of ICT in developing countries. International Journal of Education and Development using Information and Communication Technology, 2(2), 49–65.

Amichai-Hamburger, Y. (2002). Internet and personality. Computers in Human Behavior, 18(1), 1–10.

Avgerou, C., & Walsham, G. (2000). Information technology in context : studies from the perspective of developing countries. Aldershot, Eng.; Burlington, VT: Ashgate.

Bimber, B. (2000). Measuring the Gender Gap on the Internet. Social science quarterly, 81(3).

Brosnan, K., & Burgess, R. C. (2003). Web based continuing professional development – a learning architecture approach. Journal of Workplace Learning, 15(1), 24–33.

Chen, A.-Y., Mashhadi, A., Ang, D., & Harkrider, N. (1999). Cultural Issues in the Design of Technology-Enhanced Learning Systems. British Journal of Educational Technology, 30(3), 217–230.

Churches, A. (2007). Bloom's and ICT Tools. Retrieved from http://edorigami.wikispaces.com/Bloom%27s+and+ICT+tools

Churches, A. (2008). Bloom's Digital Taxonomy. Retrieved from http://montgomeryschoolsmd.org/uploadedFiles/departments/techtraining/homepage/BloomDigitalTaxonomy2001.pdf

Clancey, W. J. (1995). A tutorial on situated learning. In Proceedings of the International Conference on Computers and Education (Taiwan), 49–70.

Contu, A., & Willmott, H. (2003). Re-embedding situatedness: the importance of power relations in learning theory. Journal of Critical Postmodern Organization Science, 14(3), 283-296.

Coto, M. C. (2010). Designing for Change in University Teaching Practices. Aalborg University, Denmark.

Cousin, G., & Deepwell, F. (2005). Designs for Network Learning: A Communities of Practice Perspective. Studies in Higher Education, 30(1), 57–66.

Dewan, S., & Riggins, F. J. (2005). The Digital Divide: Current and Future Research Directions. Journal of the Association for Information Systems, Vol. 6(12), 298–337.

Dimaggio, P., Hargittai, E., Celeste, C., & Shafer, S. (2004). From Unequal Access to Differentiated Use: A Literature Review and Agenda for Research on Digital Inequality. Social Inequality, 355–400.

Durndell, A., & Haag, Z. (2002). Computer self efficacy, computer anxiety, attitudes towards the Internet and reported experience with the Internet, by gender, in an East European sample. Computers in Human Behavior, 18(5), 521-535.

Eastin, M. S., & LaRose, R. (2000). Internet Self-Efficacy and the Psychology of the Digital Divide. Journal of Computer-Mediated Communication, 6(1), 0.

Edwards, S. L., & Bruce, C. (2002). Reflective Internet Searching: An Action Research Model. Learning Organization, 9(4), 180–88.

Foster, C. (2011). ICTs and informal learning in developing countries. Manchester: University of Manchester, Institute for Development Policy and Management.

Gherardi, S., Nicolini, D., & Odella, F. (1998). Toward a Social Understanding of How People Learn in Organizations: The Notion of Situated Curriculum. Management Learning, 29(3), 273–297.

Hargittai, E. (2002). Second-Level Digital Divide: Differences in People's Online Skills. First Monday, 7(4).

Hargittai, E. (2004). Internet Access and Use in Context. New Media & Society, 6(1), 137–143.

Harrington, K. V., McElroy, J. C., & Morrow, P. C. (1990). Computer anxiety and computer-based training: A laboratory experiment. Journal of Educational Computing Research, 6(3), 343-358.

Heeks, R. (2002). Information Systems and Developing Countries: Failure, Success, and Local Improvisations. The Information Society, 18(2), 101–112.

Heeks, R. (2009). The ICT4D 2.0 manifesto where next for ICTs and international development? Manchester: University of Manchester. Institute for development policy and management (IDPM), Development informatics group.

Hill, J. R., Wiley, D., Nelson, L. M., & Han, S. (2004). Exploring Research on Internet-Based Learning: From Infrastructure to Interactions. In Handbook of Research on Educational Communications and Technology. Mahwah, NJ: Lawrence Erlbaum Associates.

Iske, S., Klein, A., Kutscher, N., & Otto, H.-U. (2008). Young People's Internet Use and Its Significance for Informal Education and Social Participation. Technology, Pedagogy and Education, 17(2), 131–141.

James, J. (2004). Reconstruing the digital divide from the perspective of a large, poor, developing country. Journal of Information Technology, 19(3), 172–177.

Joiner, R., Gavin, J., Duffield, J., Brosnan, M., Crook, C., Durndell, A., ... Lovatt, P. (2005). Gender, Internet identification, and Internet anxiety: correlates of Internet use. Cyberpsychology & Behavior: The Impact of the Internet, Multimedia and Virtual Reality on Behavior and Society, 8(4), 371–378.

Jørgensen, K. M., & Keller, H. D. (2007). Learning as negotiating identities. Management and Philosophy, no. 3, Danish Center for Philosophy and Science Studies, Aalborg University, Denmark.

Kearney, K. S., & Hyle, A. E. (2004). Drawing out emotions: the use of participant-produced drawings in qualitative inquiry. Qualitative Research, 4(3), 361–382.

Kozma, R. B. (2011). The Technological, Economic, and Social Contexts for Educational ICT Policy. In Transforming Education - The Power of ICT Policies. UNESCO.

Kumari, S. (1998). Teaching with the internet. Journal of Information Techology for Teacher Education, 7(3), 363–377.

Lave, J. (1991). Situating learning in communities of practice. In L. B. Resnick, J. M. Levine, & S. D. Teasley (Eds.), Perspectives on Socially Shared Cognition. (pp. 63–82). Washington, DC, US: American Psychological Association. Retrieved from http://content.apa.org/books/10096-003

Lazonder, A. . (2000). Exploring novice users' training needs in searching information on the WWW. Journal of Computer Assisted Learning, (16), 326–335.

Leidner, D. E., & Kayworth, T. (2006). Review: a review of culture in information systems research: toward a theory of information technology culture conflict. MIS Quarterly, Vol. 30(No. 2), 357–399.

Liaw, S.-S. (2002). An Internet survey for perceptions of computers and the World Wide Web: relationship, prediction, and difference. Computers in Human Behavior, 18(1), 17-35.

Loch, K. D., Straub, D. W., & Kamel, S. (2003). Diffusing the Internet in the Arab World: The Role of Social Norms and Technological Culturation. IEEE transactions on engineering management, vol. 50(1).

McClure, C. R. (1994). Network Literacy: A Role for Libraries? Information Technology and Libraries, 13(2), 115–25.

Mehra, B., Merkel, C., & Bishop, A. P. (2004). The internet for empowerment of minority and marginalized users. New Media & Society, 6(6), 781–802.

Nardi, B. A., & O'Day, V. L. (1999). Information ecologies : using technology with heart. Cambridge, Mass. [u.a.]: MIT Press.

Nasir, N. S., & Cooks, J. (2009). Becoming a Hurdler: How Learning Settings Afford Identities. Anthropology & Education Quarterly, 40(1), 41–61.

Norris, P. (2001). Digital Divide: Civic Engagement, Information Poverty, and the Internet Worldwide. Cambridge University Press.

Nossiter, V., & Biberman, G. (1990). Projective Drawings and Metaphor: Analysis of Organisational Culture. Journal of Managerial Psychology, 5(3), 13 –16.

Nwagwu, E. W., Adekannbi, J., & Bello, O. (2009). Factors influencing use of the internet: A questionnaire survey of the students of University of Ibadan, Nigeria. Electronic Library, The, 27(4), 718–734.

Owston, R. D. (1997). The World Wide Web: A Technology to Enhance Teaching and Learning? Educational Researcher, 26(2), 27–33.

Preece, J. (2004). Etiquette online: From Nice to Necessary. Communications of the ACM, 47(4), 56-61.

Ramayah, T., Jantan, M., & Ismail, N. (2003). Impact of Intrinsic and Extrinsic Motivation on Internet Usage in Malaysia. Presented at the The 12th International Conference on Management of Technology.

Rosen, L. D., & Maguire, P. (1990). Myths and realities of computerphobia: A meta-analysis. Anxiety Research, 3(3), 175–191.

Sam, H. K., Othman, A. E. A., & Nordin, Z. S. (2005). Computer Self-Efficacy, Computer Anxiety, and Attitudes toward the Internet: A Study among Undergraduates in Unimas. Educational Technology & Society, 8(4), 205-219.

Savolainen, R. (2002). Network competence and information seeking on the Internet: From definitions towards a social cognitive model. Journal of Documentation, 58(2), 211–226.

Schumacher, P., & Morahan-Martin, J. (2001). Gender, Internet and computer attitudes and experiences. Computers in Human Behavior, 17(1), 95–110.

Siemens, G. (2004). Connectivism: A Learning Theory for the Digital Age. elearnspace (2004), 115(12), 1–9.

Sklar, E., & Pollack, J. (2000). A Framework for Enabling an Internet Learning Community. Educational Technology & Society, 3(3), 393-408.

Straub, D., Loch, K. D., & Hill, C. E. (2001). Transfer of Information Technology to the Arab World. Journal of Global Information Management, 9(4), 6–28.

Tekinarslan, E. (2008). Computer anxiety: A cross-cultural comparative study of Dutch and Turkish university students. Computers in Human Behavior, 24(4), 1572–1584.

Thompson, M. (2005). Structural and Epistemic Parameters in Communities of Practice. Organization Science, 16(2), 151–164.

Torkzadeh, G., & Koufteros, X. (1994). Factorial validity of a computer self-efficacy scale and the impact of computer training. Educational and Psychological Measurement, 54(3), 813-821.

Tsai, C.-C., Lin, S. S. J., & Tsai, M.-J. (2001). Developing an Internet Attitude Scale for High School Students. Computers & Education, 37(1), 41–51.

Twidle, J., Sorensen, P., Childs, A., Godwin, J., & Dussart, M. (2006). Issues, challenges and needs of student science teachers in using the Internet as a tool for teaching. Technology, Pedagogy and Education, 15(2), 207–221.

Uden, L., Tearne, S., & Alderson, A. (2001). A Conceptual Model for Learning Internet Searching on the Internet (Vol. Vol.1, pp. 1058–1066). Presented at the Thirty-fourth Hawaii International Conference on System Sciences. (HICSS-33), Software Process Improvement. IEEE Computer Society Press.

UNDP. (1999). Human Development Report 1999. New York: UNDP.

Warschauer, M. (2002). Reconceptualizing the Digital Divide. First Monday, 7(7).

Wenger, E. (1998). Communities of practice : learning, meaning, and identity. Cambridge, U.K.; New York: Cambridge University Press.

Wenger, E. (2006). Communities of practice - a brief introduction. Retrieved from http://www.ewenger.com/theory/

Pre-Service Teachers' Learning Experiences with E-Portfolios for ICT and Language Development

Mahbub Ahsan Khan
Email: makhanrajib@gmail.com

Muhammad Kamarul Kabilan
Email: kabilan@usm.my

Abstract

In Malaysia, making the best use of ICT and mastering the English language are considered the two crucial enablers of economic growth and national development. However, relevant literature reveals that pre-service language teachers are lacking the expected ICT savvy and are yet to attain a reasonable proficiency in English. Since researchers advocate e-portfolios to foster teachers' tangible development, a study was carried out to explore pre-service language teachers' learning experiences and examine their perception of e-portfolios and their contribution to their language and ICT skills. 55 participants were required to create and maintain personal e-portfolios and participate in online reflective practices. For data collection, different sources were used, which include semi-structured surveys, interviews and content of the e-portfolios. Findings indicate that initially, participants were unfamiliar with e-portfolios. Later, being familiar with them at the end of the semester, participants perceived their usefulness and demonstrated commitment for further utilization in their professional careers. Regarding ICT skills, participants were generally skeptical about their contribution; however, creating e-portfolios significantly increased their language skills.

Introduction

The integration of ICT and the consequent explosion of networked communication have yielded enormous educational reform in recent years. Particularly, the computer and the Internet are fostering synchronous and asynchronous communication, allowing unlimited access to knowledge beyond time and locality and transforming traditional methods into more engaging approaches to responding to the students' needs. That is, ICT is playing a crucial role in students' educational quality, which, in turn, has a significant impact on a country's development. Therefore, it is no longer debated whether ICT should be introduced in the teaching of learning or not, but rather to what extent it should be used. In Malaysia, a road map of *Vision 2020* has been sketched to establish an innovative, scientific and progressive society for the new millennium. Mastery in English (Pandian, 2006) and making the best use of ICT (Kader, 2007) are believed to be the enablers to generate such a workforce. English proficiency is particularly focused for economic attainment (Kabilan, 2007) or national development (Sarudin et al., 2008). However, English language proficiency is alarmingly low (Sarudin et al., 2008), and ICT adaptation is yet to reach an acceptable level (Ngah & Mona, 2006). Therefore, it can be stressed that Malaysian teachers require further development to enhance their English language proficiency and hone their skills to stay updated with new ICT innovations. However, the critical question is what would be the effective way to facilitate them in this regard. Although there is no magic bullet, utilizing the multiple potentials of ICT could be valuable because it "will have, is having, has had, can have an impact on how we teach and learn" (Mehilnger & Powers, 2002. p.11).

Literature Review
Language Situation in Malaysia
As in many other Southeast Asian countries, the language situation in Malaysia is rather complicated. The main three population groups have individual languages; however, the size of the immigrant population is almost as big as that of the indigenous population. Since the country was a British colony and people are generally familiar with the English language, it is considered the second language. But, rather than a mere instrument of social interaction, fluency in English seems to be significantly connected with higher social positions as well as higher paying jobs. Students who pursue higher education abroad require higher proficiency in English. Therefore, emphasis is placed on English as an academic subject and as a tool for economic attainment in Malaysia (Kabilan, 2007). Conversely, with a gradual, strictly confined and deliberate language policy, *Bahasa Malaysia* has achieved recognition as the sole official language. This has caused a drastic reduction in the amount of time the students were exposed to the English language and deteriorated the standard as well. The acquisition of English was seen as a necessary evil (Gaudart, 1987 cited in Vethamani, 2007). It has been claimed that English language proficiency is alarmingly low and students from primary to tertiary levels lack the basics of English (Sarudin et al., 2008). Particularly, pre-service teachers demonstrate a doubtful picture of English language proficiency. Atan (2007, cited in Sarudin et al., 2008) reports that 29% of students who got a chance for higher studies achieved Band 1 (extremely limited user) or Band 2 (limited user) in admission tests. Only 13% graduate students are competent or good users of English. In such a situation, Sarudin et al. (2008) stress that Malaysia requires "quality graduates in English" (p. 40).

ICT Situation in Malaysia
In 1991 former Prime Minister Tun Dr. Mahathir Mohamad stated a few challenges which could hinder the development of the country in the new millennium. Among them, the sixth challenge was to develop a scientific, progressive, innovative and forward-looking society that was not merely a consumer of ICT, but rather a contributor to the scientific technological civilization. Therefore, he felt the necessity of ICT integration for national development and declared "no

effort must be spared in the creation of an information rich Malaysian society" (MMR, 1992). Accordingly, educationists were keen to know how to make the best use of ICT to deliver knowledge and information, what were the ways to facilitate ICT for communication and greater interaction, and how to encourage the use of ICT for innovation and creativity to improve national productivity and competitiveness (Kader, 2007). The government has taken several measures to implement ICT in education, which includes infrastructure development, policy declaration, revision of curriculum and linking educational and industrial sectors. In consequence, the country has achieved global importance to some extent as regards economy, but the technical integration is minimal and far behind compared to the developed countries (Frost & Sullivan, 2004 cited in Kader, 2007). Literature also reveals that the intense penetration of ICT for effective classroom practice is slower than expected. Teachers are generally ICT literate, using it for administrative purposes or to prepare lessons; but they seem reluctant to use it for online activities (Vethamani, 2004). Ya'acob, Nor and Azman (2005) mention that access to the Web is no longer a problem but it is not used to its fullest potential. Sivapunniam (2001, cited in Mothar & Saad, 2007) reports that 93% of teachers surf the Internet for research purposes, but only 27% use it for pedagogical exercise. Pandian (2006) also notes that teachers who are undergoing training in teacher-training colleges lack the desired ICT savvy traits which might benefit their roles as educators. Since Malaysian pre-service teachers are falling behind as regards the expected ICT and language proficiency, identifying more effective approaches is imperative in this regard. E-portfolios can be one valuable phenomenon in this regard, because the learning of specific skills is the most significant role that they can serve (Shermen, 2006).

E-portfolio

An e-portfolio is the digitized version of the traditional paper-based portfolio. However, researchers frequently and synonymously use terms like portfolio, electronic portfolio, digital portfolio, ePortfolio, e-folio, digital folio, among others. E-portfolios are categorically dependent upon their purposes (assessment, marketing, employment, or documentation of learning, among others), audiences, resources available and the technological expertise of users. Klenowski (2002) argues that the e-portfolio is the most effective approach in understanding the value of an educational model that can guide independent learning, self-evaluation, reflective practice, organization, meta-cognition and the role of teacher-learner partnership. During this process, learners would be able to feel and experience a non-threatening environment that would encourage them to evaluate personal skills and attributes. It provides appropriate criteria of evaluating actual learning outcomes (Carmen & Christie, 2006), and subsequently, it facilitates the reaching of a satisfactory level of the learners' own work (Douvlou, 2006). Thus, e-portfolios not only document learning but also demonstrate the process of learning. Evans (1995) defines e-portfolios as an:

> "evolving collection of carefully selected or composed professional thoughts, goals, and experiences that are threaded with reflection and

self-assessment. It represents who you are, what you do, why you do it, where you have been, where you are, where you want to go, and how you planned to getting there" (p. 11).

Kilbane and Milman (2005) describe four key elements of e-portfolios which include (1) must be goal-driven, (2) organized collection of materials, (3) must demonstrate expansion of knowledge and skills, and (4) should be observed over time.

Researchers argue that e-portfolios can support learning in multifold ways; for example, they are flexible to use, accessible anytime anywhere and inexpensive to reproduce (Klenowski, 2002), enhance ICT competency (Barrett, 2007), promote self-directed, collaborative and lifelong learning (Acosta & Liu, 2006), enhance cross-curricular competencies (Abrami & Barret, 2005), promote critical thinking and self-confidence (Reidinger, 2006), encourage development, reflection, assessment and showcasing (Stefani, Masson & Pegler, 2007), and represent accomplishments throughout teacher preparation programs (Sherman, 2006). Hence, they are seen as an adaptable tool currently available in teacher education contexts (Stefani, Masson & Pegler, 2007). However, in Malaysia, most of the teacher education programs are following conventional strategies which meagerly determine learners' actual accomplishments, and the use of e-portfolio is a relatively new experience in educational contexts (Kabilan & Khan, 2012). Therefore, understanding the individual's perceived attitude toward e-portfolios is essential as it can affect the implementation process in Malaysia. Particularly, exploring pre-service language teachers' perception is crucial because they seem to lack certain important qualities (Kabilan, 2007) and their progress requires more attention and careful monitoring (Genesee & Hamayan, 1991, cited in Kabilan & Khan, 2011).

E-portfolio in CoP

In this globalized epoch, the learning style of the 'net generation' is ever changing. Today's students are "more oriented to visual media than previous generations and prefer to learn by doing rather than by telling or reading" (Windham, 2007 cited in Oblinger, 2008. p. 13). Community of Practice (Wenger 1998; Wenger, McDermott & Snyder 2002), the contemporary development of sociocultural theory, has become a competing paradigm in today's landscape. It is a more intentional and systematic method to manage knowledge. Members can spend time together, share information, insight, and advice, help each other to solve problems, discuss their situations, aspirations and needs, ponder common issues, explore ideas and act as sounding boards. The combination of three fundamental elements has distinguished Community of Practice (CoP) from other learning theories: domain, community and practice. Domain is the issues or problems that members of a community have in common. Later, in pursuing common interests in a domain, members engage in a practice of joint activities to share information. However, in this epoch of ICT, developing such community online has become a norm. Since tools act as mediators to link human activities and the society (Vygotsky, 1978), their role is imperative to creating such communities. Vygotsky gives examples of cultural tools such as

printing presses, rulers, abacuses (Woolfolk 2005); likewise, e-portfolios have been used as mediators to develop pre-service language teachers' CoP, and therefore, examine their perception regarding e-portfolios and their contribution in their ICT and language skill development. Therefore, the overall aim of this study is to explore pre-service language teachers' learning experiences with e-portfolios and to examine:
1. How do pre-service language teachers perceive e-portfolios in CoP?
2. How can e-portfolios contribute to language and ICT development?

Method

Study Context & Participants
Universiti Sains Malaysia (USM), a well-known government university both locally and internationally, was considered as the study context because of the close connection between the aim of the University and the research objectives. USM demonstrates strong commitment towards the society's aspiration, the country's vision as well as universal aspirations. Awareness is expressed about their responsibility within the construct of the new economy, the commoditization of knowledge, the impact of globalization and the rapid pace of technological advancement (USM, 2008). Moreover, this university has demonstrated a willingness to implement e-portfolios for academic purposes (USM, 2008). 55 pre-service language teachers who enrolled in the second semester (2008/2009 academic year) in USM participated in this study. Participants were randomly divided into nine groups (on average six members in each group) to create an online CoP with e-portfolios.

Type of E-Portfolio
E-portfolios categorically depend upon their purposes, audiences, available resources and the technological expertise of users (Kilbane & Milman, 2003). Stefani, Mason and Pegler (2007) suggest that "one of the best ways of ensuring that students develop a portfolio is to integrate it into a course" (p. 57). Derived from such a suggestion, e-portfolios are defined as the *Course E-portfolio* in this study because this is best integrated in a course and in the objectives of a course to facilitate teachers to collect, select, reflect, and present artifacts in a pre-determined online platform. The possibility of synchronous and asynchronous communication encourages the creation of an online community where participants can mutually engage to share repertoire. The course (Teaching of English through Literature) and *Google Group* were considered as the face-to-face and online settings respectively. The study plan is graphically presented in Figure 1:

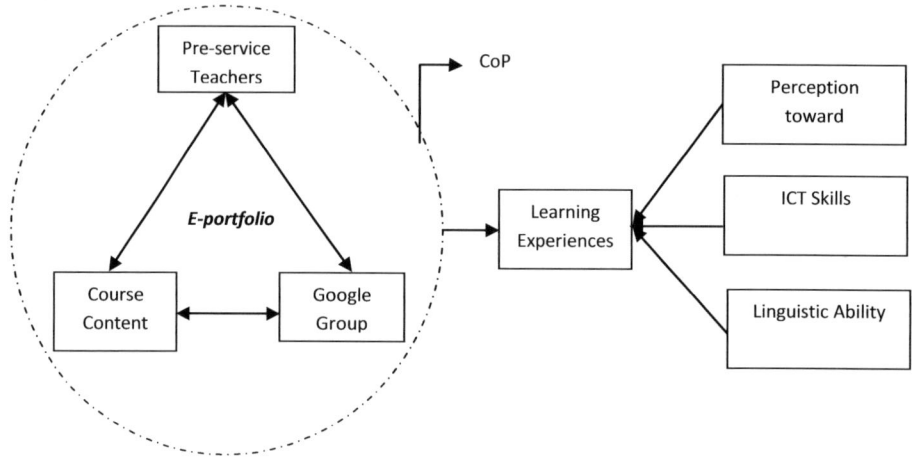

Figure 1. Study plan

Creation Procedure

The creation procedure was accomplished in two phases. In the first phase, a discussion session was arranged to (1) let participants understand what e-portfolios are and (2) demonstrate the creation procedure. For the second phase, participants were required to involve with group members through a Weekly Journal (WJ) and a Discussion Journal (DJ). The contents of the WJs were the domains which were discussed face-to-face in the classroom. Participants were required to visit other participants' e-portfolios and to read, examine and reflect on journal entries. Participants were advised to follow the four steps of Stevenson's (2006) reflection model of e-portfolios: (1) look through other participants' journals, read, study, or examine again; (2) consider retrospectively, look back on; (3) examine with an eye to criticism or correction; and (4) write a critical report mentioning individual opinion. Participants were free to include related useful materials, such as links, supplementary reading materials, examples of similar texts, or reviews of related materials. The Course Instructor (CI) played the role of E-moderator (Salmon, 2000) when participants were making incorrect conceptualization or deviating from the main discussion or even when decision-making was required on debatable issues. The researchers were not active in terms of posting messages and initiating issues to be discussed, but assumed a more passive role.

Instruments

One semi-structured 'survey questionnaire' was developed in line with the research questions. The aim of this questionnaire was to explore the initial and conclusive perceptions of the participants as a type of pre-post procedure. To conduct in-depth interviews, one flexible 'interview guide' was developed, aiming to document participants' perceptions in the middle of the semester. It was intended to gain insights of interesting or unexpected findings and to understand how and why they arrived at that particular perspective.

Data Collection
The period of data collection was limited to one semester (fourteen weeks). The process started with a semi-structured survey questionnaire at the discussion session. The aim of this survey was to see the initial perception of the participants towards e-portfolios and to compare this with conclusive perceptions at the end of the semester. In addition, nine interviews (one from each group) were conducted to gain insights of interesting or unexpected findings, and to understand how and why participants arrived at that particular perspective. Participation was voluntary, and group members themselves selected their representative for interviews. The contents of the e-portfolios (weekly and discussion journals) were considered as the source of data. Formative feedback of CI was also considered as the important source of qualitative data.

Data Analysis
The WJs and DJs were collected to analyze participants' experiences of using e-portfolios. At the beginning and end of the semester, the survey was carried out to explore the teachers' initial and concluding perceptions of e-portfolios, as well as to triangulate the data. For data analysis, the process described by Creswell (2007) was followed, which includes—firstly: preparing and organizing the data, secondly: reducing the data into themes through a process of coding and condensing the codes and finally: representing the data in figures, tables, or discussion. A coding system was used to single out the participants (e.g. A1, where A refers to the Group A and 1 is the first participant; C5 stands for the fifth participant of Group C) and data sources (WK and DJ refer to weekly journal and discussion journal respectively, and 'In' stands for the interviews). For citation, data code and participants' code were used together (e.g. WJF4—weekly journal of fourth participant of group F, DJB5—discussion journal of fifth participant of group B, InH5—opinion of fifth participant of group H in interview). Moreover, several issues were considered to avoid any unethical complexity. For example, to ensure anonymity and preserve confidentiality, participants' details and their responses were coded. It was made clear to them that collected information would be treated as confidential and used only for research purposes, and that their basic human rights would not be violated.

Findings
Demographic information reveals that among the 55 participants of this study, 34 (62%) students were female and 21 (38%) were male. Since they were from the same class, their ages did not vary widely (average 22). Most of the participants were Malays (57%), 16% Chinese, 16% Indian and 11% participants marked themselves as others. Average GPA of the students was 3.17. Only 18 students scored less than 3.00 in the last examination. In the following sections, analyzed data is presented in line with the research questions.

Initial Perception
In the demonstration session, participants commented that they had prior knowledge of using ICT for academic purposes, such as searching websites to

gather information, using emails or instant messages for sharing information, typing papers or participating in online networks for collaboration. Despite this, participants were unfamiliar with e-portfolios as they had "zero knowledge" of it before enrolling in the course (In2B7). For that reason, in the first qualitative survey, participants were not "able to answer almost all or all the questions" (WJB3). Some of their answers that portray such unfamiliarity are narrated below:

- So far, I am not sure what e-portfolio is (Sr1B2)
- I have no experience about e-portfolios (Sr1D4)
- Never heard of it before (Sr1E3)

Early Challenges
Unfamiliarity with e-portfolios stretched participants' mind initially, and they felt agony to some extent. They were 'really blurred and quite confused' (WJA6), or 'worried' (WJI2), or even 'quite uncertain' (In3D6) about e-portfolios. Some of them even felt 'angry' (WJA1) from thinking that e-portfolios 'would be very hard to use' (DJA1). One participant described such a situation:

> "When I first heard about it, I really did not know what it meant. When the lecturer explained that this course is associated with e-portfolios, I was asking myself what it was, how am I going to do it, what am I supposed to do?" (WJI5)

Consequently, the critical question arose how e-portfolios will help in this course (DJA4) or whether it is the best way to learn about this subject (DJD3). Therefore, it was argued that the implementation of e-portfolios in this course could be 'troublesome and unnecessary' (In4E1) or 'a waste of time and energy compared to our normal lecture where we depend on the black and white documents on notes' (WJA7). Moreover, it could be challenging for the participants who are uncomfortable with ICT (WJF4). One participant noted:
"It's quite hectic for me because I am not good in using web technologies. I also don't know much about computer. I need to seek help" (WJG4).

Using *Google Groups* as a platform was also new to them (In5F1), and many of them were facing difficulties. One participant shared this experience:

> "I'm confused with the Google group operations. Sometimes the page is displayed in Malay and sometimes it is displayed in English. When I try to change the language setting, nothing changes. I refresh and refresh but it is still the same. I don't understand why I have to upload a picture for group and then another picture for my profile, how come I have to upload two display pictures for one account? What is the point? What is the idea? Do the files that I upload will show up in my group? Which group should they access to view my files? Do they log into their own group or mine?" (DJA5)

Moreover, from their previous experiences, participants also anticipated that interrupted Internet connection could be a serious concern as regards the creation of e-portfolios, because –"most of the time there will be error in Internet connection and students will need to go to certain area to get connected" (WJD6). Another participant argued—"I know that trouble would arise and stress would accumulate because of the Internet" (DJB7). In such a situation, the motivational role of the CI was crucial to keep their interest up:

> "By having this e-portfolio you can express your frustrations. You are not alone, let's learn together. I tried this approach because I want students to be more active discussing things in tutorials rather than listening to your friends' presentation and then you fall asleep. Hang in there…" (CI).

Perceived Usefulness
Data indicate, however, that prior knowledge encouraged participants to search e-portfolio possibilities; consequently, they perceived its usefulness, anticipated its academic significance and took this project as a challenge. To eliminate such challenges, participants started exploring the concept—"After some research on the Internet, I got a brief idea of what e-portfolio is" (WJA2). They collected useful links relating to e-portfolios and shared these with others since they were also in the same confusing situation:

> "I have surfed internet and found lots of information about it. Apparently, other universities are utilizing e-portfolios already. I am an undergraduate, but never really knew about it" (DJB7).

It was argued that e-portfolio is quite similar to many popular online social networking platforms, although they had never used those for educational purposes (In6G1). One participant claimed:

> "I am familiar with many kinds of e-portfolios such as blog and social networking. But this is my first e-portfolio for education, because I need to have an e-portfolio to share discussions, comments and upload assignments" (DJD7).

Gradually, participants started realizing the usefulness of e-portfolios: "I began to feel that it is actually very useful" (DJB7); although this comment was made: "if we need to share our opinions, why not we just try to give our opinions face to face" (DJA6). Nevertheless, others expressed their disagreement, described face-to-face as an old style and suggested to embrace new methods (DJA5). It was anticipated that e-portfolios could be "a great way to learn new things" (In6G1). Therefore, it was asserted that they would require to do "all the works together" (WJD3) where "many people can contribute in many ways" (DJA5) and "read and look for more information to write stuffs about them" (DJA2). Such student-centered activities would provide the opportunity to know the viewpoints of others, which they might never have thought of (DJA7), and could be helpful in extending face-to-face learning (DJA1) and in "think[ing] logically in expressing views and feelings" (DJA1). It was also noted that creating e-portfolios might be useful to nurture the "correct way of writing English" (In7H1). Assuming such benefits, it was noted that e-portfolios could be a valuable way of learning to become professional teachers (DJA5).

Perceived as a Challenge
Data reveals that participants' realization is that opportunities of modern technology should be incorporated in practice. Therefore, this critical question arose: "why not we use the e-portfolio for teaching and learning?" (DJB4). Hence, one participant claimed, "we should be glad because the course gives opportunity to explore e-portfolios" (DJB7). Despite its potential, participants understood that the full use of e-portfolios depends upon the students: "what's the use of best way to learn if not trying out by ourselves" (DJA2). They have to take the responsibility for their own learning in this regard - "we must workout for it so that we can become compatible with these new technologies in future" (DJA4). It was anticipated that e-portfolios could be an opportunity for "having great fun" (DJA5), sharing thoughts and views with friends beyond the class time (DJA6) and learning the proper way to use ICT (DJA7).

Conclusive Perception
After experiencing e-portfolios, at the end of the semester it was stated "we now realize the importance of e-portfolio for future English teachers" (WJA7). It convinced them e-portfolios are "actually very interesting" (In5F1) or "a pleasant experience to learn new things" (WJA2) or even "effective activity to share opinions and weaknesses" (WJA1). Consequently, participants realized that "e-portfolios brought great change to us" (WJD5) since "everyone has a worthy impact on e-portfolios" (DJA4) or everyone can list the benefits that they achieved (DJE6). Therefore, e-portfolios were appreciated as "more than when it just begun" (WJA2). One participant noted--"I tell you from bottom of my heart that e-portfolios helped me a lot in various ways" (WJA7). It gave them a new outlook regarding "how flexible learning activities can take place" (WJE1) compared to the "usual approaches of teaching learning that is used today" (WJH2). From such experiences it was understood that "we should not deny the benefits that we can get from this application. Once you know the 'hidden' advantages, you will not miss it" (DJD5). Therefore, creating e-portfolios as part of this course was seen as "just a start" (DJF1) and described in this way: "learning is a journey and let's keep exploring" (DJB1). Indeed, there were "ups and downs while participating with e-portfolios" (WJA2) or problems were faced "here and there" (In8C4); but it was suggested that "just take the pros and leave the cons" (DJA4) since "it does have more positive aspects than the negative one" (WJH3). One participant uttered: "I personally think that no other instrument would be realistic enough except e-portfolios" (WJD1). For this reason, they felt proud to be a part of this e-portfolio journey (DJF1) and believed that such experience "will be a sweet memory in our life" (DJA4). Therefore, it was concluded: "we should thank our course teacher for introducing e-portfolios to us" (DJA5) and expected that more teachers will use e-portfolios to synchronize teaching-learning (WJB3).

ICT Skills
Data indicate that participants were concerned with the importance of ICT in the teaching learning process. One participant stressed that "students are moving forward quickly, and they never pay attention to the traditional approach-

es" (WJA6). Rather, they prefer surfing the Internet, watching television or texting for communication (In6G1). Therefore, to fulfill the needs of students, future teachers will be required to update themselves with the latest technology and gadgets, otherwise the classroom will again be dull and boring (DJC4). Surfing the internet to find relevant teaching methods and aids may help them to plan and implement new styles of teaching (DJF1).

However, participants who were more familiar with ICT found that creating e-portfolios is actually not very effective as a method to enhance ICT skills (Sr2G5) since it "just requires the basics" (Sr2E1) or the elementary skills (Sr2E6). One participant said,

> "I did not learn any new skills because all the skills required in this e-portfolio are just basic skills; such as giving opinions, open an email account, etc. All the skills required to conduct this e-portfolio have been applied by students when they open their email account" (WJE5).

In contrast, data indicate that a number of participants demonstrated reluctance since they were not ICT savvy (Sr2D1) or suffered from technophobia (Sr2D5). For example, one participant commented that "using ICT in work was the most difficult part" for her as regards the creation of e-portfolios (Sr2D5). At the beginning of the semester, one participant perceived it as expressed here: "I really hate it because I am not a person with computer literacy" (WJG3). Similarly, other participant confessed—"at first I was not confident of using ICT to post discussion because I did not have sufficient skill" (DJC4). However, after using e-portfolios for about three months, it was claimed that using ICT is "really interesting and enjoyable" (WJG3). One participant noted his experience in this way,

> "Although I have taken computer courses after my secondary school, I still have a negative perception about ICT. I prefer to do my work manually, because I think that is much easier. I only knew how to contact my friends via e-mail. I experienced e-portfolios in this course. Since that day, I started loving technology, especially e-portfolios" (WJD5).

Therefore, it was stated: "E-portfolios enhanced my ICT skill as I learnt how to create Gmail and upload videos in correct format" (WJA6). Another participant added that "e-portfolios introduced me how to become ICT literate since I learned how to post comments, take part in discussion, post comments, criticize and many more" (WJB3). Since Malaysian government is "pouring millions ringgits into ICT for better Education, incorporating e-portfolios would be valuable to upgrade the educational features" (WJD1).

Linguistic Ability

It was argued that language teachers must possess sufficient linguistic proficiency for effective teaching and learning (WJE5). Particularly, fluency and acceptable pronunciation in English would be critical in this regard (WJA4). For example, if a teacher is full of knowledge but unable to speak fluently, her knowledge will be considered as a waste (DJA4).

However, the critical question is: do the teachers possess sufficient readiness to perform such roles in future, or how do they perceive their own linguistic abilities? Data indicate that most of the participants were convinced about their linguistic abilities, although it was agreed that further development is essential for effective teaching. They have attained the level of fluency; however, accuracy is still questionable (In1A2). For example:

- I think I have (proficiency in English) but I still have to learn more. The situation I am facing at university may differ in the actual context. So I have to improve my language (Sr2A3).
- I need to improve my English first before I can teach them (DJC6 14-1).
- I need to build up my speaking skills. I need that to express myself clearly and effectively (Sr2E6).
- I can teach by using interesting teaching methods, but my English is not admirable (Sr2E4).

Content analysis of the online discussion (DJ) also demonstrates that in terms of sentence making and spelling, the proficiency level was often unimpressive. It could be noteworthy that DJs were posted in the tutorials sessions where time allocation was limited to one hour and participants were rushing at times to express individual opinions. For this reason they were not always faultless in sentence construction or written in correct spelling. However, in the WJs, which they were supposed to write in their own time and place, language was sometimes unimpressive. A few examples are as follows:

- Most of the students will not be happy if we were to literature on that day (WJG4).
- We should be use our own literature rather than using some else (WJH4).
- Which is why I say that materials for literature component are motivating (WJI5).
- Internet is very helpfulness in helping teacher to find resources and ideas in creating creative approaches in teaching literature (WJA6).

However, participants claimed that e-portfolios generated a "community language learning" environment among them (Sr2E6), and "continuous feedback and discussion within the community greatly increased the linguistic ability" (WJD1). Particularly, reading and writing skills were nurtured by the creating of e-portfolios (In4E1); because, "students need to read more to discuss or write an essay about a certain topic" (Sr2A2). One participant noted:

> "To produce good WJs, we do extra reading for information collection. Through reading, we got new words and ways of using the language. I came across with many new words during doing WJs. By reading friends' e-portfolios I was able to develop language as well" (WJA3).

Participants also noted that improving writing skills requires constant practice, and "e-portfolios ensure that we practice this regularly" (WJA2). Thus, e-portfolios inculcated the culture of writing (WJE3) and polished it continuously (WJG1). One participant expressed how e-portfolios facilitated her work,

> "I look for words in the dictionary every time I was stuck. I talk to

myself and hear if the sentences are good. I repeated them several time before I typed that particular sentence. Every time I did my WJs, I felt my language is improving" (Sr2H5).

Participants agreed that it is not difficult to find incorrect sentences at an early stage, but this improved when they received criticism from others (Sr2G1). Such a claim is evident if they compare their earlier comments and recent postings (WJD1). It was stated: "Even though it was just less than three months ago when e-portfolios were introduced, result is already evident. Responses are becoming more matured, well-written and constructive" (WJD1). Such a claim was confirmed: "My writing skill has improved. Even if it is not a big improvement, but more than I used to have" (WJG1). Another participant described "Now I have confidence that I can do well in my writing. E-portfolio has a big contribution in this case" (WJG4).

It was stated that freedom of writing underpinned participants' language development since they felt "empowered and less afraid to contact others" (WJD4). For example, one participant stated: "During the use of e-portfolio I don't feel so tied up on selecting words that make my assignment look formal. I feel relax and just go with the flow which I think made me more confident to write" (WJH3). It also gave them confidence to express feelings toward community (In7H1). Moreover, flexibility of the online platform also encouraged them to rearrange paragraphs and sentences (WJA7). It was realized that "writing is not a static action rather it continually evolves and develops" (WJA7). As a result, participants argued that e-portfolios "can be a platform for Malaysian students to develop English language and become confident to use it' (WJE5). Therefore, it was concluded that e-portfolios could be a valuable tool to groom ICT in the teaching and learning of English in Malaysia (WJG1).

Discussion

Findings indicate that e-portfolios can be a useful mediator tool to develop CoP among Malaysian language teachers. They used e-portfolios as a platform to reveal individual voices, argue with personal opinions, encourage the work and outlooks of others, and provide suggestions for implication. Initially, participants had no prior experiences with e-portfolios and experienced difficulties in handling them. Such difficulties indicate that merely providing a handout or one demonstration session was inadequate to prepare them for creating e-portfolios. Actually, the handout mostly focused on definition, types and advantages of e-portfolios, i.e. the inter-connectivity between the course content and the creation of e-portfolios was less emphasized. As a result, participants were struggling to understand the objectives of creating e-portfolios during the course. Therefore, to overcome the initial stress, it might be more supportive to offer one module with detail description, including a short workshop with hands-on activities before involving with e-portfolios.

Later on, participants who considered creating e-portfolios a challenging task gradually developed an online community with peers and started interacting with its members. Such activity in the virtual world assisted them to construct ideas from prior knowledge, change their perception of e-portfolios and reach a comprehensive understanding of language and ICT. They judged the usefulness of e-portfolios in a Malaysian context analytically, perceived them to be positive for language development and expressed commitment to continue using them in their future academic professions. A necessity of changing the existing academic practice was felt. To make such a change and face the uncharted challenges of the contemporary globalized era, participants stressed that no other instrument would be realistic enough except the e-portfolios. It was realized that e-portfolios could be a suitable platform to express the ideas which they were not able to appraise within the limited time and scope of the face-to-face classroom. Shared practices encouraged participants to feel committed to using e-portfolios in their future teaching profession. Wenger, McDermott and Snyder (2002) believe that such commitment signifies a distinction between a CoP and a group of friends.

However, innovations that have greater relative advantages, compatibility, trialability, observability, and less complexity should be adopted more rapidly than others (Rogers, 1995). Moreover, in a diffusion process, adopters learn about the innovation, become persuaded, decide to adopt, implement the innovation, and confirm the decision of adopting an innovation. In this study, participants (as the adopters) examined the relative advantages of the e-portfolio (as innovation) critically, judged its compatibility according to their needs, experienced it for one semester, identified challenges and shared their experiences with others. In this way, they learned about e-portfolio, became persuaded of its merits and decided to adopt it in future. Nevertheless, 'lack of stickiness' is the reason why, despite ample promise, e-portfolios still remained dissociated from academic contexts, although, Jafari and Kaufman (2006) believe the "stickiness problem…should not be seen as a long-term problem" (p.xxxiv). Therefore, further tracking of learning experiences is essential to understanding whether e-portfolios are implemented and confirmed or not in their professions.

Participants' positive perception toward e-portfolios may burn out because of inevitable difficulties in practical contexts, personal issues and vulnerabilities or social pressure. Hence, it is not enough to provide a positive perception toward e-portfolios and send teachers out to schools. Darling-Hammond and Bransford (2005) suggest that it is necessary to become adaptive experts who can continuously add knowledge and skills in their academic careers. Developing a teachers' community might be useful in order to become adaptive experts. Such perception of participants can be related to the literature, since Darling-Hammond and Bransford (2005) claim that e-portfolios can support teachers' development of a conceptual framework about teaching. With e-portfolios, they can link theoretical learning to classroom contexts, analyze and refine their practices and reflect upon what, how, and why they teach. Since participants perceived e-portfolios as an effective tool to create a learning community, it can be a useful way to become language adaptive experts in Malaysia.

Moreover, creating e-portfolios generated a student-centered community for language learning, and continuous feedback and discussion from peers greatly increased the participants' linguistic ability. Such findings reaffirm the notion that learner-centeredness of collaborative practices is the main attribute of communicative language teaching and learning (Nunan,1988) which maximizes interaction among students, increases language practice opportunities, improves quality of language skills, assists individualized instruction and influences positively on learning attitudes towards a second language (Long & Porter, 1985). Particularly, WJs and DJs obliged participants to practice writing, which eventually contributed to their linguistic ability. Reflective writing engages learners in a "good writerly process to explore a topic in discussion and exploratory writing; to complicate their thinking; to allow for perplexity and getting lost; to get feedback; to revise; and to collaborate" (Elbow, 1994. p. 41). Since participants required additional reading to make the discussions effective or to write a presentable essay in front of others, it was claimed in the findings that creating e-portfolios nurtured their linguistic ability, particularly their reading and writing skills.

However, content analysis demonstrates that in terms of sentence making and spelling, the proficiency levels of the participants were often unconvincing. Participants also agreed that many incorrect sentences in writing were evident at the early stage. However, it started to improve when they received criticism from others. Participants also claimed that it might not be a big improvement, but within three months, writing became more mature and constructive. This reaffirms the notion that grooming between online engagements and creating e-portfolios can result in a paradigm of language learning. However, Malaysian students often possess an examination-oriented attitude, dare not to involve in activities which require own judgment or feel comfortable to remain passive. In such a situation, the role of the CI is crucial if language development is the aim. The CI needs to provide "quality and quantity support" (Wray, 2007. p. 1139) through frequent interaction, recognition of the strengths and weaknesses of individuals, encouragement of constructive use, monitoring of participation and provision of formative suggestions. If the CI remains non-responsive or non-directive or even offers an open-ended environment, students may feel de-motivated to write in e-portfolios. Students also need to take responsibility to enhance their linguistic ability. For example, students who feel less confident in writing can be open-minded to asking for peer help, if the CI is unavailable. Most importantly, students should not consider language merely as a medium of passing an examination successfully; rather, the means to become effective teachers in future.

Regarding ICT skills, most of the participants noted that creating e-portfolios was not very helpful. One reason could be the selection of *Google Group* as an online platform in this regard. *Google Group* restricted participants' choice to decorate individual e-portfolios according to their likings since most of the features such as layout and color are controlled by the authority. However, commercial or institutional e-portfolio software is so far unavailable in Malaysia. Hence, previous e-portfolio-based studies mostly depended on free websites (Vethamani, Kabilan & Khan, 2008), *Yahoo Group* (Yassin, Mohamad & Yamat, 2007) or *Google Group* (Kabilan & Khan, 2011). In the initial stage, using such platforms is acceptable as it may provide implications for designing e-portfolios in a Malaysian context.

Indeed, plenty of commercial e-portfolio software is available. However, purchasing such software might not be practical as it demands sufficient financial capacity, technical support and the ability of continuous maintenance. Moreover, technological systems should be socially produced, culturally informed, and therefore, must be relevant to the local users. But commercial software is shaped by the creators' values, appreciations, ideologies, beliefs or aesthetics, which may differ between cultures. Nowadays, many institutions have been designing their own platforms for e-portfolios in line with the aim and objectives of the academic programs. Besides, few participants surprisingly noted their difficulties to maintain such basic ICT tasks and consented that they possess inadequate skill of ICT. This indicates that for language teachers to attain sufficient ICT skills remains a matter of concern. Oblinger (2008) believes "becoming net savvy isn't a one-time affair– it is a lifelong educational process" (p. 20). Participants were in a learning process, perhaps they will become ICT-savvy before they enter into the in-service phase.

Conclusion

The aim of this study was to explore language teachers' perception toward e-portfolios and how these can contribute to their language and ICT skills. Although generalization of this study was neither the intention nor in the scope, findings have yielded several considerable implications. One of the major implications is that meaningful utilization of e-portfolios in teacher education contexts may confer additional dimensions in the efforts of contemporary web-based language learning in Malaysia. Since the present efforts of the governments are, in general, mainly confined to the quality in education, findings from the study may assist the policy-makers to modify the conventional teaching and learning method and phase in more technology-based education. It must be acknowledged that the reality of the world is progressing faster than the teacher education institutions. Nowadays, learners do not use technologies less than face-to-face communication, but possibly more. Hence, teacher education programs need to adapt to the rapid changes of new technologies and stay aligned with the contemporary era. Oblinger (2008) argues, "Time changes. Technologies change. Students change. And so does education" (p. 29). Since the institutions of developed countries are frequently encouraging students to utilize e-portfolios, the Malaysian Government can also implement these to meet the specific needs of local contexts, in order to remain abreast with the evolvement of the contemporary era and foster language teachers' development in multifold ways. Fullan (2001) believes that teachers' capacities to handle such change, learn from it and help students learn from it are critical for the future development of societies.

Despite such implications, this study was elementary in nature, involved only a subset of participants, and data collection was limited to one semester. For extensive implementation, such baseline information is inadequate since several fundamental queries remain unresolved. For example, participants experienced challenges initially to cope with the e-portfolios; therefore, an understanding of the methodological aspects of creating e-portfolios is essential.

Exploring the experiences of the CI as 'e-moderator' requires serious consideration as well, because the success of such online teaching learning depends largely on her effective involvement until the participants become reasonably comfortable with the technology and the online culture. This means that more issues remain unanswered than have been answered in this study. Therefore, it can be concluded that further extensive research is required which can guide the diffusion, adoption and implementation processes of e-portfolios and establish these as a pedagogical and technological tool in Malaysia.

References

Abrami, P. C. & Barrett. H. (2005). Directions for research and development on electronic portfolios. Canadian Journal of Learning and Technology. 31 (3), 1-15

Acosta, T. & Liu, Y. (2006). ePortfolios: Beyond assessment. In Jafari, A. & Kaufman, C. (Eds) Handbook of research on ePortfolios, p. 15-23. USA/UK: Idea group Inc.

Barrett, H. (2007). Researching electronic portfolios and learner engagement: The reflect initiative. Journal of Adolescent & Adult Literacy, 50(6), 436-449

Carmean, C. & Christie, A. (2006). ePortfolios: Constructing meaning across time, space, and curriculum. In Jafari, A. & Kaufman, C. (Eds.) Handbook of research on ePortfolios. (pp. 33-43). USA/UK: Idea group Inc.

Creswell, J. W. (2007). Qualitative inquiry and research method: Choosing among five approaches (2nd Ed.). Thousand Oaks, CA: Sage Publications.

Darling-Hammond, L. & Bransford, J. (2005). Preparing teachers for a changing world: What teachers should learn and be able to do (Eds.). San Francisco, CA: Jossey-Bass Inc.

Don, Z. M. (2007). The English language proficiency of Malaysian public university students. In Enhancing the Quality of Higher Education through Research: Shaping Future Policy. (pp. 1-8). Malaysia: The Ministry of Higher Education.

Douvlou, E. (2006). Effective teaching and learning: Integrating problem based learning in the teaching of sustainable design. CEBE Transactions. 3 (2), 23-37

Elbow, P. (1994). Will the virtues of portfolios blind us to their potential dangers? In Stillman, P. (Ed.) New directions in portfolio assessment. Portsmouth, NH: Boynton/Cook Publishers.

Evans, S. M. (1995). Professional portfolios: Documenting and presenting performance excellence. Virginia Beach, VA: Teachers' Little Secret

Fullan, M. (2001). The new meaning of educational change (3rd Ed). New York: Teachers College Press.

Jafari, A. & Kaufman, C. (Eds.) (2006). Handbook of research on ePortfolios. USA/UK: Idea group Inc.

Kabilan, M. K. & Khan, M. A. (2011). Assessing pre-service English language teachers' learning using e-portfolios: Benefits, challenges and competencies gained. Computers & Education, 58 (4), 1007-1020

Kabilan, M. K. (2007). English language teachers reflecting on reflections: A Malaysian experience. TESOL Quarterly, 41(4), 681-705.

Kader, B. K. B. A. (2007). Malaysia's experience in training teachers to use ICT. In Meleisea, E. (Ed.), ICT in Teacher Education: Case Studies from the Asia-Pacific region. (pp. 10-22). Bangkok: UNESCO.

Kilbane, C. & Milman, N. (2003). The digital teaching portfolio handbook: A how-to-guide for educators. Boston: Ally and Bacon.

Kilbane, C. & Milman, N. (2005). The digital teaching portfolio handbook: Understanding the digital teaching portfolio process. Boston: Ally and Bacon

Klenowski, V. (2002). Developing portfolios for learning and assessment: Processes and principles. London: Routledge Flamer

Long, M. H. & Porter, P. A. (1985). Group work, interlanguage talk and second language acquisition. TESOL Quarterly, 19 (2), 207-227.

Mehlinger, H. D. & Powers, S. M. (2002). Technology and teacher education. Boston, New York: Houghton Miffilin Company.

MMR (Malaysiam Management Review) (1992). 'Malaysia: The Way Forward' by Prime Minister of Malaysia Dato' Seri Dr. Mahathir Mohamad. 27 (3).

http://mgv.mim.edu.my/MMR/9209/frame.htm [Viewed 14 April 2008]

Mothar, T. M. T. & Saad, M. (2007). Enhancing reading through Internet. In Kabilam, M. K. & Vethamani, M. E. (Eds.) Vithamani, M. E. (General Editor) Internet and the English language classroom. (pp. 31-52). Pj: Sasbadi Press

Ngah. N. A. & Mona. M. (2006). Development of ICT instructional materials based on needs identified by Malaysia secondary school teachers. Proceedings of the 2006 Informing Science and IT Education Joint Conference. http://proceedings.informingscience.org/InSITE2006/ProcNgah164.pdf [Viewed 2nd March 2013]

Nunan, D. (1988). The learner-centered curriculum. Cambridge: Cambridge University Press.

Oblinger, D.G (2008). Growing up with Google. What it means to education. Emerging Technologies for Learning, 3 (2008), 11-29

Pandian, A. (2006). Information technology challenges: Practice and views of language teachers. In Kabilan, M. K., Razak, N. A., Embi, M.A. (Eds.). Online teaching and learning in ELT. (pp. 202-221). Pulau Pinang: Penerbit Universiti Sains Malaysia.

Riedinger, B. (2006). Mining for Meaning: Teaching students how to reflect. In Jafari, A. & Kaufman, C. (Eds.) Handbook of research on ePortfolios. (pp. 90-101). USA/UK: Idea group Inc.

Rogers, E. (1995). Diffusion of innovations. New York: Free Press.

Salmon, G. (2000). E-moderating, the key to teaching and learning online. London: Taylor & Francis.

Sarudin, I., Zubairi, A., Nordin, M. & Omar, M. (2008). The English language proficiency of Malaysian public university students. In Enhancing the quality of higher education through research: Shaping future policy (pp. 40-65). Ministry of Higher Education of Malaysia

Shermen, G. (2006). Instructional roles of electronic portfolios. In Jafari, A. & Kaufman, C. (Eds) Handbook of Research on ePortfolios. (pp. 1-14). USA/UK: Idea group Inc

Stefani, L., Mason, R. & Pegler, C. (2007). The Educational potentials of e-portfolios: Supporting personal development and reflective learning. London & NY: Routledge publications.

Stevenson, H. (2006). Using ePortfolios to foster peer assessment, critical thinking, and collaboration. In Jafari, A. & Kaufman, C. (Eds.) Handbook of research on eportfolios. (p. 112-124). USA/UK: Idea group Inc.

USM (2008). The official website of Universiti Sains Malaysia. http://www.usm.my/en/profil.asp?s=4 [Viewed 2 March 2013]

Vethamani, M. E. (2004). A new CALL: Computer applications for literature learning. Internet Journal of e-Language Learning & Teaching, 1(2), 58-72

Vethamani, M. E. (2007). The ebb and flow of english language education in Malaysia. In Vethamani, M. E. & Perumal, R. (Eds.) Teaching English in Malaysia: A special 25th MELTA anniversary publication. (pp. 1-10). Pj: Sasbadi Press.

Vethamani, M. E., Kabilan, M. K. & Khan, M. A. (2008). E-Portfolios and English language teacher development. In Kabilan. M. K. & Vethamani. M. E. (Eds.) Qualitative studies in teacher development. (pp. 88-104). Pj: Sasbadi Press

Vygotsky, L. S. (1978). Mind in society: The development of high psychological process. Cambridge, Massachusetts: Harvard University Press.

Wenger, E. (1998). Communities of practice: Learning, meaning, and identity. New York: Cambridge University Press

Wenger, E., McDermott, R., & Snyder, W.M. (2002). Cultivating communities of practice. Boston: Harvard Business School Press.

Woolfolk, A. (2005). Educational psychology (9th Ed.). Boston: Pearson education Inc.

Wray, S. (2007). Teaching portfolios, community, and pre-service teachers' professional development. Teaching and Teacher Education, 23, 1139-1152

Ya'acob, A., Nor, N. F. M. & Azman, H. (2005). Implementation of the Malaysian smart school: An investigation of teaching-learning practices and teacher-student readiness. Internet Journal of e-Language Learning & Teaching, 2(2), 16-25.

Yassin, S. F. M., Mohamad, N. S., Yamat, H (2007). Developing w-portfolio culture in computer education for teacher education. http://www.eifel.org/publications/eportfolio/proceedings/ep2007/papers/eportfolio [Viewed 23 July 2010]